D0931379

# Heinrich von Kleist

# PLAYS

# The German Library : Volume 25

Volkmar Sander, General Editor

EDITORIAL BOARD
Peter Demetz (Yale University)
Reinhold Grimm (University of Wisconsin)
Jost Hermand (University of Wisconsin)
Walter Hinderer (Princeton University)
Victor Lange (Princeton University)
Frank Ryder (University of Virginia)
Volkmar Sander (New York University)
Egon Schwarz (Washington University)
Peter Wapnewski (Institute for Advanced Study, Berlin)
A. Leslie Willson (University of Texas)

PT 2378 .A2 E5 1982
Kleist, Heinrich von, 1777-
1811.
Plays

# Heinrich von Kleist

# PLAYS

Edited by Walter Hinderer

Foreword by E. L. Doctorow

CONTINUUM · NEW YORK

RITTER LIBRARY
BALDWIN-WALLACE COLLEGE

1982

The Continuum Publishing Company
575 Lexington Avenue, New York, NY 10022

Copyright © 1982 by The Continuum Publishing Company

Introduction © 1982 by Walter Hinderer
Foreword © 1982 by E. L. Doctorow

All rights reserved. No part of this book may be reproduced, stored
in a retrieval system, or transmitted, in any form or by any means,
electronic, mechanical, photocopying, recording, or otherwise, without the
written permission of The Continuum Publishing Company.

Printed in the United States of America

*Library of Congress Cataloging in Publication Data*

Kleist, Heinrich von, 1777–1811.
Plays.

(The German library; v. 25)
Contents: The broken pitcher / translated by Jon
Swan—Amphitryon / translated by Charles E. Passage—
Penthesilea / translated by Humphrey Trevelyan—[etc.]
I. Hinderer, Walter, 1934–     .  II. Title.
PT2378.A2E5   1982        832'.6        81-22060
ISBN 0-8264-0253-4        AACR2
ISBN 0-8264-0263-1 pbk

For acknowledgments of published material, please see page 342,
which constitutes an extension of the copyright page.

# Contents

# Foreword

Amphitryon, the great Theban commander, returns from war to find his palace, and his wife, in the possession of an imposturing double. Struggling to reclaim his identity he rages against the impostor as a

> . . . lying spirit up from hell, who wants
> Me out of Thebes, and out of my wife's heart,
> Out of the world's remembrance, if he could,
> Out of the fortress of my consciousness.

A Kleist play may be set in ancient Greece, in Holland, or in seventeenth-century Prussia, but the fortress of consciousness is where the action occurs; inevitably, the walls are breached and the ramparts overrun. We feel Kleist's heroes and heroines are entitled to the trances, fainting fits, and visions to which they are continually subject, for in his universe everything is simultaneously its opposite—a man's identity is not his own, love is murder, military heroism is treason, the sitting judge is the guilty party. Kleisteans struggle monumentally with their perceptions; something else than what they expected is happening to them. That may be why, almost two centuries after these plays were written, we find them disturbingly current. In our century we acknowledge the genius of Isaac Newton but know that the universe we live in is, irrevocably, Einstein's. Similarly we give homage to Goethe but recognize ourselves as denizens of Kleist. No wonder Franz Kafka loved this writer and read him aloud to friends.

Perhaps the most stunning feature of Kleist's work is its faculty of narrative advance. This is as true of his plays as it is of his prose. No matter what he writes for the stage, rustic comedy, high tragedy, the tempo of consequential event is unfailing, the action is headlong and unceasingly generative. Typically, some sort of infernal proposition launches the work, some disorder of the world's logic: It powers its way through the lives of the characters as a demonic animation that possesses them and, like the god Jupiter who has come to earth in the form of Amphitryon, appropriates their very being.

In *Prince Frederick of Homburg,* for example, the young Prince wins the day against the Swedes at Fehrbellin, but his triumph comes of a reckless disregard of his battlefield orders from the chief of state, the Elector of Brandenburg. So two Prussian values—personal courage and military obedience—are mounted in one self-contradictory event. The Elector accepts the Prince's victory and sentences him to death. The heroic Prince expresses the most abject cowardice as he pleads for his life—even to the point of bartering his fiancée's love for it. Then he finds a stoic, statist rationalization for his death, and thereby wins a last minute reprieve.

In Kleist things change and they change fast. The protagonist's mind undergoes an alternation of ecstasies and despairs as it spins on the axis of Kleistean paradox. *Penthesilea* begins with the young warrior queen of the Amazons sweeping down indiscriminately on Greeks and Trojans alike, disrupting their warfare with a furious campaign. Why? She wants the great Achilles as a prize of war. He allows himself to be taken, whereupon her ferocity gives way to her love and she becomes the most demure of women and agrees to follow him. Has she won Achilles or has he won her? Rebuked by the High Priestess of her nation, Penthesilea recovers her sense of honor. She cannot reconcile her feelings, she can only suffer them in turn. This is not true of Achilles, who is pragmatic. He makes the mistake of wooing her in the language of war. Penthesilea kills him and falls on his body like a ravening dog.

The excess of self, the irrepressible force of individual love and passion and desire, is always present in Kleist, and always portrayed as a threat to the ruling order. Even in the earliest of these plays, the genuinely farcical *Broken Pitcher,* in which the lascivious and bumbling Judge Adam must hear a case in which his own sexual scandals come to light, there is a district examining judge to uphold the claims of society. We begin to perceive the structure of Kleist's imagination as a repertory company of players whose costumes and titles and gender change from work to work, but who stand in fixed relation to each other and to the argument. Amphitryon, Prince Frederick, the beautiful Queen Penthesilea, and even the randy Judge Adam, all hold high rank in their respective societies and command a following. Typically, one of the followers is a trusted aide or servant who will attempt to intercede and mediate in a voice of practicality and reason when the problem arises. The problem arises when someone of even higher rank than the hero or heroine, someone older who is himself or representatively the source of all rank and position—Jupiter, or the Elector of Brandenburg, or the High Priestess of Diana, or District Judge Walter—moves to impose the will or judgment of God or state.

One way or another God and state always win in the end. This outcome is perhaps most troublesome to us in *Prince Frederick of Homburg*. Here Kleist seems clearly to be arguing the virtue in the submission of the individual to totalitarian rule—Frederick, after all, affirms the justice of his own death sentence. And the end of the play seems celebratory. But is it? The constant shifting of Prince Frederick's fortunes, and with it his mind's conditioning, proposes itself as Kleist's real vision. If there is any rule of life, he seems to say, it is volatility. What has the Prince undergone if not a form of brainwashing? Is the state anything more than his delusion? Kleist's Germanic passion was for an objective order or truth, a system of certainty that could not be sabotaged by his thought. This passion was never satisfied. And so, at the moments of resolution in his plays, odd or ambiguous things happen, irrepressibly, as if to suggest the lie involved even in bringing a piece of work to conclusion. "No, tell me," says the Prince, his life and love and glory given back to him, "is it a dream?" He may here be using a metaphor for incredible happiness. Or he may be suggesting life's ephemeral insubstance. In any event, he is assured that a dream is what it is, and that is the way the play ends.

Even more ambiguous is the ending of the comedy *Amphitryon*. At the very moment of happy resolution—Amphitryon's soul reseated, his rights and privileges returned by the god Jupiter—his wife Alcmena lets out a guttural cry of despair. It is the last word of the play, the woman's realization that she has had the love of a god, but from now on will only have Amphitryon.

In the embattled fortress of consciousness there is no end to warfare, only the incessant flow of the contending forces of subjectivity as they advance and fall back, occupy or give up the blasted structure. Kleist's dramas are beautifully constructed, each is informed by a shrewd stagecraft and skillful use of convention. (Even his employment of props—a lady's glove, the bent plume of a helmet, a bloodied arrow, a broken pitcher—is consummate.) If you were preparing any of these works for stage production you would be hard pressed to find a scene, or even a passage, that is extraneous—so elegantly are they put together. But it is a final Kleistean irony that the overwhelming sense of his plays is of immense disorder, teeming madness, an infernally wild fluctuation of feeling and event. Kleist makes excessive demands on his characters and gives them excessive responses that call up his greatest powers as a metaphorist and dramatic poet. He leaves us with a body of work which, though small and neatly made, seems to enlarge and grow jagged in our contemplation.

E. L. DOCTOROW

# Introduction

A critic of the *New York Times* wrote with regard to the first play of our volume; "There are no surprises in *The Broken Pitcher,* only an endless series of excuses, subterfuges and delays as Adam tries to shift the blame," and he drew the hasty conclusion: "Many of the jokes deal with his wig . . . and his clubfoot, not exactly the most mirthsome subjects for laughter. The biblical and Greek parallels—the judge as both Adam and Oedipus—seem forced." However, the critic confessed at the end that he vastly preferred "the dramatic von Kleist of *The Prince of Homburg.*"

Since Jean Vilars' remarkable 1951 staging of *The Prince of Homburg* in Paris (with Gérard Philipe in the title role), this last drama of Kleist's has become very well known abroad. Yet why should *The Prince of Homburg* seem any less strange to a French, English, or American audience than *The Broken Pitcher?* In what sense is the prince of Homburg a hero? He fears for his life and in order to save it is willing to renounce his beloved Natalie. What kind of officer believes in spontaneous intuition, the world of dreams, and the "order of the heart" instead of betting on the battle plan, reality, and the order of war?

In all of Kleist's plays, his comedies as well as his tragedies, the conflict is based on the mysterious nature of the individual and the continual discrepancy between personality and society. Goethe once remarked in reference to *Amphitryon,* "Kleist, in his delineation of the main character, aims for a confusion of emotions." His dramatic figures are mysterious to themselves and to the world around them, and out of this mystery comes the dramatic complexity, the exposition and development of his plays. Man, for Kleist, has no means of orientation, since "we cannot decide whether that which we call truth is really truth, or whether it only seems that way to us" (a letter of March 22, 1801). Any belief in permanence he considers futile. He shares neither Goethe's faith in the harmonic development of the personality nor Schiller's in the autonomous powers of the human self. Only in the dream, in the unconscious, in "the heart's core" (*Homburg,* II,6) does Kleist find certainty and identity of the self; outside this, we live in a condition of deception and confusion. Thus he develops in his essay *On the Marionette Theater* the private mythology of the second fall from grace, according to which "we again have to eat from the tree of knowledge in order to fall back into the state of innocence."

During the short time that Kleist could be considered part of the German Enlightenment and Classicism, he searched for his happiness in the "gratifying contemplation of moral beauty" and believed in the possibility of planning his life, in the power of science and education. But the doubts multiplied and finally this optimistic structure collapsed.

Kleist experienced the decay of values, the modern phenomenon of alienation, loss of identity, a vacuum of ideas; he despaired of finding meaning in life, in society, and in the political situation of his time. To his cousin, Marie von Kleist, in June 1807, he related the following insight from his prison in France: "What times are these. In my withdrawn way of life they always thought me isolated from the world, and yet nobody was probably more intimately connected to it than I. How desolate are the prospects open to us." Such insights help to explain the lasting appeal and modernity of his dramas. It is not the comic situations that give Kleist's comedies their impact, but rather the brilliant fireworks of his linguistic and formal virtuosity.

But who was Bernd Heinrich Wilhelm von Kleist, born on October 18, 1777 in Frankfurt-on-the-Oder? He was descended from an old and well-known Prussian-Pommeranian noble family that brought forth many officers, generals, marshals, and also a poet,

Lessing's friend Ewald von Kleist. In spite of this, Kleist thought little of his social class and would rather have resigned from "the whole splendid lot of nobility, and class, and honor, and wealth" in order to find love and happiness (from a letter to his fiancée, Wilhelmine von Zenge, November 13, 1800).

At the age of 14 he joined the regiment of guards in Potsdam and reached the rank of second lieutenant before asking the Prussian king to relieve him of his duties in 1799. The military profession was as unpleasant to him as it had been to his uncle Ewald von Kleist. Instead he strove for a "most complete training of [his] spiritual and physical powers" (letter of March 18, 1799). Therefore he wanted to devote himself totally to the sciences; he studied physics, mathematics, philosophy, Greek and Latin, in order to complete his life-plan. Without such a "firm destination," he informed his sister Ulrike (May 1799), man is "subject to the caprice of chance, a puppet on the strings of fate." At the same time, he already feared that he would become "useless for social life" like "most professional scholars." Thus he finally came to the conclusion that he was not made for a profession. He did not want to submit to the role-expectations of his family or society; it was unthinkable for him to structure his life according to goals, and so he preferred an independent and private existence to that of the secure civil servant.

After his discharge from the army on April 4, 1799, Heinrich von Kleist diverted himself by studying (in Frankfurt-on-the-Oder), taking short trips, and making new social acquaintances. But soon he again attempted to live up to the demands of his family and the expectations of the society of his day by considering the career of a civil servant in Berlin. He came into contact with the then Prussian minister Karl Gustav Struensee and undertook, with his friend Ludwig von Brockes, a mysterious journey that led him, among other places, to Wittenberg, Leipzig, Dresden, and Würzburg. The pair registered under fictitious names at the University of Leipzig in order to obtain false passports. From a letter Kleist sent to his sister it appears that the two had been sent by Prussia to engage in industrial espionage in foreign plants. Heinrich von Kleist complains in the letter that "proprietors of foreign factories do not let experts inside their workshops. The only possibility of getting in is through flattery and hypocrisy, in short, through fraud." He felt the task to be an imposition and accused the Prussian king and his government of demanding from their servants total subjugation and irresponsible surrender of autonomy. On this journey, however, he discovered where his abilities really lay. After briefly considering a visit to Paris to acquaint France with "the newest philosophy," above all Kant's, he decided to begin training himself for the "literary profession."

In 1801 Kleist gave up the long-cherished dream of studying science, philosophy, and education. The specialization, one-sidedness, and alienation from life that were characteristic of the academic disciplines disturbed him. But he became, in consequence, not only a despairing intellectual skeptic, but also a poet. In a letter of July 21, 1801, he drew some preliminary conclusions: "Confused by the maxims of a morbid philosophy, incapable of applying for a position, I had left Berlin only because I feared that peace in which I found no peace at all; and now I find myself intent on a trip abroad without aim and purpose, incapable of comprehending where all this might lead me." Already he toyed with the idea of leaving his fiancée, Wilhelmine von Zenge, and felt that he was drifting toward an abyss.

The experience of cosmopolitan Paris intensified in Kleist the desire to withdraw to the country. In 1802 he found seclusion in Switzerland on an island in Lake Thun. He had contact with local writers and found a degree of satisfaction. He worked on *The Broken Pitcher* and the drama *Robert Guiscard* and finished his first tragedy, *The Schroffenstein Family*. He wanted to buy land and live in these idyllic surroundings, enjoying, like Rousseau, the life of a contented country gentleman with his Wilhelmine. But Wilhelmine declined and Napoleon, as Kleist saw it the greatest danger in Europe, threatened an invasion. Kleist became ill.

In 1803 Kleist joined the circle of the famous writer Christoph Martin Wieland, in Weimar and Ossmannstedt. He fell in love with Wieland's "pretty daughter" Luise and read to the father from his *Guiscard,* which the latter praised with unusual enthusiasm. In spite of all this Kleist fled this idyll, went to Paris, and in a fit of despair burnt the nearly completed manuscript of *Robert Guiscard*. Kleist's general discontent grew; he contemplated suicide and considered entering French military service in order to be killed in battle. But the Prussian envoy in Paris sent him back to

Germany where he first toyed with the idea of becoming a car-
penter and then applied once again for a position in the Prussian
civil service. Through his adjutant general the King, angry, severely reprimanded Kleist; however, the compassionate Minister
Karl Freiherr von Stein zum Altenstein employed him in the
finance department and gave him a post in the Königsberg administration. But again the attempt at a renewed social integration
failed; Kleist complained about his "ruined health," and, on June
30, 1806, asked for a prolonged leave. Even in his letters to his
understanding superior he was severely critical of Prussian politics
for leaving the "maniac" Napoleon too much of a free hand. (In a
farewell letter to his cousin Marie on November 10, 1811, he
mentioned, among other reasons for suicide, the political one:
"The Alliance," he explained, "which the king now concludes
with the French is not designed to encourage me to cling to life.")

On his way from Königsberg on January 30, 1807, Heinrich
von Kleist was arrested by the French as an alleged spy and taken
to Fort de Joux near Pontarlier. After several attempts, his sister
Ulrike finally succeeded in having him released in August. He then
settled in Dresden where he was caught up in frenetic literary activity. Besides the conception and completion of several dramatic
and prose works, he was full of journalistic projects. With his
friend Adam Müller, he started the journal *Phöbus*. His social suc-
cesses as a writer did not pass unnoticed. It culminated in his
being crowned poet laureate by the Austrian envoy. He completed
*Penthesilea, Käthchen of Heilbronn, The Battle of Arminius,* and
started preliminary work on the *Prince of Homburg* which was
completed on June 21, 1811 in Berlin.

In Prussia's capital, where he settled in 1810 after the confusion
of war and the dislocation of travel, he started the newspaper *Ber-
liner Abendblätter*. Very successful at the beginning, it lost sub-
scribers because of government restrictions. Like the protagonist
of his famous story *Michael Kohlhaas,* Kleist stubbornly de-
manded financial restitution for his losses. The restless struggle for
a secure existence, the many confrontations, journalistic and literary failures, quarrels with his family and what seemed to him a
hopeless political situation, drove him increasingly into a state of
extreme despair. On November 10, 1811, he wrote to his
confidante Marie von Kleist: "But I swear to you it is quite impos-

sible for me to live any longer. My soul is so sore that I would almost say that the daylight hurts my nose when I stick it out the window." With his friend and companion in suffering Henriette Vogel, he prepared, with an almost eerie composure, their joint suicide. On November 21, 1811, at approximately 4:00 p.m., by the Wannsee, he ended their lives with two pistol shots.


Heinrich von Kleist's work consists, apart from some minor poems, a few political writings and literary essays, mainly of the much admired stories of which volumes 30 and 31 of the German Library will contain a selection, and the following dramas: *The Schroffenstein Family* (first version at the beginning of 1802 in Switzerland); *Robert Guiscard* (first version, 1802, in Switzerland; the almost completed version destroyed in Paris in 1803. In 1807/08 he returns to the theme and publishes the fragment in the journal *Phöbus*); *The Broken Pitcher* (the first three scenes written in Berlin in 1805. Work continues 1803 in Dresden, 1805 in Berlin and in Königsberg where he finishes the manuscript at the end of 1806 and the beginning of 1807); *Penthesilea* (begun 1806 in Königsberg, continued 1807 as a French prisoner of war and completed in the fall of 1807 in Dresden): *Käthchen of Heilbronn* (begun 1807 in Dresden, reworked several times until the book edition of Berlin in 1810): *The Battle of Arminius* (written 1808 in Dresden, published first in 1821 by Tieck in Berlin); *Prince Frederick of Homburg* (presumably begun 1809 in Dresden and finished 1811 in Berlin).

The four plays selected for this volume—*The Broken Pitcher* and *The Prince of Homburg* have been especially translated for this edition—undoubtedly represent the most important and characteristic contributions Heinrich von Kleist made to world dramatic literature. In Weimar, Wieland, who was well-informed in literary as well as critical matters, saw in Kleist the fulfillment of his expectations: an original synthesis of Greek classical, Elizabethan, and French classicist dramatic accomplishments. But beyond that Kleist points in his work to a modern self-understanding. Literature had become an existential necessity for him. The crack that runs through Kleist's image of world and society is constantly reflected in the disturbed human relationships of his fictionalized characters. Even his comedy *The Broken Pitcher* portrays in the end the loss of a former wholeness, a "broken" wholeness. The tensions between the Elector and the Prince of Homburg reveal not only a conflict between uncle (father) and nephew (son), but also the questionable nature of the Prussian state, which is examined as to its human qualities. Colonel Kottwitz does not plead "for a myopic statesmanship," but for a state which leaves room for human feelings, dignity, and freedom. The trial and the interrogation that Kleist's major figures must undergo are intended to demonstrate how the individual, deceived by his consciousness, becomes a victim of an ostensible reality. Kleist's works are directed against the fetishism of consciousness, typical of the Enlightenment; he makes a new appeal to spontaneous feelings and the "infallibility of the unconscious." His dramas as well as his stories are in the end an inventory of the "fragile nature of the world," especially the world of modern man, whose cognitive powers, in his view, must again "go through the infinite." Only in this way can man regain the lost natural grace and self-identity which Kleist describes so eloquently in his well-known essay *On the Marionette Theater,* * the centerpiece of his Romantic hope and belief.

W.H.

* This essay can be found in Vol. 21 of THE GERMAN LIBRARY, *German Romantic Criticism,* edited by A. Leslie Willson.

# THE
# BROKEN
# PITCHER

*A Comedy*

## Characters

Justice Adam
Court Clerk Link
District Judge Walter
Eve
Mrs. Martha, *Eve's mother*
Ruprecht
Veit
Mrs. Bridget
Constable
Manservant. Two Maids.

# Scene 1

*Adam, seated, is bandaging his leg. Link enters.*

LINK: Ay, what the devil! What a sight you look!
  What happened to you, Adam? What befell?

ADAM: Well, look. All it takes to stumble is a pair
  Of feet. The floor itself is flat—or no?
  Still, here I stumbled. For each man bears,
  Within himself, his own stumbling block.

LINK: Oh, come now, friend. You say that each man
                                          [bears . . . ?

ADAM: Ay, in himself . . .

LINK:                    Block be damned!

ADAM:                                   Beg pardon?

LINK: You take your name from an unsteady sire who,
  When things were just beginning, fell,
  And still is famous for his fall.
  Surely you wouldn't . . .

ADAM:                     Well?

LINK:                          Follow suit?

ADAM: You? You are asking me . . . if I . . . ? I think . . .
  *Here* is where I fell, I tell you, Link.

LINK: You literally fell, you mean.

ADAM:                              I did.
  And must have cut a wretched figure doing so.

LINK: When did this accident occur?

ADAM:                               When? Now!
  In the very act of climbing out of bed.
  My morning song was still upon my lips
  When head over heels I stumble into day.

And so, before I'm altogether up,
  I'm down—and the good Lord sprains my ankle.
LINK: And, to top it all, your left one.
ADAM:                  My left?
LINK: This one? Your game leg?
ADAM:                Yes. Of course!
LINK:                        Good Lord.
  The one that made perdition's path
  Such heavy going in the past!
ADAM:               My foot?
  What? Heavy? How?
LINK:             Your club foot.
ADAM:               Club foot?
  A foot's a foot, whichever side it's on.
LINK: Begging your pardon, Adam, but you wrong
  Your right foot by clubbing it with the left.
  For the right one lacks the other's gravity
  And so dares venture onto thin ice first.
ADAM:               Rubbish.
  Where one leads, the other follows. They're both game.
LINK: And what put your face so out of joint?
ADAM: What? My face?
LINK:           You mean you did not know?
ADAM: I'd be a liar if I said . . . How does it look?
LINK: How it looks?
ADAM:         Yes, friend. How?
LINK:               Horrible.
ADAM: Explain yourself. Enlarge!
LINK:             It's scratched.
  A grisly sight. A piece gone from the cheek.
  How large? Without a scale I couldn't say.
ADAM: The devil you say!
LINK (*bringing a mirror*): Here. Look for yourself.
  A ram that, chased by hounds, plunges through brambles,
  Leaves no less wool behind than you left skin—
  Though God knows where you left it.
ADAM:             Hm. Yes. True.
  A cheerless sight. And my nose, too, has suffered.
LINK: *And* your eye.

ADAM:                    The eye not, friend.
LINK:                                          Yes, here.
  Don't you see this cut? A bloody swipe,
  As if some furious farm boy had let fly.
ADAM: That, Link, is the cheekbone, not the eye. Imagine.
  All that damage and I never felt a thing!
LINK: No. One never does in the heat of battle.
ADAM: Battle? What? Ay, with that blasted ram
  Jutting from the stove I strove in battle,
  If you would have it so. It comes back now.
  I lose my balance, yes, and, at the same time,
  Reach out, arms flailing like a drowning man,
  Clutch at my trousers which, last night, I'd hung
  All wet to dry upon the rack, clutch hold
  Of them, you see, believing, like a fool,
  That they will hold me up, when—*rip*—my waistband
  Tears; and waistband, trousers, me, all three
  We fall, and there, smack on the corner
  Of that stove, where a ram sticks out his nose,
  I come hurtling headfirst down.
LINK (*laughing*):                    Well done!
ADAM: Well done, my foot!
LINK:                              No Adam fell before
  By slipping out, instead of into, bed.
ADAM: 'Pon my soul!—But what I meant to say was,
  What news?
LINK:            News? Damn, I had almost forgot.
ADAM: Well?
LINK:        Prepare for an unexpected visitor
  From Utrecht.
ADAM:              Oh?
LINK:                        The District Judge is coming.
ADAM: Who?
LINK:          Judge Walter is on his way from Utrecht,
  Inspecting courts throughout the province. *And*
  He's due to turn up here today.
ADAM: Today? Have you gone mad?
LINK:                                    As I live,
  He was in Holla, on the border, yesterday,

And has already finished with that court.
A farmer saw the lead team hitching up
To start the journey here to Howzem.
ADAM: Here? Today? The District Judge, you say?
  Him? Inspect *us*? That worthy fellow
  Who fleeces his own flock, but has no use
  For meddlers? What? He's coming all the way
  To Howzem just to bully us around?
LINK: If he came as far as Holla, he'll come
  To Howzem. So take care.
ADAM:                          Pah.
LINK:                              I'm telling you.
ADAM: And I tell you I don't believe your fairy tale.
LINK: The farmer saw him with his own two eyes!
ADAM: Who knows who the blear-eyed loafer saw?
  These yokels, they see a bald man walking by,
  They can't tell which side his face is on.
  Stick me a three-cornered hat on my cane,
  Toss a cloak on its crook and add boots,
  These simpletons would say it's God knows who.
LINK: Doubt on then, in the devil's name, until
  He walks in through the door.
ADAM:                              Him? Walk in? Here?
  Without slipping us word ahead of time?
LINK: What simplicity! Have you forgotten?
  Inspector Tipplegin has since retired.
  It is Judge Walter who will inspect us now.
ADAM: Judge Walter. Puh. Go. Leave me in peace.
  The man has sworn to uphold his office
  And deals out justice, as we do,
  As it's defined by law *and* local custom.
LINK: Well, I assure you that Judge Walter did appear,
  Unheralded, in Holla yesterday;
  Examined that court's records and accounts,
  And then suspended clerk and justice both.
  Why? I wouldn't know. *Ab officio*.
ADAM: The devil you say! The farmer said that?
LINK: That, and more.
ADAM:                  More?

LINK                              If you must know:
  This morning, early on, they seek the justice,
  Who, confined to house arrest, is gone,
  And find him in his barn, high up, hanging
  From a rafter.
ADAM:            What's that?
LINK:                            Help arrives.
  They cut him down, rub and slap and douse him
  And manage, just, to bring him back to life.
ADAM: What? They bring him?
LINK:                              Yet now, his house sealed up
  And locked, and inventory taken, it is
  As if the poor man were a corpse already.
  His vacant post already has been filled.
ADAM: Ah, hang it. Easygoing, that he was.
  Yes, but honest, as I live and breathe.
  A stout fellow, good company. A sloven,
  True. No doubt about it. A dreadful sloven.
  If the judge was, indeed, in Holla today,
  It must have been rough weather for the poor sod.
LINK: And but for this affair, the farmer said,
  Judge Walter would long since be here. By noon,
  You can be sure he will arrive.
ADAM: By noon! Splendid, friend! Now show your friendship.
  You know how one hand scrubs the other clean?
  And you, I know, would like to be—and, by God,
  You deserve it, too—to be the justice here.
  And yet, today, the occasion does not suit.
  May this bitter cup, today, be spared me, Link.
LINK: I, the justice here? You think that of me?
ADAM: You are a scholar of the rhetoric
  And know your Cicero as well
  As any he who schooled in Amsterdam.
  Today, though, curb me your ambition, hear?
  There will be other and more suitable
  Occasions for you to show your skills.
LINK: We two. As close as kin. Come now, Adam.
ADAM: The great Demosthenes, in his time, too,
  He held his tongue. Make him your example.

And though I'm not the king of Macedon,
  I can, in my own way, show gratitude.
LINK: Enough of your suspicion. Have I ever . . . ?
ADAM: And, look you, Link, I for my part, I, too,
  Will heed the noble Greek's example. One could,
  Of course, work up a fine oration on
  Public monies, interest rates, and taxes.
  But why waste prose on such stuff, eh?
LINK:                        Well then!
ADAM: No. Far be it from me to stoop so low,
  The devil take it! While, as to other
  Mischief, 'tis but a prank that, hatched by night,
  Would shun the nosey light of day.
LINK:                  I know.
ADAM: My soul! There is no reason why a judge,
  When he's not sitting on the bench, must be
  As icy-solemn as the polar bear!
LINK: I quite agree.
ADAM:         Well then. Come, my friend,
  We'll step into the registry awhile.
  I'll sort the documents, for they,
  They lie there like the Tower of Babel.

# Scene 2

*A manservant enters. Later, two maids.*
MANSERVANT: God save you, Justice Adam. Justice Walter
  Sends his greetings, and soon he will arrive.
ADAM: Ye just heavens! He's already finished up
  In Holla?
MANSERVANT: Yes. He is already in Howzem.
ADAM: Hey! Liza! Margaret! Hey!
LINK:                Calm now. Keep calm.
ADAM: My dear friend!
LINK:         Return his greetings with thanks.
MANSERVANT: And tomorrow we set off to Hussahey.
ADAM: What should I do? What shouldn't I . . . ?
          *(He reaches for his clothes.)*

FIRST MAID *(entering):*                              You called,
[sir?

LINK: What? You'd put *those* trousers on? Are you mad?
SECOND MAID *(entering):* You called, Your Honor?
LINK:                                          Your coat.
  Here. Take it.
ADAM *(glancing around):* Who? His Honor? Judge Walter?
LINK:                                                    Just
[the maid.

ADAM: My bands! My coat! My collar!
FIRST MAID:                            Your vest first.
ADAM: What? Coat off. Quick!
LINK *(to manservant):*          His Honor the judge
  Will be most welcome. We shall be prepared
  To receive him instantly. Tell him this.
ADAM: The devil! Tell him Justice Adam begs to be
  Excused today.
LINK:          Excused?
ADAM:                    Excused. He's on
  His way?
MANSERVANT: He's biding at the tavern, Sir.
  He sent out for the smith. The coach broke down.
ADAM: Good! My regards. The smith's a lazy dog.
  Tell him I beg to be excused. Tell him
  I nearly broke my neck and legs. Look
  For yourself: a spectacle, the way I look.
  And each new shock works like a purgative.
  Say I am unwell.
LINK:          Have you lost your wits?
  —We'll be most pleased to receive His Honor.
  Would you . . . ?
ADAM:              Hang it!
LINK:                    What now?
ADAM:                              My guts rebel, Link,
  As if I'd swallowed a peck of physic.
LINK: That's all you need—to start him on your trail.
ADAM: Margaret! Hey! The bag of bones! Liza!
BOTH MAIDS: Here we are! What do you want?
ADAM:                              Move!

The butter, bottles, sausage, cheese, the ham—
Get them out of the registry—and quick!
Not you. The other. Gooseface! You! Yes.
God's blisters, Margaret, it's Liza I want
To clean up the mess in there.
*(The first maid exits.)*
SECOND MAID: If only you
Would talk so we could underst . . .
ADAM: Wench,
Shut your mouth. Away. Fetch me my wig.
Hup! It's in the bookcase. Scat, snail. Move!
*(The second maid exits.)*
LINK *(to manservant):*
Your master's journey went, I hope, smoothly?
MANSERVANT: Hardly. The coach tipped over in a pothole.
ADAM: A pox on my sprained ankle. Can't get my boot . . .
LINK: Good heavens! Tipped over, you say. No . . .
Further damage, I hope?
MANSERVANT: Nothing of consequence.
My master wrenched his wrist a bit, that's all.
And the shaft broke.
ADAM: A pity it wasn't his neck.
LINK: Sprained his wrist? Good Lord. And did the smith come?
MANSERVANT: For the shaft, yes.
LINK: What?
ADAM: You mean, Link,
Did the doctor come.
LINK: What?
MANSERVANT: To fix the shaft?
ADAM: Rubbish, man! The wrist.
MANSERVANT: Farewell, gentlemen.
*(aside)*
I think these clowns are mad.
*(The manservant exits.)*
LINK: I meant the smith.
ADAM: You give yourself away, friend.
LINK: I do? How so?
ADAM: You betray confusion.

LINK:                           What?
                    (*The first maid enters.*)
ADAM:                               Hey, Liza!
   What's all that?
FIRST MAID:        Sausages, Your Honor.
ADAM: These are my files on foster children, goose.
LINK: I, confused?
ADAM:               Take them back to the registry.
FIRST MAID: The sausages?
ADAM:                           The sausages? Nonsense. The
                                    [wrapping, fool.
LINK: It was all a misunderstanding.
                    (*The second maid enters.*)
SECOND MAID: Your wig's not in the bookcase, Your Honor.
ADAM: And why not?
SECOND MAID:        Because—hm—you . . .
ADAM:                                   Because?
SECOND MAID: Because at eleven last . . .
ADAM:                                   Well, out with it!
SECOND MAID: Well, you came in, remember?—without your wig.
ADAM: I? Wigless?
SECOND MAID:        Indeed you did.
   And here's Liza too, who can vouch for it.
   Your other wig was sent out for repair.
ADAM: I came home how?
FIRST MAID:               God's truth, Justice Adam!
   Your head was bare when you came home last night.
   You spoke about a fall—don't you remember?
   Your head was bloody. I had to wash it off.
ADAM: Baggage, you lie!
FIRST MAID:               On my word of honor.
ADAM: Shut your mouth, I say. Not a word is true.
LINK: You've had this wound since yesterday?
ADAM:                                   Today.
   The wound today and yesterday the wig.
   I wore it, powdered white, and, on my honor,
   When I doffed my hat I doffed my wig, as well,
   By accident, when I came in last night.

Whatever it might be she washed it wasn't me.
—Oh, go to the devil where you belong!
There. In the registry!
(*The first maid exits.*)
Go, Margaret.
Go ask the sexton if he'll lend me his wig.
Tell him, tell him the cat—the swine—littered
In mine this morning. Tell him it lies
—Ah yes, that's where—beneath my bed, befouled.
LINK: The cat? What? Are you . . . ?
ADAM: God's truth. Just so.
Five kits in all—yellow and black and one
That's white. I'll drown the black ones in the pond.
Well, Link, what would *you* do? D'*you* want one?
LINK: In the wig?
ADAM: The devil take me, in my wig!
I'd hung the thing up when I went to bed,
On a chair, you know, and, tossing in my sleep,
I must have bumped the chair and floored the wig.
LINK: Whereupon Puss picks the wig up in her mouth . . .
ADAM: I swear.
LINK: . . . and, dragging it beneath your bed,
Casts her litter in it.
ADAM: In the mouth? No.
LINK: No? How then?
ADAM: The cat?
LINK: You mean—you . . . ?
ADAM: In the mouth? I think—! I shoved it with my foot
Beneath the bed when I saw it.
LINK: Well. Well.
ADAM: Canaille! Rabble! They rut and litter
Wherever the yen hits 'em.
SECOND MAID (*giggling*): Shall I go then?
ADAM: Do. And give
[my greetings

To the sexton's wife. Tell the old dame
She shall have the wig back, in good shape,
Before nightfall. No need for her husband
To know. You understand?

SECOND MAID:               I'll tell her.
            (*The second maid exits.*)

# Scene 3

ADAM: Ah, Link, this day, I fear, bodes little good.
LINK: Why so?
ADAM:         Everything tripping me up, head over heels.
   Also, is court not in session today?
LINK: Indeed it is. A crowd of plaintiffs has
   Already gathered outside by the door.
ADAM: Hm. I had this dream: a plaintiff seized
   And hailed me into court, and there I stood
   And at the same time there I sat as justice
   On the bench, scolding, tongue-lashing
   My other self—then sentenced me to irons.
LINK: What? Sentenced yourself?
ADAM:                   Link, I swear it.
   Then the two of us turned into one and fled
   And had to sleep the night beneath the stars.
LINK: Well then? And you think this dream . . . ?
ADAM:                     Devil take it!
   If not the dream, then some plot, trick, curse, spell—
   Be what it may, Link, it's working against me.
LINK: A foolish fear. Do but mete out justice
   During the District Judge's visit here,
   According to the rules, to each in turn,
   So that your dream in which the judge is judged
   Will not come true in some other way.

# Scene 4

*District Judge Walter enters.*
WALTER: God greet you, Justice Adam.
ADAM:                    Ay, welcome!
   Welcome, gracious lord, to humble Howzem.
   Who could have thought—by all that's just, who could

Have dared to hope for such a pleasing visit!
No dream as recent, say, as eight o'clock today
Would brashly have aspired to such joy.

WALTER: I come, I know, a bit abruptly, and must,
On such a journey, made in service of the state,
Be content if, when I depart,
My hosts' farewells are well intended.
As for my greeting now, on my arrival,
Be assured it is sincere.
The Provincial Court in Utrecht is determined
Here in these remoter regions to improve
The administration of justice which,
In sundry ways, falls far short of the mark,
And abuses must expect their sharp correction.
Still, my present business in itself
Is not severe. I come to see, not punish,
And, say I find not all in order here,
If things go middling well, I shall be glad.

ADAM: By God, a noble, an exalted, thought.
Your Grace will chide us, now and then,
For still abiding by the old procedures,
Although they've served the Netherlands
Quite well since Charles the Fifth was emperor.
Newfangled notions, who can keep them down?
The world, they say, grows daily wiser,
And all the world, I know, reads Puffendorf.
But Howzem is a little piece of it
And so can claim no more, and no less
Either, than its share of the common knowledge.
Enlighten justice here with mercy, Sir,
And, rest assured, so soon as you have turned
Your back, you will be fully satisfied.
But should you find such justice here today,
Upon my soul, 'twould be a miracle,
Since we but darkly know what you expect.

WALTER: We lack regulations, very true.
Or, rather, suffer from a surfeit
Of them. They should be sifted.

ADAM: Ay, in a huge sieve. Chaff. Mountains of chaff!

WALTER: This, I take it, is your clerk?

LINK:                              Court Clerk Link,
  At your most gracious worship's service, Sir.
  I shall have served the bench nine years come Whitsun.
                  *(Adam brings up a chair.)*

ADAM: Sit down.

WALTER:          Let it be.

ADAM:                     You've come from Holla
  In good time.

WALTER:          Two short miles.—You know then? How?

ADAM: How? Why, Your Grace's servant . . .

LINK:                              A farmer
  Who just now returned from Holla told us.

WALTER: A farmer?

ADAM:          Exactly.

WALTER:                     Yes. It was
  A most unpleasant case, damping
  The good spirits that should escort us
  On such journeys. You've heard, then, of the incident?

ADAM: Is it true, Your Grace? That Justice Slack,
  Put under house arrest, he lost his head—
  The fool. He hung himself?

WALTER:                     He did.
  Making what was already bad, worse yet.
  For what at first appeared excusable
  Confusion in his affairs now looks more like
  Embezzlement, which, as you know,
  The law cannot condone. Tell me:
  How many funds do you administer?

ADAM: Five, so please Your Grace.

WALTER:                     What? Five?
  I had been led to . . . Active funds?
  I had been led to think but four.

ADAM:                     Beg pardon.
  With the Rhine-Flood-Allocation Fund?

WALTER: The Rhine-Flood-Allocation Fund? You have . . . ?
  But nowhere these days is the Rhine in flood,
  And thus no funds have been collected either.
  Tell me. Are you holding court today?

ADAM: If we . . . ?
WALTER:             What?
LINK:                          Yes. First session of the week.
WALTER: And that throng of people that I saw outside
   Crowding the hallway, they are . . . ?
ADAM:                                      They would be . . .
LINK: The litigants, Your Grace, already gathered.
WALTER: Splendid. Gentlemen, the occasion suits.
   So, if it please you, let these people enter,
   And I'll sit by t'observe how here in Howzem
   You customarily proceed.
   Later, when this session's done,
   We'll look into your funds and records.
ADAM: As you will.—Constable! Hey, Ned!

# Scene 5

*The Second Maid enters.*
SECOND MAID: The sexton's wife sends greetings to Your
                                    [Honor.
   Though she would like to lend the wig . . .
ADAM:                                      What? No?
SECOND MAID: She says her husband's wearing one himself
   Because they're holding morning service now,
   And his second wig is so unfit, she says,
   It's being sent off for repair today.
ADAM: Be damned!
SECOND MAID:      But as soon as church lets out,
   And he gets back, she'll send his good wig over.
ADAM: Upon my soul, gracious sir . . .
WALTER:                              What is it?
ADAM: A fluke of fate, an evil fluke, has robbed me
   Of both my wigs. And now a third that I
   Had hoped to borrow likewise escapes me.
   I shall be forced to preside bareheaded.
WALTER: Bareheaded?
ADAM:                 Ay, even so. And, God knows,
   Without my wig's help, I'll be hard put to it

To preserve the dignity of this court.
I'd best go look around my farm in case
—Who knows?—my tenant . . .

WALTER: Your farm? But surely
Someone in the village has a wig . . .

ADAM: No. Not a soul.

WALTER: Well. Perhaps the parson?

ADAM: The parson? That . . . ?

WALTER: The schoolmaster then.

ADAM: Ever since the old tithes were abolished
—A reform, Your Grace, that I administered
With zeal—neither church nor school can be
Relied upon.

WALTER: Well then. And your session?
Or would you wait until your hair grows in?

ADAM: Yes. With your permission, I'll send someone
To the farm to fetch it.

WALTER: How far is this farm?

ADAM: A stone's throw. Half an hour at the most.

WALTER: Half an hour? And the official hour
Long since struck? Do something! I still must
Visit Hussahey today.

ADAM: Do! But what?

WALTER: Oh, powder your head if nothing else.
Where the devil did you leave your wigs?
Do what you can. I'm pressed for time.

ADAM: Will do.

*(The Constable enters.)*

CONSTABLE: Your constable is here!

ADAM: Might I
Meanwhile suggest a hearty breakfast:
Sausage and a sip of gin.

WALTER: Thank you.

ADAM: Not at all.

WALTER: No, I say. I've had my breakfast.
Go now. Use well your time which I, in turn,
Will use to jot some observations down.

ADAM: Well, if that's your will. Come, Margaret.

WALTER: But you are badly injured, Justice Adam!
Did you fall?

ADAM:       I took a mortal tumble, ay,
  Early this morning, getting out of bed.
  A bad spill, Your Grace, across the room
  And, as I thought, headfirst into my grave.
WALTER: I am sorry. It will, I hope, not cause
  You further trouble?
ADAM:       Hardly. Hardly.
  Nor hinder me in my court duties either.
  If you'll excuse?
WALTER:     Go. Go.
ADAM:        Constable! Ho!
  You there! Get those plaintiffs! March!
         *(Adam, the Maid, and the Constable exit.)*

# Scene 6

*Enter Mrs. Martha, Eve, Veit, and Ruprecht.*
MRS. MARTHA: You feckless pitcher-smashing rabble, you!
  You'll pay for this!
VEIT:       Calm down, Mistress Martha.
  Calm. The matter will be settled here.
MRS. MARTHA: Oh, yes. Settled! You hear this glib-mouth?
  My broken pitcher will be settled on me.
  And who—pray—will settle on me—how?—
  My undone pitcher. Piece by piece may be?
  Here this only can be settled: that I
  May keep what's gone for good—a settlement
  I wouldn't pay a shattered shard to win.
VEIT: If you can prove your case, look here—
  I will replace it.
MRS. MARTHA:    Replace my pitcher?
  Replace, you say, if I can prove my case?
  Replace it on its shelf at home. *Re*place?
  It? My pitcher? That knew its place far better
  Than some people I could mention? It can't be done!
VEIT: You heard! Why babble? What more can one do?
  If any one of us broke you your pitcher
  We will gladly make amends.

MRS. MARTHA:                    Amends, he says,
  Sounding as dumb as my cow Nell.
  You think that Justice is a master potter?
  Oh, if the rulers of this earth themselves
  Tied aprons on and slipped it in the kiln,
  Better they use it for a chamber pot
  Than try to amend me the damage done.
RUPRECHT: Let her be, Father. The old dragon. Come.
  It's not the broken pitcher's rankling her.
  It's the marriage that has sprung a leak
  And that she hopes, by force, to patch up here.
  As for me, though, I'd gladly kick her crock
  To kingdom come, since I'll be damned if I
  Will ever marry that slut now.
MRS. MARTHA: Vain pup! Me patch that marriage here? Not I!
  That marriage isn't worth a single piece
  Of my crashed pitcher, and if that wedlock
  Sparkled here as bright as stood my pitcher
  On its shelf but yesterday, me, I'd swing
  It up and crack it clanging on his head.
  But here—to pick and patch those pieces up?
  Patch that?
EVE: Ruprecht!
RUPRECHT:      Keep away!
EVE:                            Dearest Ruprecht!
RUPRECHT: Out of my sight!
EVE:                              I implore you, Ruprecht!
RUPRECHT: You miserable . . . I won't say what.
EVE: Just let me say a single word, in secret.
RUPRECHT:                                        No!
EVE: You'll soon be called to your regiment.
  Oh, Ruprecht, who knows, once you've shouldered arms,
  If I shall see you alive again?
  War it is—remember—war to which you go.
  Would you part with me in anger then?
RUPRECHT: Anger? No, God forbid, I won't do that.
  God grant you as much prosperity as
  He can spare. But when I come home from war,
  Sound in body and tempered hard as steel,

And if I live to eighty here in Howzem,
Even on my deathbed, I will call you whore!
You've come to testify to that—or no?
MRS. MARTHA *(to Eve)*:
　Away! I warned you, Eve. You relish
　More of his abuse? The corporal now,
　The worthy Pegleg, there's a catch for you—
　A man who caned his way up through the ranks
　Unlike that dolt there whose back will shortly
　Feel the cane. Today we'll make the match
　And have the wedding, too, and if there be
　A christening as well, that's fine with me,
　And gladly I'd be buried, too, if but,
　Today, I crush this haughty cock whose pride
　Swells up to such a pitch he cracks my crocks.
EVE: Mother. Forget the pitcher. Or let me see
　If I can find some craftsman hereabout
　Who can mend it to your satisfaction.
　And if he fails, take all that I have saved
　And buy yourself a new one. But who would
　Cause such turmoil or so much mischief
　For the sake of a pitcher made of clay,
　And had it come down from the days of Herod.
MRS. MARTHA: What you say shows what you know: nothing.
　Are you so eager, then, to sit in stocks;
　To do penance in the church next Sunday?
　Your good name, girl, with this pitcher fell
　And, with it, broke in the eyes of all,
　If not in the Lord's nor in yours or mine.
　The only craftsman I can turn to now
　Are judge and constable; the pillory,
　The whip, that's what's needed here,
　And that whole rabble burning at the stake
　For our good name to get its luster back
　And this my pitcher to be glazed again.

# Scene 7

*Adam enters in his robes of office, but without his wig.*

ADAM *(aside):* Oh, Eve! And look. That burly-shouldered ox,
   Young Ruprecht. Ay, look. The whole pack is here!
   Surely they wouldn't dare charge me, their judge,
   In my own court?

EVE:                Oh, Mother, come. I beg you.
   Let's flee this room where we but court disaster.

ADAM: Tell me, Link, my friend, what's their complaint?

LINK: God knows. Much ado about little or nothing.
   From what I gather a pitcher's been broken.

ADAM: A pitcher? So? Ay, ay, and who broke it?

LINK: Who broke it?

ADAM:                Yes, Link, who?

LINK:                                Sit down. You'll learn.

ADAM *(to Eve, secretly):* Eve?

EVE *(also secretly):*          Keep away!

ADAM:                                One word.

EVE:                                        Don't talk
                                                [to me!

ADAM: What brings you here?

EVE:                        I told you, keep away.

ADAM: I beg you, Eve—what does all this mean?

EVE: If you don't . . . I said, leave me alone!

ADAM *(to Link):*
   Listen, friend. My soul! I'll never get through this.
   My shin-bone bruise, it's turned my stomach sour.
   I'll leave this case to you. I'm going to bed.

LINK: To bed? You want to . . . ? I do believe you're mad.

ADAM: Hang it, Link, my whole supper's surging up.

LINK: Stark, raving mad! What? No sooner come than . . .
   Oh, as you wish. Go tell the District Judge.
   He may allow it. God knows. What's wrong with you?

ADAM *(to Eve):* By the world's wounds, Eve, I beg you tell me—
   What brings you here?

EVE:                         You'll find out soon enough.
ADAM: Is it just that pitcher there your mother
   Holds, that I . . . ?
EVE:                    Yes. Only the broken pitcher.
ADAM: And nothing else?
EVE:               Nothing.
ADAM:                      You're sure? Nothing?
EVE: Go, I said. Leave me in peace.
ADAM:                         By God, Eve,
   And I say, watch your step. Be prudent.
EVE: I? For shame!
ADAM:           The certificate is all made out:
   "Ruprecht Puddle" writ in big black script.
   It's in my pocket, this one, signed and sealed.
   Hear it crackle? I'll give it to you, Eve,
   I promise you, a year from now, to use
   As pattern paper for your mourning clothes
   When word arrives that Ruprecht died out there
   In Indonesia, laid low by some fever—
   Scarlet, yellow? Or was it jungle rot?
WALTER: There will be no speaking, Justice Adam,
   Before the session, with the litigants.
   Here sit and put your questions.
ADAM: What's that? What's he say?—Your Grace commands?
WALTER: What I command? I plainly stated that,
   Before this session opens, you must not engage
   In dubious parley with the litigants.
   Here is the place befits your office
   And the public hearing which I await.
ADAM *(aside):* Be damned. I can't make up my mind!
   I did hear something crash just as I turned to . . .
LINK *(rousing him):* Your Honor! Are you . . . ?
ADAM:                                Me? On my
                                      [honor, no!
   I'd hung it up there with the utmost care.
   Only an oaf would have . . .
LINK:               What?
ADAM:                   What?
LINK:                      I asked . . . !

ADAM: You asked if I . . . ?
LINK:                              If you were deaf, I asked.
  His Grace has called on you to open session.
ADAM: I thought . . . Who called?
LINK:                              District Judge Walter did.
ADAM *(aside):* Devil take it. It can only turn out
  One way or the other.—Coming! Coming!
  Your Grace commands? The session should commence?
WALTER: You are marvelously distraught. Why so?
ADAM: Why, yes! Beg pardon. A guinea hen of mine
  —Bought from a sailor in the Indies fleet—
  It has the pip. Now, cramming is the cure,
  But how to do that I don't know, so I
  Was asking this lass for advice. When it
  Comes to such things, I'm a fool, you see,
  And my hens are dear to me as children.
WALTER: Here. Sit down. Call and question the plaintiff.
  And you, Clerk, record what's said here.
ADAM: Your Grace wishes the trial carried out
  In accordance with all the forms of law
  Or as is customary here in Howzem?
WALTER: With due regard, as customary here,
  To the law's fixed forms, and no whit different.
ADAM: Good. Good. Your least wish will be catered to.
  Clerk, are you prepared?
LINK:                              I am at your service.
ADAM: Then Justice, take thy course!
  Plaintiff, step forward.
MRS. MARTHA:                    Here, Your Honor.
ADAM: Who are you?
MRS. MARTHA:          Who?
ADAM:                         You.
MRS. MARTHA:                      Who I . . . ?
ADAM:                                         Who you are!
  Name, rank, place of domicile, and so on.
MRS. MARTHA: Surely Your Honor's jesting.
ADAM:                                         Jesting, am I?
  I sit here in the name of Justice and,
  Mistress Martha, Justice must know who you are.

LINK *(sotto voce):* Drop your pointless questioning!

MRS. MARTHA:                                    But you,
Each Sunday as you walk out to your farm,
You look in my window!

WALTER:                    You know this woman?

ADAM: She lives, Your Grace, if you take the path
Between the hedges, just around the corner.
Widow of a gate-keeper. She midwifes now;
Otherwise she's honest, of good repute.

WALTER: Seeing that you know all this, Justice Adam,
Such questions are superfluous.
Enter her name in the record, Clerk,
And simply add: "Known to the Court."

ADAM:                                    Better yet!
You've little patience with formalities.
You, Clerk, do as His Grace commands.

WALTER: Ask now after the substance of her complaint.

ADAM: Now? Ask now . . . ?

WALTER *(impatiently):*        Ay. Elicit the substance!

ADAM: The substance, likewise, is a pitcher, if,
Sir, you'll excuse.

WALTER:            What? Likewise?

ADAM:                            A pitcher.
A common pitcher. Write down: "Pitcher,"
Clerk, and simply add: "Known to the Court."

LINK: You mean Your Honor accepts my conjecture
Based on hearsay as . . . ?

ADAM:                        My soul! If so I say,
So write. It is a pitcher, isn't it?

MRS. MARTHA: Yes. This pitcher here.

ADAM:                        You see?

MRS. MARTHA:                        My
                                    [broken . . .

ADAM: Pedantical punctilio!

LINK:            I beg your . . .

ADAM: Who broke it then? I trust that scoundrel was . . .

MRS. MARTHA: Yes. Him! That scoundrel there!

ADAM *(to himself):*                    That's all I
                                    [need.

RUPRECHT: But that's not true, Your Honor!
ADAM *(to himself):*                     Arise! Revive and
                                          [thrive, old Adam!
RUPRECHT: She's lying through her teeth!
ADAM:                                     Silence, oaf!
   You'll thrust your neck in irons quick enough.
   Clerk, enter "One pitcher" as I said before,
   Together with the name of him who broke it.
   This case will be concluded in a trice.
WALTER: Your Honor! A vehement procedure!
ADAM: How so?
WALTER:          Will you not formally . . . ?
ADAM:                                     Nay, not I.
Your Grace abhors niggling formalities.
WALTER: If, Justice Adam, you do not know
   How to preside at a court of law,
   Now is not the time nor here the place
   To instruct you. If you can preside but so,
   Step down. Perhaps your clerk knows better.
ADAM: Beg pardon. I started off the Howzem way,
   As Your Grace commanded.
WALTER:                          I what?   .
ADAM                                     'Pon my honor.
WALTER: I bade you, sir, conduct this trial
   With due regard to the law which, I take it,
   Is here the same as elsewhere in the Netherlands.
ADAM: Most humbly begging Your Grace's pardon,
   We have here, with your permission,
   Certain statutes peculiar to our village—
   Not written down, I grant you, but rather
   *Hand*ed down through time and by tradition.
   From this local code, I'm bold enough to hope,
   I have till now strayed not a jot today.
   And yet I also know your other form
   As it is practiced nowadays throughout the realm.
   You ask for proof? Just say the word! I can
   Deal justice this way, that way, as you please.
WALTER: Scarcely reassuring, Justice Adam.
   So be it. Reopen the proceedings.

ADAM: My oath on't. You'll see, and you'll be satisfied.
—Mistress Martha Rull. State your complaint.
MRS. MARTHA: My complaint, as I was saying, has to do
 With this pitcher. Before I tell what happened
 To it, though, allow me to describe
 Just what this pitcher meant to me.
ADAM: The floor is yours.
MRS. MARTHA:                    You see this pitcher,
 Worthy gentlemen? See you this pitcher?
ADAM: Ay, we see it.
MRS. MARTHA:            Nothing's what you see,
 If you'll permit. You see pieces only.
 The fairest among pitchers—smashed to bits.
 Here on this hole, where there's nothing now,
 These our Netherlandish Provinces
 Were handed over to the Spanish Philip.
 Here, in regal robes, stood Charles the Fifth;
 Of him—look you—his legs alone still stand.
 Here Philip kneeled to receive the crown.
 He lies inside, but for his buttocks,
 And they, too, suffered a rude blow.
 There his two cousins, the Queens of France
 And Hungary, moved to tears, dabbed them
 From their eyes, and if you can make out, here,
 This lonely hand lifting its handkerchief,
 It is as if, poor thing, it mourns its fate.
 Here, among the retinue, Sir Philibert
 Leans on his sword, though he, by rights, should fall,
 And Maximilian too, the rogue, since both
 Their swords are broken off from hilt to tip.
 Here, in the middle, with his holy hat,
 The Archbishop of Arras stood, but him
 The Devil took—both man and mitre—
 Leaving his shadow only, stretched out black
 Along the cobblestones. In the background,
 Here, the royal guard stood tightly ranked,
 With upright pikes and clustered halberds thick.
 Here houses—look you—fronting the Great Square
 Of Brussels; and here's a face still gazing

From a window, though what there's now to see
I wouldn't know.

ADAM: Mistress Martha!
  Spare us, please, the broken treaty, unless
  You think it pertinent to your complaint.
  It is the hole—and not the provinces
  Therein handed over—that concerns us.

MRS. MARTHA: Beg pardon, no! The pitcher's beauty *is*,
  Your Honor, pertinent to my complaint!
  'Twas claimed as booty when the Prince of Orange
  And his quick men took Brill, by Childeric,
  The tinker. A Spaniard had just hoisted it,
  Filled with wine, to drink from, when this tinker
  Strikes him from behind, snatches up the pitcher,
  Drinks it dry, and forges on.

ADAM: A worthy patriot!

MRS. MARTHA: It next passed on, when the tinker died,
  To Gravedigger Godfear, who drank from it
  But three times in his life, the sober man,
  Each time watering his wine. The first was when
  —Sixty if a day—he wed a wife
  As young as he was old. The second when,
  Three years pass by, she bears a bouncing babe.
  But then she bore him fifteen more, and so
  He drank from it the third time when she died.

ADAM: Well! And well done, too!

MRS. MARTHA: Whereat the pitcher fell into the hands
  Of one Zacchaeus, tailor of Tirlemont,
  Who told my late departed—rest his soul—
  With his own lips, what I will tell you now.
  He threw this pitcher, when the French were looting,
  With all his movables, out his window,
  Then leapt himself and broke his neck, the oaf,
  While this, this earthen pitcher, this thing of clay,
  Came down, foot-first, without a crack.

ADAM: To the point, Mistress Martha! Come to the point!

MRS. MARTHA: So when the Fire of Sixty-Six broke out,
  My husband had it then—God rest his soul . . .

ADAM: Blast it, woman. Are you not finished yet?

MRS. MARTHA: If, Your Honor, you don't wish me to speak,
I'm out of place here, so I'll take me off
And search me out a court that *will* listen.
WALTER: You should indeed speak here, but not of things
That have no bearing on this case. Simply
Tell us the pitcher's worth to you, and that,
For us to judge your case, will be enough.
MRS. MARTHA: How much you need to know to judge a case
I wouldn't know nor won't inquire into.
But this I do know, that I, to plead my case,
Must be allowed to tell you a thing or two.
WALTER: Well then. Briefly. What happened to the pitcher?
What? What in Sixty-Six did happen
To the pitcher? Shall we ever hear?
What happened to that pitcher?
MRS. MARTHA:                              What happened?
Nothing—begging your pardons, gentlemen—
Nothing happened to it in Sixty-Six.
Not a single thing. It remained, Sirs,
Even in the midst of all the flames,
Whole, and when, the morning after, I
Plucked it from the ashes, it was glazed
And gleaming as if taken from the kiln.
WALTER: Now then. Now we're acquainted with your pitcher
And know all that has or has not happened
To it. And now?
MRS. MARTHA:     Now, this pitcher here, which,
Lo, though cracked, yet remains a pitcher
Fit for a lady's lip to touch nor unfit
Either for a regent's wife to sip from,
This my pitcher, you two noble judges,
Has been broken by that scoundrel there.
ADAM: Who?
MRS. MARTHA: Him there. Ruprecht!
RUPRECHT:                              That's a lie,
Your Honor!
ADAM:        Silence until you're questioned, you!
Your turn will come in time today, young man.
—You have this in the record, Link?

LINK:                                        Yes, yes.
ADAM: Describe the incident, worthy Mistress Martha.
MRS. MARTHA: It was eleven yesterday . . .
ADAM:                              When's that?
MRS. MARTHA: Eleven.
ADAM:                  In the morning!
MRS. MARTHA:                        Beg pardon, no.
   At night, and I in bed about to snuff
   The wick, when suddenly I'm frighted by
   This din of quarreling men, of tumult,
   As if the Fiend himself had broken in,
   That comes up to me from my daughter's room.
   I rush downstairs, I find her door burst open,
   A flood of furious curses pouring out,
   And when I lift my candle to throw light
   On all these goings-on, what, Your Honor,
   Do I find now? What now I find? I find
   That pitcher lying shattered all across
   The room, a piece in every corner;
   That girl wringing her hands, and that dolt there
   Fuming, frenzied, in the middle of the room.
ADAM (*shattered*): Ay. Damn it.
MRS. MARTHA:                What say?
ADAM:                                Just think of it!
MRS. MARTHA:                                      [Yes!—
   Then it's as if such righteous fury
   Grew me ten new arms, the fingers clawed as sharp
   As vultures and I dig right in and ask:
   What business had he there, at this late hour,
   Smashing my pitchers like a madman, pray?
   And he to this replies—now you just guess.
   The shameless ruffian, that rascal there.
   Oh, I'll see him stretched upon the rack
   Or take no pleasure on my back again!
   He says it was another who toppled me
   My pitcher off its shelf—another, if you please—
   Who'd slipped away the moment he rushed in.
   Then heaps abuse on my poor daughter's head.
ADAM: It smells. It smells. Whereat?

MRS. MARTHA:                              Whereat, Sir,
   I stare my questions as the girl, who stands
   There like a corpse, and, "Eve," I say.
   She sits. I ask, "Was it another, then?"
   And, "Joseph and Maria!" cries the child,
   "What did you think then, Mother?"—"So? Who then?"
   —"Who else?" says she—"and who else could it be?"
   And swears to me that *he* it was who did it.
EVE: What did I swear? What did I swear to you?
   Nothing did I swear.
MRS. MARTHA:          Eve!
EVE:                              No. You lie . . .
RUPRECHT: There! You hear?
ADAM:                              Dog! Damn your hide! Shut up,
   Or see this fist? I'll ram it down your throat.
   Your time will come. But later. Not quite yet.
MRS. MARTHA: You say you did not . . . ?
EVE:                                        Mother, you twist
                                             [the truth.

   God knows it hurts me to my soul's core
   That I must publicly declare this here.
   But I swore to nothing, to nothing did I swear.
ADAM: Now, children, let's be reasonable.
LINK: This is strange.
MRS. MARTHA:          Eve! Did you not assure me—
   Not call on Joseph and Maria then?
EVE: Not as an oath. Not swearing! To this, now,
   I *do* swear by Joseph and Maria.
ADAM: Ay, neighbors. Ay, Mistress Martha, what's afoot?
   There is no need to bully the poor child.
   Give her a moment to mull things over,
   Calmly to recollect what did occur—
   I say, what *did* occur and, I might add,
   What still, should she speak injudiciously,
   Still *can* occur—why then, you'll see, she'll say
   The very same today as yesterday,
   Whether she swears to it or not.
   Leave Joseph and Maria out of this.

WALTER: No, Justice Adam, no! How can you give
   Your witness such dubious instruction?
MRS. MARTHA: If she can boldly tell me to my face—
   Shamelessly—the young slut, her there,
   That it was another man than Ruprecht,
   She can, so far as I'm concerned—can—
   Oh, I won't say what she can do. But I,
   I, Your Honor, do assure you—
   Though I can't swear she swore to it—
   That yesterday she said he was the one.
   And to that, by Joseph and Maria, I do swear!
ADAM: Well, but that's all the girl herself . . .
WALTER:                              Justice!
ADAM: Your Grace?—What's he say?—Aren't I right, dear Eve?
MRS. MARTHA: Out with it! Is that not what you said?
   Did you not yesterday not say that to me?
EVE: Who denies I said it?
ADAM:                    There you have it!
RUPRECHT: The whore!
ADAM:               Clerk, take note.
VEIT:                          Fie. Shame. Shame on
                                          [you!
WALTER: Your performance, Justice Adam—I simply
   Know not what to think of it. If you
   Yourself had smashed that pitcher you could not
   Display more zeal than now you do
   To fix the blame on that young man.
   Clerk, you will, I trust, enter this only—
   The girl admits to her yesterday's
   Confession, not though to its truth.
   Is it now time to call the girl as witness?
ADAM: Upon my soul, if it's not her turn yet
   Men are fools and the law needs mending.
   Who else should I question? The accused?
   Faith, I'll gladly listen to good counsel.
WALTER: *Sancta simplicitas!* Yes, question the accused.
   Question and be done. Just question him.
   This is the last case that you'll ever try.

ADAM: The last? What? Ay, of course! The accused!
  What, indeed, old judge, were you thinking of?
  Damn that pip-sick guinea hen of mine!
  Why couldn't she have croaked in Djakarta
  Of some native plague? It's that noodle dumpling—
  It sticks in my wits like glue.

WALTER:                  What sticks?
  What sort of dumpling's this?

ADAM:                  Noodle, Sir.
  The noodle dumpling I should cram my hen with.
  If she won't swallow the pill—the cluck—
  She . . . Why, there's no telling what she'll do.

WALTER: Damn your pips and pills, man. Do your task.

ADAM: Accused! Stand forward.

RUPRECHT:              Here stands, Your Honor,
  Ruprecht, Veit the crofter's son, of Howzem.

ADAM: You heard what Mistress Martha there just now
  Accused you of before this bench?

RUPRECHT: I did, Your Honor.

ADAM:                And you make so bold
  As to offer objections to her charge—what?
  Dare you then, like a godforsaken sinner,
  Go so far as to plead innocent?
  Or do you confess?

RUPRECHT:        You ask, Your Honor,
  If I have objections. Well! If you'll permit:
  Not a word of what she said is true.

ADAM: So? And you think you can prove that here?

RUPRECHT: I do.

ADAM:        The worthy Mistress Martha, you there . . .
  Just be calm. There is no need to worry.

WALTER: And why, Your Honor, this concern for *her*?

ADAM: Why? By God, must I, as a good Christian,
  Sit idly by while . . . . ?

WALTER:            State what you know
  In your defense.—Clerk, can you preside?

ADAM: Hah! Rubbish!

LINK:          If I . . . ? Well, should Your Grace . . .

ADAM: Why do you stare? You've something to depose?

—Does not this ass look more like an ox?—
What have you to depose?
RUPRECHT:                            Depose? Who, me?
WALTER: You, yes, should now relate what happened.
RUPRECHT: My God, if you would only let me speak!
WALTER *(to Adam):* In truth, sir, 'tis not to be endured.
RUPRECHT: Close on ten it must have been last night—
   And this one January night as warm
   As May—when I say to Father: "Father,
   I'll go have another word with Eve,"
   Because I wanted then to marry her,
   You understand. A sturdy girl. I saw
   Her once at harvest time; the men below
   Were pitching hay to her and she was laying it
   As quick as if bewitched, and so I said,
   "Well, yes or no?" And she said, "Oh, go take
   Your cackle elsewhere!" But later she said yes.
ADAM: Stick to the point! "Cackle?" What? "I said,
   'Yes or no,' and later she says yes."
RUPRECHT: Ay, God's truth, Your Honor.
ADAM:                               Proceed! Proceed!
RUPRECHT:                                         [Well—
   So then I said: "Father, did you hear me?
   Let me go. It's just to chat a while
   By her window."—"Well then," he said, "go.
   But you'll remain outside and not go in?"
   "I give my word," I say. "Then go," he says,
   "But you be back here by eleven, son."
ADAM: "He said," "I said," and so on and no end.
   Will you soon have had your say?
RUPRECHT:                               "Well," say I,
   "I will be back by then," and take my cap
   And leave and set off down the footbridge path,
   But the brook's so high the bridge is out,
   So I turn back toward town when suddenly,
   Damn, I think, you've botched it, Ruprecht.
   The gate at Mistress Martha's house—it's locked,
   Since Eve knows if I haven't come by ten
   I won't be coming, so she locks it then.

ADAM: A shady business that.

WALTER:                          And then?

RUPRECHT:                               So then
  I'm heading up to Martha's on Linden Lane,
  Where the trees in rows arch overhead
  And make it dark as Utrecht cathedral,
  When up ahead I hear the gate hinge squeak.
  Thank God, I think, that means Eve's still there;
  And look ahead with joy to where my ears
  First heard this news, and then I curse my eyes
  As blind for seeing what they see, and pack
  Them off again to take a better look
  And this time call them rotten slanderers,
  A pair of good-for-nothing scandalmongers,
  And drive them out a third time, thinking when
  They've done their job they'll wrench loose and take
  Up service elsewhere. It's Eve they see.
  I recognize her dress. And someone's there beside her.

ADAM: So? Someone else? Who then, Know-it-all?

RUPRECHT: Who? My God, you ask me . . . ?

ADAM:                               Well, what else?
  Uncaught is unhung, as the old saw has it.

WALTER: Go on. On with your tale.—Let the man talk!
  Why these constant interruptions, Justice Adam?

RUPRECHT: Now I can't take a Bible oath on this,
  Since when it's dark all cats look gray,
  But you should know that Cobbler Lebrecht who
  Not long ago got his deferment—
  He's been after Eve. Last fall I told her:
  "Look, Eve, I don't like the way he prowls
  Around your house. Tell him you've got other
  Fish to fry, because if you don't warn him off,
  By God, I'll hurl him out of here myself."
  —"You can't be serious," she says, and tells him
  Something—who knows?—neither flesh nor fowl.
  So then I pick him up and throw him out.

ADAM: So? Lebrecht is his name?

RUPRECHT:                     Lebrecht, yes.

ADAM:                              Good.

We have a name. Proceeding nicely now.
You've got this in the record, Clerk?
LINK: Oh yes, and the rest as well, Your Honor.
ADAM: Then speak, Ruprecht. Speak on, Ruprecht, my son.
RUPRECHT: It hits me—it's eleven when I see
These two; I always left at ten—hits
All at once. I think, "The nick of time.
Your antlers haven't sprouted yet. But feel
Your forehead now: is something horny
Pushing through?" I slip quiet through the gate
And crouch behind a hedge, and hear a whisper
Get a teasing answer, hear a pull
Away from and a tug back to, Your Honor,
Until, my soul, I think that I will die of . . .
EVE: Wretch. Oh, how low and mean of you!
MRS. MARTHA: Scoundrel!
You, when I get you alone, I'll teach you
I have teeth! You wait! I'll pick a bone
With you, pup, that will make you yelp!
RUPRECHT: A quarter of an hour this goes on.
I think: What now—will wedding night be next?
And there I am, still wondering, when, *whisht,*
Not waiting for the parson, into the house
They go.
EVE: Go, Mother. Let happen here what will.
ADAM: Hush you there, I say, or thunder strike you,
Impudent chatterbox! Wait until
I bid you speak.
WALTER: Most strange, by God!
RUPRECHT: And then
It wells, Your Honor Adam, it wells up
In me like a burst of blood. Give me air!
Off pops a button from my chest: Now. Air!
I rip my collar open. Give me air!
And run, shove, kick, batter—because I find
The slut's door locked—stand back a step,
Then boot the door once more, hard, and in.
ADAM: Ay! Blazes, boy!
RUPRECHT: And as it bangs wide open

That pitcher topples from its shelf in there
And—*whoosh*—out the window this figure leaps.
I see those coattails flapping even now.
ADAM: And that was this Cobbler Lebrecht?
RUPRECHT:                               Who else?
Eve just stands there. I shove her aside
And, rushing to the window, find him snagged,
Hanging from the trellis that the grapevines
Climb to reach the roof. The handle to the door,
It's in my hand from when I yanked it out,
So now I bring it down and thump his skull, which,
Your Honor, was all that I could reach from there.
ADAM: A handle, you say?
RUPRECHT:                What?
ADAM:                          You used . . . ?
RUPRECHT:                                    Door
                                          [handle, yes.

ADAM: So.
LINK:      You thought it was a dagger, I suppose?
ADAM: A dagger? I . . . ? Why so?
RUPRECHT:                          A dagger?
LINK:                                    Ah well,
One's hearing can play tricks on one. Besides,
One can so easily confuse the two.
ADAM: I think . . .
LINK:               Why yes. The handle's shaft, Your Honor?
ADAM: The shaft?
RUPRECHT:        No. Not the shaft, but turned around.
ADAM: The other end? Turned? The handle?
LINK:                                    Mm hm!
RUPRECHT: Well, yes. There was a lump of lead on it,
Which, I'll admit, you could take for a hilt.
ADAM: Yes, for a hilt.
LINK:                  A dagger's hilt, for instance,
Yes, it had to be a fearsome weapon
Of some sort. I was convinced of that.
WALTER: Gentlemen. To business here. Proceed.
ADAM: Nothing but claptrap, Clerk.—You there, proceed!
RUPRECHT: So he falls down and then, about to turn,

I see this shadow scramble to its feet.
"You're still alive down there?" I think, and leap
Onto the sill to stop him in his tracks
When, Sirs, as I'm about to jump, up flies
Into my face this sand, a handful of it,
And him, the night, the world, that window sill
I'm standing on—all, so help me God,
When that hail hits me in the eyes and stings,
Then everything at one fell swoop goes black.

ADAM: Be damned! And who did that?

RUPRECHT:                       Who? Why, Lebrecht!

ADAM: The villain!

RUPRECHT:         By God! *If* it was the cobbler.

ADAM: If? Who else?

RUPRECHT:            So then, as if a storm
Had swept me off a cliff ten fathoms high,
I fall back off that sill into the room
And think I'll go right through the floor, but no,
My neck, it isn't broken after all,
Nor back, nor hip, nor anything, though he
For sure had meanwhile got clean away,
And I sit up and rub my eyes and there,
She's coming toward me and "Oh, God," she says,
And "Ruprecht, are you hurt?" Me? Good Lord!
I cock one leg and kick. Where I kicked
I couldn't see, and a good thing too.

ADAM: Still blinded by the sand?

RUPRECHT:                 The sand? Oh. Yes.

ADAM: Be damned! A bullseye, eh?

RUPRECHT:                   Then I get up.
What's the point of dirtying my knuckles?
So I tongue-lash her, call her a filthy whore,
And think: that's all that she deserves.
But tears, you know, keep me from saying more.
Then in comes Mistress Martha, lifts her lamp,
And now, in front of me, I see that girl,
Trembling like a leaf, pitiful—she
Who was so lively and so full of cheer;
And so I think: being blind is not so bad.

I'd gladly given both my eyes away.
Agates—take them—for a game of marbles.
EVE: He, he is not worth . . . Wretch!
ADAM: You there! Silence!
RUPRECHT: The rest you know.
ADAM: What? The rest?
RUPRECHT: Oh, well,
    Mistress Martha, she began to rave,
    And Rolph the neighbor came, and Henk, another,
    And then Aunt Nell and Bess, they came in, too,
    And man and maid and cat and dog ran in—
    A huge to-do—and Mistress Martha asked
    That girl there who had smashed her pitcher,
    And she, she said—well, you know—that I had.
    And, on my soul, she wasn't far wrong, either.
    The pitcher she brought to the well I broke,
    And the cobbler has a hole in his head.
ADAM: Mistress Martha, what say you to this?
    Speak!
MRS. MARTHA: What say I, you say, to this? I say,
    Your Honor, that his words sneak like weasels,
    Killing the truth as 'twere a cackling hen,
    And that whosoever loves Justice should
    Reach for a stout club and do this night-fiend in.
ADAM: You will have to prove your charge against him.
MRS. MARTHA: Prove my charge? Gladly. Here is my witness.—
                               [Speak.

ADAM: Your daughter? No, no, Mistress Martha.
WALTER: No? Why not?
ADAM: As witness, gracious Sir? Is it not written
    In *titulo quarto* of the codex—
    Or is it *quinto*—that when pitchers—
    Or something anyway, who knows what?—
    Are broken by young scallawags,
    No daughter may bear witness for her mother?
WALTER: Within your head, ignorance and knowledge
    Lie kneaded into one, as in some dough.
    With each slice you cut, you give me both.
    The young woman is not speaking now

As witness, but merely to inform the court.
If and for whom she will or may bear witness
Will be determined by her deposition.
ADAM: Deposition, yes. Good. *Titulo sexto.*
  But what she says is not to be believed.
WALTER: Step forward, child.
ADAM:                          Hey, Liza!—If I may!
  My tongue's dried out on me.—Margaret!


# Scene 8

*A maid enters.*
ADAM: A glass of water!
THE MAID:                 Yes, Sir!
                          *(Exits.)*
ADAM:                              Perhaps you'd care . . . ?
WALTER: Thank you.
ADAM:                 French? Moselle? Whichever you
                                              [prefer.
  *(Walter merely bows. The maid brings water and exits.)*


# Scene 9

ADAM: If I may be so bold, Your Grace, to venture
  An opinion, this case seems well suited
  For a settlement to which both sides agree.
WALTER: Settlement? In this case? I have my doubts.
  Reasonable people can settle their disputes,
  It's true, but how *you* can do so now,
  With the case as yet entirely unsolved,
  I would be truly pleased to hear from you.
  Tell me, Justice Adam, how would you
  Arrange it? You've settled on the culprit?
ADAM: Upon my soul! If I, seeing that the law
  Has left me in the lurch, turn to philosophy
  For help, then it was . . . Lebrecht.

WALTER:                              Who?

ADAM:                                        Or Ruprecht . . .

WALTER: Who?

ADAM:             Or Lebrecht, ay, who broke the pitcher.

WALTER: Which was it, then? Ruprecht here, or Lebrecht?
  It seems you grope for your decision
  Like a hand thrust into a sack of peas.

ADAM: With your permiss . . .

WALTER:                         Shut up. Shut up, I beg you.

ADAM: As you wish. On my honor, it would be fine
  With me if it had been the both of them.

WALTER: Ask there. And you will learn the truth.

ADAM:                                        Glad to.
  Still, if *you* can solve this, call me a knave.
  —The record is prepared for deposition?

LINK: It is.

ADAM:     Good.

LINK:             I turn a new leaf over,
  Eager to learn what I shall write on it.

ADAM: A new leaf? Well done.

WALTER:                       Speak now, child.

ADAM: Speak, Eve. You heard the man. So now, speak up.
  Yield unto the Lord—you hear me, child?—
  To Him and to the world yield up a morsel
  Of the truth. Think that in this court you stand
  Before God's Judgment Seat and so must not
  Deceive your judge with lies and pointless babble.
  But, fah. You are no fool. You know
  A judge remains to judge again,
  And this Jack needs him one day, and the next
  Another. Say you say 'twas Lebrecht. Fine.
  Or say you say 'twas Ruprecht. That's fine, too.
  Say thus or so and, if things turn not out
  As you would wish them to, I'm no honest man.
  But should you prate here of some other he,
  Some third, perhaps, and name another name,
  Why, who in Howzem would believe you, girl,
  Or who in all the Netherlands? The walls,
  They say, have ears, but make poor witnesses,

And him you might accuse can well defend
Himself, or no? While Ruprecht, what of him?
WALTER: If you would only cease this gibberish
Which lacks all rhyme and reason!
ADAM:                              Your Grace?
You failed to follow me?
WALTER:               Oh, proceed!
You've spoken from this bench quite long enough.
ADAM: It's true, Your Grace, I never studied,
But though to such learnèd men of Utrecht
As yourself my speech is all a jumble,
It could be different with these simple folk.
I'll wager you that girl understood me.
MRS. MARTHA: What's this now? Straight talk, and out with it!
EVE: Oh, dearest Mother!
MRS. MARTHA:              You—I'm telling you!
RUPRECHT: My soul, straight talk comes hard, Mistress Martha,
When your conscience sticks in your craw.
ADAM:                              Enough,
Jackanapes! Hold your tongue!
MRS. MARTHA:                 Who was it?
EVE: O Jesus!
MRS. MARTHA: That dolt there? That wretched crook!
O Jesus, as if she were a common whore.
Was it our Lord Jesus?
ADAM:               Mistress Martha!
What a thing to . . . ! Leave the poor girl be!
To fright the child so! "Whore"?—Nitwit!—
Such talk won't help. In time she will remember.
RUPRECHT: Ay, she'll remember.
ADAM:                     Dummox! Clod! Silence!
RUPRECHT: The cobbler will be on the tip of her tongue.
ADAM: Satan take him! Call the constable! Ho! Ned!
RUPRECHT: Now, now. I'll keep my peace. Leave it be.
She'll give you my name soon enough.
MRS. MARTHA: Listen, you. Don't make me a scandal here.
For nine and forty years I've been of good
Repute. My birthday is on February three.
Today's the first. So make it short. Who was it?

ADAM: Well said, I say! Good, Mistress Martha Rull.

MRS. MARTHA: Your father's dying words were these: "Martha?
    You find our daughter a good man, you hear?
    But should she turn into a common slut,
    Then pay a guilder to the gravedigger
    To turn me on my back again, because,
    Upon my soul, the thought would spin me over.

ADAM: And that's not bad, either.

MRS. MARTHA:                          If now, Eve,
    You honor, as the Fourth Commandment bids,
    Your father and your mother, then say: I,
    Eve, admitted to my room the cobbler,
    Or some other man—not, though, my intended.

RUPRECHT: Leave her alone! Forget your pitcher.
    I'll gladly lug it off to Utrecht.
    That old crock? I only wish I *had* smashed it.

EVE: Mean-spirited boy! Fie. You should be ashamed
    You cannot say, "It's true. I broke that pitcher"—
    Ashamed you cannot trust in what I do.
    Did I not give my hand to you and say,
    "I will," when you asked, "Will you have me, Eve"?
    You think the cobbler a better man than you?
    And even had you through the keyhole seen
    Him drinking with me from that pitcher,
    Still you should have thought: My Eve is honest
    And all will turn out well and to her honor,
    If not in this life, then hereafter, and when
    We rise again there'll be another day.

RUPRECHT: By my soul, Eve, that's too long for me to wait.
    What I can lay my hands on, I'll believe.

EVE: Say that Lebrecht had been in my room
    —Why, may I die an eternal death—
    Why could I not confide in you, my love?
    But there, before those neighbors, servants, maids?
    Or say that I had reason to conceal
    His or whoever's visit—why, then—
    Oh, Ruprecht, say—why could I not,
    Trusting in your trust in me, say it
    Was you? Why not? Why could I not do so?

RUPRECHT: Oh, devil take it. Say it. I don't mind—
   If that will keep your neck out of the stocks.
EVE: Oh, what a monster! What ingratitude!
   That's all that you deserve: that I be spared
   The stocks. *And* this: that I, with one small word,
   Should get my honor back, but send *you* off
   To your destruction.
WALTER:                    What? And this one word?
   So it was not Ruprecht after all?
EVE: No, gracious Sir, since he will have it so.
   For his sake only, I kept silent.
   The earthen pitcher Ruprecht did not break.
   If he himself denies it, it is so.
MRS. MARTHA: Eve! Not Ruprecht?
EVE:                         No, Mother. No.
   And if I said so yesterday, I lied.
MRS. MARTHA: I'll crack you every bone in your body!
                    *(She sets the pitcher down.)*
EVE: Do what you will.
WALTER: *(threateningly):* Mistress Martha!
ADAM:                              Ho! Constable!
   Pitch the old hag out of here!
   —And why, pray, did it have to be Ruprecht
   And none other? Were you under the bed? What?
   I trust the girl herself should know who it was.
   If it wasn't Lebrecht, call me a rogue.
MRS. MARTHA: Don't tell me it was Lebrecht! Tell me—was it?
ADAM: Speak, Eve, dear girl. Was it not Lebrecht, child?
EVE: You shameless creature! Base and wretched man!
   How can you say that Lebrecht was . . . ?
WALTER:                              Girl!
   How dare you? Is this, then, the respect
   You owe this court and him your justice?
EVE:                              I owe?
   That justice there? Ha! That poor sinner who
   Himself deserves to stand before a judge?
   He, who knows too well what man it was?
                    *(She turns to face Justice Adam.)*
   Did not you yourself send Lebrecht into

Town to the Commission of Conscription
In Utrecht yesterday? Did you not send
With him his papers of deferment, signed?
How can you say that it was Lebrecht, then,
Knowing full well that he was gone all day?
ADAM: Well, but who else then? If it isn't Lebrecht
—Devil take it!—nor this Ruprecht, nor
That Lebrecht, nor . . . What are you up to?
RUPRECHT: My soul, Your Honor, if I may speak,
The girl's not lying about this at least,
Because I myself met Lebrecht early
Yesterday, just setting off for Utrecht,
And unless he stole a horse, that lad,
With his bandy legs, could never hope
To be back here by ten o'clock at night.
ADAM: Nonsense! Bandy legs? Dunce, that fellow,
He can hoof it as quick as the next man.
May my bunghole grow together if
A sheep dog—oh, about so high, say—wouldn't
Have to pant hard to keep pace with him.
WALTER: Tell us what occurred.
ADAM:                                       Your Grace's pardon.
On this point, Sir, the girl will serve you ill.
WALTER: Ill serve? Ill serve *me*? And why's that?
ADAM: Slow-witted, poor thing. Good heart, but slow.
A child, really. Only just confirmed.
Blushes when she sees a beard. Her sort,
They'll do it in the dark, but let the sun
Come up, they'll swear they never did.
WALTER: You are, Justice Adam, in all things
Touching the girl, most considerate.
ADAM: Truth to tell, Judge Walter, Sir, her father
Was a friend of mine. Should Your Grace
Be merciful today, we'll do no more
Than is our duty, and let his daughter go.
WALTER: I feel a growing inclination, Justice,
To plumb this matter to the very bottom.
—Speak up, child. Tell us who broke the pitcher.
You stand before no person now who,
Had you erred, would not forgive you.

EVE: Worthy, worshipful, and gracious Sir,
   Spare me the telling of a full account.
   Read no mischief into my refusal.
   Providence, the law of heaven, bids
   Me keep silent in this case. I shall,
   However, if you command, testify
   And swear to this on any altar,
   That Ruprecht did not break that pitcher.
   The events of yesterday, however,
   And all that they entail, are private.
   My mother has no right here to demand
   —In order to unravel the one sole strand
   That is her own—the entire skein
   Of this long yarn. I cannot say, not here,
   Who broke that pitcher, because to do so
   I would have to speak of others' secrets
   Which have no bearing on the pitcher.
   Soon or late, I will let my mother know,
   But this tribunal, Sir, is not the place
   For her to exercise her right to ask.
ADAM: No right at all. Upon my honor, no.
   The lass knows all the loopholes! If she swears
   To what she said just now before this court,
   The complaint her mother lodged is void,
   And no objection can be raised to that.
WALTER: What say you, Mistress Martha, to what she said?
MRS. MARTHA: If, if, if, Your Worship, I say nothing
   To the point at once, if I can't speak,
   I beg you to believe it is because
   A stroke this minute paralyzed my tongue.
   History provides examples by
   The score of wretches who, to save their honor,
   Perjured themselves before the judgment seat,
   But that any should, before a holy altar,
   Swear to a lie to win a seat in the stocks—
   Whoever heard of such a thing before?
   Had it been proven here that someone else,
   Not Ruprecht, but another, had slipped
   Into her chamber yesterday—if such
   A thing were possible, you understand—

I would not waste another minute here.
I'd go and, home, first thing I'd do, I'd put
A chair before the door for her to start
Another trade and cry: "Go, my child.
The world is wide, you're free to roam;
There's a living on the streets for those,
Like you, who have inherited long hair,
To hang yourself with when the time is ripe."

WALTER: Be calm. Calm now, Mistress Martha.

MRS. MARTHA:                              Since, though,
I can bring forward proof, by other means
Than her who refuses me that service,
And since I am convinced that he, and not
Some other man, broke me my pitcher,
This sudden eagerness of hers to swear
He's innocent now brings to mind a foul
Suspicion. The night of yesterday cloaks
Yet another crime than that of this
My pitcher's devastation. Know then,
Gracious Sir, that Ruprecht has been called up
In this draft and soon must hie him off
To Utrecht to take his oath of service.
The young sons of the fatherland, they steal away.
Suppose last night that he had said to her:
"What think you, Eve? Come. The wide world beckons,
And to both chest and coffer you have keys,"
And say that she at first refused—
Why, then, when I barged in on them, would not
The two of them—he for revenge and she
Still out of love—have acted as they did?

RUPRECHT: You old crow! What kind of talk is that?
"To both chest and coffer . . ."

WALTER:                              Silence!

EVE:                                        He?
Ruprecht a deserter? Never!

WALTER:                         Stick
To the facts! The subject is the pitcher.
Prove, prove that Ruprecht broke it!

MRS. MARTHA: Very well, Your Grace, I first will prove,

Here, that Ruprecht broke my pitcher;
Then, at home, I will look into this.
I can, you see, fetch me a tongue to prove false
Each and every word he said,
And had I dreamt she would refuse me hers,
I would have here assembled troops of tongues!
But if you'll summon Mistress Bridget now—
His aunt there—she'll be enough for me,
Since she will blast the scoundrel's main defense
Because—at half-past ten, when, mark you,
This my pitcher still was whole—she heard him
In the garden chatting up my Eve,
And how this whole tall tale he has puffed up
Will be brought crashing down by this one tongue,
This, noble judges, I leave to you to see.

RUPRECHT: Who heard?

VEIT:                          Sister Briggy?

RUPRECHT:                                    Me with Eve?
In the garden?

MRS. MARTHA:  Him, in the garden, yes,
With Eve, at half-past ten—full half an hour
Prior to the time he says he broke
That door to storm into her room—she heard
Exchange of words, now sweet, now bullying,
As if he would persuade her to some deed.

ADAM *(aside):* Be damned! The Devil's on my side now!

WALTER: Fetch that woman here.

RUPRECHT:                          I beg you, Sirs,
Not one word is true. It is not possible.

ADAM: You wait, bounder!—Constable, ho! Ned?—
Pitchers soon break that try to run away.—
You, Clerk, go. Fetch Mistress Bridget here.

VEIT: What's this now, you misbegotten rascal?
I'll break every bone in your body.

RUPRECHT:                          Why?

VEIT: Why told you not your father that you had
Snuggled with that slut at half-past ten
In Martha's garden? Why did you not?

RUPRECHT:                                    Why not?

God's thunder, Father, because it is not true!
If Bridget says it is, then hang me and,
For all I care, string her up, too!
VEIT:                              If, though,
Boy, if she proves you were—oh then, beware!
You and your dainty virgin there, despite
This show you're putting on in court, I know
The two of you are working hand in glove.
And there's another shameful secret here,
Of which she knows and, to save your skin, says naught.
RUPRECHT: Secret? Which?
VEIT:                              Why did you pack to leave?
Eh? Yestereve, why packed you your things?
RUPRECHT: What things?
VEIT: Jacket, trousers, yes, and underwear.
Just such a bundle as the wayfarer
Over his shoulder slings.
RUPRECHT:                              Because I must
Set off for Utrecht to join my regiment.
God's thunder! You thought I . . . ?
VEIT:                              To Utrecht, eh?
So, in a rush to get to Utrecht, were you,
When only yesterday you knew not if
You would be called up in five days or six?
WALTER: Have you information, Father, which we should know?
VEIT: Mighty Sir, as yet I'll make no statement.
I was at home the night the pitcher broke,
And as to other matters I confess
That when I weigh what I have heard thus far
I find no shadow of suspicion cast
Upon my son. Convinced of his innocence,
I came here, this strife once settled,
To dissolve his vow of marriage and get
Me back the little silver chain and fine
Commemorative coin he gave that girl
Last fall as token of their plighted troth.
This news of flight and treason, though, thus sprung
On me in my old age, it is as new
To me, Sirs, as it is to you. And, oh,
If true, then may the devil crack his neck!

WALTER: Justice Adam, have Mistress Bridget brought.
ADAM: Does not Your Grace grow tired of this case?
  It ekes itself out so. Then, too, Your Grace
  Still has the chore of sifting all those funds,
  Accounts, and records . . . —Clerk, what's the clock?
LINK: It just struck half.
ADAM:                Half eleven?
LINK:                          Beg pardon. Twelve.
WALTER: No matter.
ADAM *(to Link):*      Either the clock's gone mad,
  Or you have.    *(looks at his pocket watch)*
             I could have sworn . . . —Your pleasure, Sir?
WALTER: I propose that we . . .
ADAM:                Recess? A good idea.
WALTER: No, Sir. I propose that we proceed.
ADAM: You propose that we . . . ? And that's fine, too.
  Otherwise, I would, I swear, conclude
  This case at nine o'clock tomorrow,
  To Your Grace's perfect satisfaction.
WALTER: You know my will.
ADAM:               And speed to do it, too!
  Clerk, send out the constables. Tell them:
  Deliver Mistress Bridget here without delay!
WALTER *(to Link):*
  And would you please take time—of which I've none
  To spare—to see that this is promptly done.
              *(Link exits.)*


# Scene 10


*Later, maids enter.*
ADAM *(rising):* Meanwhile, if it pleased, might one stretch
  And air one's seat a moment?
WALTER:             Hm. Oh, yes.
  What I wished to say . . .
ADAM:              Would you allow,
  Until Mistress Bridget comes, the litigants . . .
WALTER: What? The litigants?

ADAM:                              Yes, to step outside.
WALTER *(aside):* Confound it!
                              *(to Adam)*
                              Justice Adam, it occurred
   To me that, while we wait, a glass of wine . . .
ADAM: With heartfelt pleasure!—Hey, Margaret!—
   Your Grace, you cheer me up.—Margaret!
                              *(A maid enters.)*
THE MAID: Here I am.
ADAM:                     Which would you like?—You there,
   Out!—A French wine . . . —Get out! The hall!—Or Rhine?
WALTER: Our native Rhine.
ADAM:                         Splendid!—Until I call! Hup!
WALTER: Out? Where?
ADAM:                     Quick, Meg. The choicest from the rack.—
   What say? Oh, just out there in the hall.—Here. The key.
WALTER: Hm. Stay.
ADAM:                 Be off. March, I say.—Go, Margaret,
   And bring the butter, freshly stamped. And cheese.
   The ripest Limburg. And a slice or two
   Of that smoked goose.
WALTER:                 Hold. A moment. Please.
   There is no need, Your Honor.
ADAM:                              You there,
   The devil take you. Do what you're told. Go!
WALTER: You would send them out, Justice Adam?
ADAM:                                        Your Grace?
WALTER: I say . . .
ADAM:             They withdraw, with your permission,
   Until such time as Mistress Bridget's brought.
   Or no? You'd rather not . . . ?
WALTER:                         Hm! As you wish.
   But is it worth the effort, do you think?
   Will it take so long before she's found?
ADAM: It's Kindling Day, Your Grace. Our womenfolk,
   They're far out in the forest, picking twigs
   And branches.
RUPRECHT:      Aunty Bridget's home.
WALTER:                              At home?
   Then bid these people stay.

RUPRECHT:                     She'll be here soon.

WALTER: She will soon be here. Bring the wine.

ADAM *(aside)*: Damn!

WALTER:              Be quick. But I'll decline the food,
  With thanks, save for a piece of bread, and salt.

ADAM *(aside)*: Oh, for two seconds with that slut alone!
                          *(aloud)*
  What? Dry bread? Salt? You jest.

WALTER:                          No, Sir.

ADAM: Just one tiny slice of Limburg cheese?
  The cheese instructs the tongue to savor wine.

WALTER: Well then, a slice of cheese, but nothing more.

ADAM: Be gone, girl. And bring the damask tablecloth.
  —Simple fare, but honest.
              *(The maid exits.)*
                          Such are the blessings
  We disreputable bachelors enjoy:
  What others scrape and scrounge to share with wife
  And child, we, with one good friend, may tuck
  Away with gusto when occasion suits.

WALTER: I would like to know—how, Your Honor,
  How came you by your wound, a fearful gash,
  Indeed, upon your forehead.

ADAM:                  I fell.

WALTER:                  You fell.
  Hm. So. When? Last night?

ADAM:                  Today. Half-past five,
  To be exact, as I was getting out of bed.

WALTER: Over what?

ADAM:              To tell the truth, Your Grace,
  I fell over, if you will, myself.
  Head over heels and head against the stove,
  Though to this hour I know not how.

WALTER: Backward?

ADAM:              How's that? Backward?

WALTER:                          Or forward?
  You have two wounds—one front and one behind.

ADAM: Both fore *and* aft.—Ho, Margaret!
              *(Both maids enter with wine, etc.*
              *After setting the table, they exit.)*

WALTER:                                        How?

ADAM: First so, then so. First against the corner
   Of the stove, which left this dent in front;
   Then, reeling from this blow, I topple over
   On the floor, and so am cracked behind, as well.
                     *(He pours wine.)*
   Allow me.
                     *(Walter takes the glass.)*
WALTER:      Were you a married man,
   I might conclude all sorts of things, Your Honor.
ADAM: How so?
WALTER:         Why, by my faith, because your head
   Is scored and scratched.
ADAM: *(laughing):*         No, thank God. No woman's
   Nails did that.
WALTER:           I'm sure. Another blessing
   Of the bachelor's life.
ADAM: *(still laughing):*  Silkworm twigs,
   Hung by the stove to dry. Your Grace's health!
                     *(They drink.)*
WALTER: And today, of all days, to lose your wig.
   It would, at least, have concealed your wounds.
ADAM: True. True. But troubles come in pairs, they say.
   Here.—And now some cheese.—May I?
WALTER:                                        A sliver.
   Limburg?
ADAM:      Fresh from Limburg, ay, Your Grace.
WALTER: But, tell me, how the devil did it happen?
ADAM: What?
WALTER:       That you lost your wig.
ADAM:                                        Well, you see,
   Last night I sit to read this document
   And, because I have mislaid my spectacles,
   I bend so close, engrossed in that dispute,
   My candle flame sets me my wig on fire.
   Good Lord, I think, here's fire from heaven
   Visited upon my sinful pate,
   And clutch my wig and try to fling it off,
   But while I struggle to undo the strings

The whole thing blazes up in flame like Sodom
And Gomorrah, so that I barely 'scape
With these few hairs.
WALTER:                    Lord! And your other wig's
  In town?
ADAM:      Yes. Being mended.—But, to business.
WALTER: Not so quick, I beg you, Justice Adam.
ADAM: Ah, tush. Time flies. A wee glass. Here.
                    *(He pours.)*
WALTER: This Lebrecht—if one is to believe
  That fellow's story—took a bad spill, too.
ADAM: 'Pon my honor.
                    *(He drinks.)*
WALTER:                    If, then, this case should
  Go unsolved today—as I fear it may—
  It should, in such a village, not be hard
  To tell who is the culprit by his wound.
                    *(He drinks.)*
  Niersteiner?
ADAM:      What?
WALTER:                    Or a fine Oppenheimer?
ADAM: Nierstein. By God, well done. A taster's tongue.
  From Nierstein, yes, indeed, it is, Your Grace,
  As sure as if I'd fetched it thence myself.
WALTER: I drank it, at the press, three years ago.
                    *(Adam pours again.)*
  —How high is your window? You, Mistress Martha.
MRS. MARTHA: My window?
WALTER: The window in your daughter's room.
MRS. MARTHA: That room is only one floor up, above
  The cellar, so that from sill to ground
  Is no more than a nine-foot drop, I'd say.
  And yet the whole affair makes leaping risky,
  For, two feet from the wall, you see, a grapevine
  Twists its gnarly branches up the trellis
  And it spreads out the whole span of that wall,
  So that her window is roped in with vine
  So thick a wild boar would be hard-pressed,
  Despite his tusks, to break that thicket through.

ADAM: Still, none got stuck in it.
        *(He refills his own glass.)*
WALTER:              You think not?
ADAM:                     Pah. No.
        *(He drinks.)*
WALTER *(to Ruprecht):* Where did you strike the culprit? On the
                                            [head?
RUPRECHT: Here.
WALTER:         Hold.
ADAM:         A drop.
WALTER:              'Tis still half full.
ADAM:                       I'll fill it.
WALTER: You heard me.
ADAM:              For the number's sake.
WALTER:                      No more.
ADAM: Nay, come. The rule of old Pythagoras.
        *(He fills Walter's glass.)*
WALTER: *(to Ruprecht):* How often did you strike the culprit's
                                        [head?
ADAM: One is God; two, chaos; and three's the world.
  Three glasses I salute. The third glass,
  Ah, with each drop you drink bright suns,
  And with the rest, whole firmaments.
WALTER: The culprit's head—how often did you strike it?
  You, Ruprecht, I'm asking you!
ADAM:                   Out with it!
  How often did you pound the scapegoat, eh?
  God's bolts, does this fellow even know . . . ?
  You've forgotten?
RUPRECHT:           With the handle?
ADAM:                  Don't ask me.
WALTER: From the window. As you swung down at him.
RUPRECHT: Twice, Your Honor.
ADAM:                   Scoundrel. *That* he does recall!
        *(He drinks.)*
WALTER: Twice? You realize you might have killed him
  With two such blows?
RUPRECHT:          And if I had
  I would have had him, and a good thing, too.

If he lay here dead, then I could say,
   That's him, gentlemen; what I said was true.
ADAM: Yes, dead. I well believe it. But now . . .
                    *(He pours.)*
WALTER: You could not recognize him in the dark?
RUPRECHT: Not a stitch, Your Worthy Grace. How could I?
ADAM: How? Can't you open up your eyes?—Your

                                              [health!

RUPRECHT: My eyes? I had them opened wide, but then
   That devil blinded me with sand.
ADAM: *(muttering):*              Sand, yes,
   To stop you staring with those bulging eyes.
                    *(aloud)*
   So. To what we love and cherish, gracious Sir!
WALTER: To what is upright, good, and true, Justice Adam.
                    *(They drink.)*
ADAM: Now then, let's finish off, if you agree?
                    *(He pours.)*
WALTER: I trust you visit Mistress Martha
   On occasion. Tell me, Justice Adam,
   Who, Ruprecht aside, also comes and goes there?
ADAM: I rarely call, Your Grace, begging your pardon.
   Who comes and goes there, I couldn't tell you.
WALTER: What? Do you not occasionally stop
   To see the widow of your departed friend?
ADAM: No, indeed. Or seldom.
WALTER:                      Mistress Martha!
   Have you fallen out with Justice Adam?
   He tells me that he rarely visits you.
MRS. MARTHA: Hm. Fallen out, Your Worship? Hardly.
   He still, I think, calls himself a friend,
   Though that I often see him in my house
   I could not boast of in his presence, no.
   Nine weeks it's been since last he called on me,
   And even then only for a quick chat.
WALTER: What's that you say?
MRS. MARTHA:                  What?
WALTER:                              It's been nine
                                        [weeks . . . ?

MRS. MARTHA: [Nine.
    Yes. Come Thursday, ten. He stopped in then
    To ask for seed—cowslip and carnation.
WALTER: And on Sundays, when he steps out to his farm?
MRS. MARTHA: Oh well, yes—he'll look in at the window
    To bid me and my daughter a good day,
    But then he's off again and on his way.
WALTER *(aside):* Hm. Could it be I've wronged the man . . . ?
                 *(He drinks.)*

                                I
                              [thought,
    Because you need at times the girl's assistance
    In your husbandry you might express
    Your gratitude by calling on her mother?
ADAM: How's that, Your Grace?
WALTER:                How? Why, you told me
    That the girl had cured your hens. Did she not,
    Today, advise you on this matter here?
MRS. MARTHA: Indeed she does, Your Honor, do just that.
    Two days ago he had a hen sent over
    To the house that looked already dead.
    Last year she saved him one that had the pip
    And this hen, too, she'll noodle back to life.
    He hasn't shown his face to thank us yet.
WALTER: *(bewildered):* Pour, Justice Adam, if you would be so
                               [kind.
    Pour. Fill my glass. We'll have one more together.
ADAM: At your service. I am delighted. Here.
               *(He pours.)*
WALTER: To your prosperity!—Justice Adam
    Surely will stop by to see you soon.
MRS. MARTHA:             You think?
    I wonder. If, though, I could set out
    A Nierstein wine like that you're drinking now
    And which my dear departed also stored,
    At times, in our own cellar, if, I say,
    I could but set such wines before our friend
    The justice, we would see more of him.

But, poor widow that I am, I lack
The means to lure him.

WALTER:                    So much the better.


# Scene 11

*Link, Mistress Bridget, and maids enter. Mistress Bridget carries a wig in one hand.*

LINK: Here, Mistress Bridget. This way, please.

WALTER: This is the woman, then, Clerk Link?

LINK: This is Mistress Bridget, yes, Your Grace.

WALTER: Well then, let us conclude this case quickly.
  Maids, clear. Here.

                    *(The maids exit with glasses, etc.)*

ADAM *(as they clear):* Now listen to me, Evie.
  You fix me up a pill will do the job
  And I'll drop in to sup with you tonight.
  But, mind: the cluck has got to gulp it whole.
  If it's too big to swallow, let her choke.

WALTER *(seeing the wig):* What wig is this that Mistress Bridget
                                        [brings?

LINK: Your Grace?

WALTER:                    What wig is that this woman brings?

LINK: Hm.

WALTER:   What?

LINK:                    With respect . . .

WALTER:                              Will I ever learn?

LINK: Should Your Grace permit the woman to
  Be questioned by His Honor, the owner of the wig,
  And much besides, would soon be clear.

WALTER: I do not want to know whose wig it is.
  How came she by it? When found she it?

LINK: She found it in Mistress Martha's trellis.
  There it hung, nest-like, in the vine
  Close by the window where the young girl sleeps.

MRS. MARTHA: What? Where? In my trellis?

WALTER *(to Adam, privately):*       Justice Adam,
  If there is aught you would confide in me,
  I ask you, for the honor of this court,
  Be so good and tell me now.
ADAM: Me? You?
WALTER:       You haven't . . . ? Nothing?
ADAM:                  Upon my honor!
          *(He snatches up his wig.)*
WALTER: Is that wig there not yours?
ADAM:             Gentlemen,
  This wig here is mine. Which is to say,
  By thunder, it is the one I gave
  That lad eight days hence to take to Utrecht,
  To take it to the shop of Master Bleedum.
WALTER: Who? What?
LINK:       To Ruprecht?
RUPRECHT:           Me?
ADAM:               Did I not, rogue,
  Eight days ago when you set off for Utrecht,
  Charge you to take this wig to Master Bleedum
  To have it dressed?
RUPRECHT:       Well yes, you . . .
ADAM:              Then why, clod,
  Did you not deliver it? Why did you not,
  As I charged you, deliver to his shop
  In Utrecht my wig to Master Bleedum?
RUPRECHT: Why did I not? God's . . . oh, hell's blazes—damn!
  I did deliver it to him in his shop.
  Master Bleedum himself took . . .
ADAM:           Delivered?
  And now it's nesting in Martha's trellis?
  Just you wait, hoodlum. You can't fool me.
  I sniff impersonation here and—
  Who knows?—mutiny as well.—So please Your Grace,
  I will proceed at once to question the woman.
WALTER: You say you sent the wig . . . ?
ADAM:           So please Your Grace,
  When that lad there, last Tuesday, started off
  For Utrecht, behind his father's oxen,

He stepped in here and said, "Justice Adam,
Have you something to be done in town?"
—"My son," I say, "if you would be so kind,
Pray take this wig, which needs be combed and dressed."
I did not, though, say: Go, boy. Keep my wig.
Use it to disguise yourself, then leave it,
Please, hung up on Mistress Martha's trellis.

MRS. BRIDGET: Your Honors, Ruprecht couldn't, if you please,
Have done it. No. For when, last night,
I go to see my cousin on her farm—
She's due now any day—I hear Eve's voice.
She's in the garden, scolding someone, but
Fury seems, and fear, to rob her of her voice.
"Fie! You should be ashamed, you wretch.
What *are* you doing? Go. I'll call my mother,"
As if for all the world the Spaniards had
Returned. Then: "Eve!" I call out through the hedge.
"Eve," I say, "what is it?" And all grows still.
"Well, will you answer?"—"What is it, Auntie?"—
"What are you doing, child?"—"What would you think?"—
"It's Ruprecht then?"—"Ay, oh, yes, Ruprecht.
So now run along."—"And you go spin."
Now there's a love, I think, that feeds on fighting.

MRS. MARTHA: And then?

RUPRECHT: And then?

WALTER: Silence. Let her proceed.

MRS. BRIDGET: So later then, returning from the farm,
Near midnight, I take the Linden Lane
That leads past Martha's house, when, *whish,*
There rushes past me, Sirs, this fellow
Whose head is bald, who has a horse's hoof
And trails behind a stench of pitch and brimstone.
I say a prayer, turn, terrified, around,
And, Sirs, upon my soul, I see that pate
Before me still, for as it scuttles off
Into the dark it glows like foxfire,
Lighting up the lane.

RUPRECHT: What? Good God!

MRS. MARTHA: Have you gone mad, Briggy?

RUPRECHT:                                    You mean you
                                                    [think—
  You think you saw the Devil?
LINK:                        Quiet! Quiet!
MRS. BRIDGET: My soul, I know what I saw and sniffed!
WALTER *(impatiently):* Woman, whether the Devil was the culprit
  Is a line of inquiry I'll not pursue.
  Against him one does not press charges.
  If you can tell us of some other, good.
  But that old sinner, kindly spare us him.
LINK: Would Your Grace allow her to conclude?
WALTER: Oh, what a pack of fools!
MRS. BRIDGET:                    If you say so.
  But Court Clerk Link will bear me witness, Sir.
WALTER: What? You, a witness?
LINK:                        In a manner, yes.
WALTER: Really!
LINK:            I must humbly beg Your Grace
  Not to interrupt the woman's statement.
  That it was the Devil I shall not claim;
  As for the hoof, the pate, and the attendant
  Stench, however, she is, unless I'm much
  Mistaken, wholly accurate.—Proceed.
MRS. BRIDGET: So when today, to my astonishment,
  I hear of these events at Martha's house,
  And I—to spy out who this pitcher-breaker
  That I met at night there by the trellis was—
  Look close at where he jumped, I find you, Sirs,
  A track there in the snow. What sort of track?
  The footprint to the right is sharp and clear—
  A proper human foot. But to the left,
  What's this? All crude and botched and blundering,
  It is a monstrous clumsy horse's hoof.
WALTER: *(irritated):* Prattle, ranting, and mad blasphemy!
VEIT: Woman, that's impossible!
MRS. BRIDGET:                        'Pon my honor!
  First by the trellis where he leapt, look you—
  A circle, so wide, churned up in the snow,
  As if a sow had wallowed in it.
  Then, from there, human foot and horse's hoof

And human foot and horse's hoof and human foot and horse's
                         [hoof,
  Out of the garden into the whole wide world.
ADAM: Damn!—You think that scoundrel dared disguise
  Himself as Satan?
RUPRECHT:        Who? Me?
LINK:               You! Silence!
MRS. BRIDGET: He who hunts the badger and comes, at last,
  Upon the spoor, knew no such joy as I
  Knew then. "Clerk Link," I say, for even now
  I see that worthy man, by you dispatched,
  Advancing toward me. "Clerk Link," I say,
  "Adjourn your session. This pitcher-breaker
  Cannot be judged by you; he dwells beyond
  Your reach in Hell. Behold, here is his trail."
WALTER: And in this wise you were convinced?
LINK:                       Your Grace,
  What she says of this is true.
WALTER:           A hoof?
LINK: A foot, a human foot, so please Your Grace,
  Yet, *praeter propter,* most like a hoof.
ADAM: 'Pon my soul, Sirs, the case looks grave to me.
  There is no lack of biting pamphleteers
  Who won't admit there is a deity,
  And yet, so far as I know, no atheist
  Has blown away the Devil with his proofs.
  The case before us merits, it would seem,
  Special review. I propose, therefore,
  That we defer decision and first ask
  The High Court in the Hague if *this* court
  May not justifiably assume it was
  Beelzebub broke Mistress Martha's pitcher.
WALTER: Just the proposal I would expect of you.
  And what say you, Clerk Link?
LINK:                  Your Grace will not
  Require such review to judge this case.
  Conclude—with your permission!—your account,
  You there, Mistress Bridget. By hearing all
  We shall, I trust, disclose the full event.
MRS. BRIDGET: So then I say: "Clerk Link, let us awhile

Pursue this track to see if we can trace
The Fiend to where he fled."—"Fine," says he,
"And we shall not go far astray, I wager,
If we go straight to Justice Adam."
WALTER: Well. And you found what?
MRS. BRIDGET:                       First thing we find,
Across from Martha's, there on Linden Lane,
Is where that brimstone-leaking Devil, dodging
Around me, veered, stamping in the snow
A curve, such as a startled dog might make
Coming upon a bristling cat.
WALTER:                And then?
MRS. BRIDGET: A stone's throw farther, lo, a foul memento
Lies behind a tree, from which, appalled,
I turn away.
WALTER:       A what?
MRS. BRIDGET:          What? You would be . . .
ADAM *(aside):* Oh, my confounded guts!
LINK:                     Oh, leave that be.
Leave that be, I beg you, Mistress Bridget.
WALTER: Where that trail led you—that I want to know.
MRS. BRIDGET: Where? My faith, straight here to you,
Just as Clerk Link predicted.
WALTER:                 To us? To here?
MRS. BRIDGET: From Linden Lane across the common, yes,
And then along the pond, across the bridge,
Across God's acre, straight here to Justice Adam.
WALTER: To Justice Adam?
ADAM:               Here, you mean, to me?
MRS. BRIDGET: To you, yes.
RUPRECHT:             You mean you think the Devil
Lives here, in this courthouse?
MRS. BRIDGET:          Faith, I know not
Whether here he lives or no, but here—
As I'm an honest woman—he dismounted.
The trail leads to the back door and there ends.
ADAM: Could he, perhaps, have passed through here?
MRS. BRIDGET:                        Passed
[through?
Yes, that could be, too. The tracks out front . . .

WALTER: Were there tracks in front?

LINK: No trace, Your Grace,
Of tracks.

MRS. BRIDGET: Yes. The snow was trampled down.

ADAM: Trampled down. Passed through. Well, I'll be damned.
The rogue has slipped one over on this court,
You'll see. Call me a villain if now
The registry of records does not reek
Of his foul stench. If my accounts are found
Disordered, as I doubt not they will be,
Upon my honor, I'll not answer for it.

WALTER: Nor I.

(*aside*)
Hm. I can't recall. Was it the left foot?
Or the right? One of them.—

(*aloud*)
Justice Adam.
Your snuff box, if you would be so kind.

ADAM: Snuff box?

WALTER: The snuff box. Hand it. Here.

ADAM (*to Link*): Bring this
To the district judge.

WALTER: Why such a fuss,
When all that's needed is a single step?

ADAM: It's been arranged. Here. Hand it to His Grace.

WALTER: I had a word to whisper in your ear.

ADAM: Later, perhaps, there will be time for . . .

WALTER: Fine.
(*after Link has sat down again*)
Tell me, gentlemen, does some villager,
Perchance, have a misshapen foot?

LINK: Hm. There is,
To be sure, a person here in Howzem . . .

WALTER: So? Who?

LINK: Your Grace may wish to ask His Honor.

WALTER: Ask Justice Adam?

ADAM: Who? Me? Not a clue.
Ten years I've held this post in Howzem and,
So far as I know, nothing's grown up crooked.

WALTER (*to Link*): Well then, whom did you mean?

MRS. MARTHA:                                                    Leave your
[feet stretched out!
You tuck them in under the table there
In such a stew you'd almost think that *you*
Had made those tracks!
WALTER:                          Who? Justice Adam?
ADAM:                                                    Me?
Those tracks? Am I the Devil? Is this a hoof?
                    *(He shows his left foot.)*
WALTER: Upon my word. The foot looks sound.
                         *(privately, to Adam)*
Adjourn this session now, without delay.
ADAM: A foot that, if the Devil had its like,
The scamp would dance at all the finest balls.
MRS. MARTHA: Amen, say I. How could Justice Adam . . . ?
ADAM: Me? Rubbish!
WALTER:                          Adjourn at once, I say.
MRS. BRIDGET: The only thing that makes me wonder, Sirs,
Is this one piece of formal gear.
ADAM:                                   One which?
MRS. BRIDGET: Here. The wig. Whoever spied the Devil
In such gear? A towered, tallow-spattered
Fixture such as city preachers don on Sunday.
ADAM: We know so little in these parts of what
The fashion is in Hell, Mistress Bridget.
Down there, they say, he rarely dons a wig.
But here on earth, I am convinced, he wears
The wig to mingle with the upper crust.
WALTER: Undeserving wretch! Deserving only
To be driven out in public from this bench!
All that protects you now is the honor
Due the court. Adjourn!
ADAM:                          I hope you won't . . .
WALTER: You hope nothing. Find your own way out
Of this affair.
ADAM:               What? You think that I,
The justice, lost my wig in that vine?
WALTER: God forbid! Your wig went up, like Sodom
And Gomorrah, in a burst of flame.

LINK: Or rather—if Your Grace permit—the cat
   Cast her litter in it yesterday.
ADAM: Gentlemen, although appearances
   Connive against me here, do not, I pray,
   Act rashly. Honor or disgrace hang
   In the balance. So long as the girl keeps
   Silent, I cannot see what right you have
   To find me guilty. Here, upon the bench
   Of Howzem, here I sit and set this wig
   Upon the table. Whoever claims it's mine
   I'll hail before the district court in Utrecht.
LINK: Hm. 'Pon my soul. The wig does fit you, though,
   As snug as if it grew upon your scalp.
      *(Link sets the wig on Adam's head.)*
ADAM: Slander!
LINK:       No?
ADAM:          Even as a shoulder cape
   It's big on me, so it would ill fit my head.
      *(He looks at himself in the mirror.)*
RUPRECHT: By God, he would outfox the Devil!
WALTER:                 Silence!
MRS. MARTHA: Ay, a foxy judge. A pox upon him!
WALTER: Once again, will you or must I now conclude
   This case?
ADAM:     At your service—what?
RUPRECHT *(to Eve):*       Eve. Speak.
   Is he the one?
WALTER:      What's this? You. Hold your tongue.
VEIT: Shut up, I say!
ADAM:       You wait, brute. I'll fix you.
RUPRECHT: Blast you, hoof-foot!
WALTER:          Ho. Constable!
VEIT: Shut up, I say!
RUPRECHT:      You wait. This time I'll get
   My hands on you. You won't throw sand today.
WALTER: Have you not sufficient wit, Justice Adam . . . ?
ADAM: Yes, if Your Grace permit, I shall pronounce
   The verdict.
WALTER: Good. Do that. Pronounce it.

ADAM: The facts have been established. Ruprecht there,
 The villain, is the culprit.
WALTER:      Well done. Go on.
ADAM: His stiff neck I hereby sentence to wear
 Irons, and, in addition, for contempt
 Of court I pack him off to prison.
 How long a term? I'll figure that out later.
EVE: Send Ruprecht off . . .
RUPRECHT:      To prison? Me?
EVE:            In irons?
WALTER: Do not worry, children.—Are you done?
ADAM: As to the pitcher, he can replace it,
 As far as I'm concerned, or not.
WALTER:      Well then.
 I rule this session closed. And Ruprecht shall
 Appeal his sentence to the District Court.
EVE: *He* appeal? He first must go to Utrecht?
RUPRECHT: Who? Me?
WALTER:    Damn it, yes. And until then . . .
EVE: And until then . . . ?
RUPRECHT:    Go off to prison? Me?
EVE: And thrust his neck in irons? Are you, too,
 A judge? He, that shameless one who sits there,
 He himself is . . .
WALTER:    Damn it! You heard me! Silence!
 Till then no harm will come to him.
EVE:       Rise, Ruprecht!
 Rise up. Justice Adam broke the pitcher.
RUPRECHT: Oh, you wait, you!
MRS. MARTHA:    Him?
MRS. BRIDGET:      Him there?
EVE:          Him, yes. Rise,
 Ruprecht. He was with your Eve last night.
 Up! Seize him! Hurl him where you will!
WALTER *(rises):*    You! Back!
 Those who disturb the court will be . . .
EVE:       Who cares now?
 Earn your irons, Ruprecht! Go. Pitch him down
 From his tribunal.

ADAM:                 Excuse me, gentlemen.
                     *(He starts to run off.)*
EVE: After him!
RUPRECHT:      Stop him!
EVE:                 Be quick!
ADAM:                     What say?
RUPRECHT: Blasted limp-foot Devil!
EVE:                         You've got him?
RUPRECHT:                         Blast!
   His cloak, that's all I've got.
WALTER:                 Quick! The constable!
RUPRECHT *(beating the cloak):* Take that. And that. And this. One
                                     [more. And,
   For lack of a back, take this as well!
WALTER: Unruly boor!—Bring order to this court!—
   If you do not calm down at once, you yet
   Today will find yourself in irons.
VEIT: Calm down, confounded madcap. Calm you down!


# Scene 12


*Preceding characters, minus Adam. All come down to the front of
the stage.*
RUPRECHT: Oh, Eve!
   How shamefully I've treated you today!
   Ay, God's bolts, and yesterday as well.
   My golden girl, my heart's own bride, will you
   Be able to forgive me ever, Eve?
                     *(Eve kneels before Walter.)*
EVE: Sir! Unless you help us, we are lost!
WALTER: Lost? How so?
RUPRECHT:             Good God. What now?
EVE:                                 Spare Ruprecht
   From this present draft! For these recruits—
   I know, for Justice Adam told me so
   In confidence—these recruits will be sent off
   To Indonesia, and, as you know,

From there for every three who go, but one
Comes back alive.

WALTER: What? To Indonesia?
Have you gone mad?

EVE: To Bantam, gracious Sir.
Do not deny it! Here I have the letter,
The secret silent edict, concerning
The militia newly issued by the government.
I am, you see, fully informed.

*(Walter takes and reads the letter.)*

WALTER: Oh, unheard-of cunning and deceit!
The letter's false!

EVE: False?

WALTER: False, upon my life!
Clerk Link, say: Is this the edict newly
Sent from Utrecht to this court?

LINK: The edict?
This? The sinner, oh. A scrap, no more,
Drawn up in his own clumsy hand! The troops
Called up in this present draft will see
Home service only; there is no thought
Of shipping them to Indonesia.

EVE: No, gentlemen? None and never?

WALTER: I swear.
And, in earnest of my word, say it were
As you have said, I will buy your Ruprecht free.

EVE *(rises)*: O Heaven! How that villain lied to me.
This was just the terrifying care
He used to twist my heart, and came that night
To say that Ruprecht might yet be deferred,
Explaining that some fabricated illness,
Duly certified, would grant exemption—
Explained, assured, and slipped—at once to draw
This false paper up—into my room,
There to demand such favors of me, Sir,
As no maid's mouth would dare to speak of.

MRS. BRIDGET: Ay, the good-for-nothing vile deceiver!

RUPRECHT: Forget, forget about that horse's hoof,
My darling child. And if a horse had smashed

That pitcher, look, I would be just as jealous
As I am now.

*(They kiss.)*

VEIT: Amen to that. So kiss,
Make up, and love each other well. Come Whitsun,
If you want, let's hear the wedding bells!
LINK *(at the window):* Look at Justice Adam, look, I pray—
How he goes stomping o'er the furrowed fields,
Up hill, down dale, as if for all the world
Rack and gallows both were hot upon his heels.
WALTER: What? That is Justice Adam?
LINK: It is indeed!
SEVERAL: Now he's nearly reached the road! Look! His wig
Is flapping, lashing Justice Adam's back!
WALTER: Quick, Clerk. Go and fetch the justice back,
Lest he make what is bad enough, worse yet.
I shall, of course, suspend him from his office,
Which you shall occupy in the interim.
Yet if his funds are found to be in order,
As I hope they will, I will not force him
Into exile. Do, I beg you, fetch him.

*(Link exits.)*

# Scene 13

*Preceding characters, minus Link.*
MRS. MARTHA: Now then, Your Worship, tell me this: where
[will I find
This government of ours in Utrecht?
WALTER: Why so, Mistress Martha?
MRS. MARTHA *(touchily):* Hm! Why so? Well,
But shall justice not be done my pitcher?
WALTER: Forgive me. So it should. The Great Square.
On Tuesday and on Friday the court convenes.
MRS. MARTHA: Good! Today a week, I will be there.

*(All exit.)*
**Curtain.**

(Fragments)

# Scene 1
The courtroom in a Dutch village.

*First entrance.*

*Adam sits, binding up his leg. Link enters.*

LINK: Ay, what the devil! What a sight you look!
  What happened to you, Adam? What befell?

ADAM: Well, look. All it takes to stumble is a pair
  Of feet. The floor itself is flat—or no?
  Still, here I stumbled, and each, within himself,
  Bears his own cursed stumbling block.

LINK: How do you . . . ? What the devil does that mean?
  You're telling me each bears a stumbling block . . . ?

ADAM: Ay, that makes him fall.

LINK *(fixing him with a sharp glance):*
                    Be damned.

ADAM:                                What say?

LINK: You take your name from an unsteady sire who,
  When things were just beginning, fell,
  And still is famous for his fall.
  And now you . . . ?

ADAM:              What?

LINK:                    Follow suit?

ADAM:                                I? I think . . .
  Here is where I fell, I tell you, Link.

LINK: You literally fell, you mean.

ADAM:                          I did.
  And must have cut a wretched figure doing so.

LINK: By my faith! A figure none would copy.
  —But when befell this accident?

ADAM:                          When? Now,
  In the very act of climbing out of bed.
  My morning song was still upon my lips
  When head over heels I stumble into day.
  And so, before I'm altogether up,
  I'm down, and to boot I sprain my ankle.

LINK: And, to top it all, your left one?

ADAM:                                    What?

LINK: Here, your game foot, the weighty one which,
As it was, made perdition's path hard going.

ADAM: Fah. Weighty! How so?

LINK:                              The club foot?

ADAM:                                    Club foot? What?
A foot's a foot, whichever side it's on.

LINK: Beg pardon, but you do your right foot wrong.
The right cannot boast this one's . . . gravity,
And so dares venture onto thin ice first.

ADAM: Nonsense. Where one leads, the other follows.

LINK: And what has put your face so out of joint?

ADAM: What? My face?

LINK:                    You mean you did not know?

ADAM: I'd be a liar if I said I did . . . How does it look?

LINK: How it looks?

ADAM:              Yes, friend. How?

LINK:                                    Horrible!

ADAM: Explain yourself. Enlarge.

LINK:                              It's scratched.
A grisly sight. A piece gone from the cheek.
How large? Without a scale I couldn't say.

ADAM: The devil you say.

LINK *(fetching a mirror)*:  Well. Look for yourself.
A ram that, chased by hounds, plunges through thorns,
Leaves no less wool behind than you left skin,
Though God alone knows where you left it.

ADAM:                                          Hm.
Yes. It's true. A cheerless sight. And my nose
Has not escaped unscathed.

LINK:                          And the eye.

ADAM: The eye not, friend.

LINK:                        But yes. A bloody swipe
Runs here across your face, and all puffed up,
Big as a fist in size, the devil take it.
No farmhand hereabouts could do better.

ADAM: That is the cheekbone, not the eye.—Imagine.
All that damage and I didn't feel a thing!

LINK: No. One never does in the heat of battle.

ADAM: The heat of battle? What sort of talk is that?
  With that blasted ram's face I did battle
  That sticks out from the corner of the stove.
  It comes back now. When I, while getting up,
  Lose my balance and, like a drowning man,
  Flail about me, I clutch—first my trousers
  Which I'd hung all wet the night before to dry
  Upon the rack; clutch them, you see, thinking,
  Fool that I was, they'll hold me up, when, rip,
  The waistband tears, and rack and trousers fall,
  I fall—and forehead-first come crashing down
  Smack on the corner of that stove where
  That damn ram sticks out his nose.
LINK *(laughing):*                Well done!
ADAM: Well done, my foot!
LINK:                Well, let it be, friend.
ADAM: And so I must.—But what I meant to ask you,
  Link, what news do you bring?
LINK:                What news?
  Why, I had almost forgotten!
ADAM:                Well?
LINK: Prepare yourself for an unexpected
  Visitor from Utrecht.
ADAM:                So? From whom then?
LINK: Judge Walter.
ADAM *(stunned):* Who?
LINK:                District Judge Walter
  Is on his way from Utrecht even now.
ADAM: What's that?

*(And so on)*

# Scene 6
Opening lines.

(NOTE: *Before Justice Adam has recovered from his shock, District Judge Walter arrives to inspect the court and lets in the litigants, whom he finds in the hall outside the courtroom. Justice*

*Adam, who has no idea who the litigants are, starts to don his robes of office, while District Judge Walter sits at a table toward the rear of the stage, where he busies himself with his writing tablet.)*

*Mrs. Martha, Eve, Veit, and Ruprecht enter.*

MRS. MARTHA: You feckless pitcher-smashing rabble, you!
  You fickle pack, who topple me my tankards
  And jar the pillars of society!
  You'll pay for this!

> *(And so on)*

# Scene 7

First five lines of Mrs. Martha's speech, in which she describes
the pitcher.

MRS. MARTHA: Nothing's what you see,
  If you'll permit. You see pieces only.
  The fairest among pitchers—smashed to bits.
  Here on this hole, where there's nothing now,
  These our United _____ Provinces
  _____ were handed over.

> *(And so on; then, following the description of the pitcher):*

WALTER: Well, good. Now we know the pitcher.

(Original version of the final scene.)

# Scene 12

*Preceding characters, minus Adam. All come down to the front of the stage.*

RUPRECHT: Oh Eve!
  I've shamefully insulted you today!
  Ay, God's bolts, and yesterday as well.
  My golden girl, my heart's own bride, will you
  Be able to forgive me ever, Eve?

EVE: Go. Leave me alone.

RUPRECHT:                Ay, damned fool that I am!
  If I could pummel me with my own hands!
  Take—you know what? Listen. Do this for me—
  Take your little hand, damn it, and make a fist
  And thump me hard behind my ear. Will you
  Do that for me? My soul, I'm not at peace.

EVE: You heard. I want no more to do with you.

RUPRECHT: Oh, what a fool! It's Lebrecht, I think,
  Blockhead, and go to Justice Adam then,
  And he who hears my case did it himself.
  What's more, he sentences my neck to irons.

WALTER: If, yesterday, the maid had promptly told
  Her mother all, as duty bade she should,
  She might then have spared this court disgrace and
  Spared herself these doubts about her honor.

RUPRECHT: She was ashamed. Pardon her, gracious Sir!
  He was her justice. She had to spare him.—
  Now let's go home. Things will turn out all right.

EVE: Yes, ashamed!

RUPRECHT:            Good. So there was something more.
  Keep that to yourself. Why need we to know?
  One day, on the lilac bench, with vespers
  Ringing from the tower, you'll tell me.
  Come. Just be good now.

WALTER:                    Why need we to know?
  I see it otherwise. If Eve would

Have us now accept her innocence,
She must present a full account of how
That pitcher came to be broken. A single
Careless word let drop does not, in my eyes,
Make the justice guilty of any sin.

RUPRECHT: So, take heart! You're innocent! Tell us
What that hoof-foot wanted of you, Eve.
Look, and if a horse had smashed that pitcher,
I would be just as jealous as I am now.

EVE: How can it help to prove my innocence?
We both are hapless evermore.

RUPRECHT: Hapless? Who, us?

WALTER:                              You two hapless? Why?

RUPRECHT: What it has to do with, it's this draft.

EVE (*throwing herself at Walter's feet*):
Sir, if you do not help us, we are lost.

WALTER: If I . . . ?

EVE:                    Eternal God!

WALTER:                                   Rise, my child.

EVE: Not, Sir, before those human qualities,
Which shine forth from your countenance, have shown
Themselves in an act of human kindness.

WALTER: My dearest child, when you to me have proved
Your innocence, as I doubt not you will,
I will not fail to prove humane to you.
Rise.

EVE:    Yes, Sir, I will.

WALTER:                      Good. So, speak.

EVE: You know that recently an edict called
To arms, this spring, ten of every hundred sons,
The fittest, from each village in the land.
The Spaniard cannot let the Netherlander
Live in peace; the tyrant's rod, once broken,
He seeks to mend and wield again. Armies
March on every road; the fleets he sent
To block the coastlands of our provinces
Ring us about; and our militia strives
To hold the now-deserted city gates.

WALTER: So it is.

EVE:        So they say, I know.

WALTER:                Well? And so?

EVE: So we had just sat down, Mother, Father,
   Ruprecht, and I, around the hearth, to fix
   The date—this Whitsun or the next—on which
   To celebrate our marriage, when in steps,
   Suddenly, into the room, the recruiting
   Officer, and Ruprecht is called up,
   And with that blade-sharp dictum he decides
   The outcome of our happy quarrel just when
   Whitsun seemed to be the choice, but which—
   God only knew which Whitsun it would be.

WALTER: My child . . .

EVE:              Yes. Yes.

WALTER:                'Tis the common lot.

EVE: I know.

WALTER:      Which Ruprecht cannot well refuse.

RUPRECHT: I wouldn't think of it.

EVE:                    He would not, Sir,
   Think of doing so, and God preserve me
   If ever I should try to change his mind.
   We may thank God that in the breast of each
   Of us free Netherlanders we preserve
   Something holy that is worth fighting for.
   So let each go forward to protect it.
   Must he do battle with the enemy,
   I still would say: go, and God be with you.
   Why then should I oppose his leaving when
   All that he must do is guard the leveled
   Walls of Utrecht from naughty boys at play?
   Meanwhile, good Sir, be not angry with me:
   When I see the birch trees in our garden
   Nigh on Whitsun start to bud out red,
   Oh, I cannot keep the tears from flowing,
   Since otherwise I do and think what's right.

WALTER: God forbid I should be angry with you.
   Speak on.

EVE:        So yesterday my mother sends
   Me on some errand to see Justice Adam,

And as I walk into this room he says:
"Good morning, Eve. Ah, why look you so sad?
Your head droops like a lily of the valley,
Which you must know looks very well on you.
It's Ruprecht, eh? Your Ruprecht!"—"Yes," I say,
"Of course it's Ruprecht; when one loves something
One must expect to suffer on this earth."
Then he: "Poor thing. Hm. What then would you give
If I arrange to have him freed from service?"—
And I: "If you could free him? Well, I would
Be glad to give you something. How would you
Go about it, though?"—"You little fool,"
He says. "The doctor, he can write, and so
Can I. Hidden ailments can't be seen.
The recruiting officer must have a signed
Certificate of disability.
Ruprecht hands it to him; they let him go.
It's simple as a horse trade."—"So," I say.—
"That's right."—"Then, no, leave matters as they are,
Your Honor. That God created Ruprecht
As if for my delight alone I will
Not hide from the recruiting officer.
God sees the wound within my heart, and no
Physician's statement, duly signed, would trick him."
WALTER: Well done. Good.
EVE:                          "Well then," he says. "As you wish.
So let him go his way. One little thing—
Those hundred guilders he came into
Not so long ago, you'll have him deed them
To you before he leaves?"—"The hundred guilders?"
I ask. "Why? What danger should he face
That you should mention them? Will he be sent
To any farther place than Utrecht?"—"Oh,
Good Lord, my child," he says then, "how can I know
Where he'll be sent? Let him follow the drum:
The drummer goes where the sergeant says,
Sergeant where the captain says, captain
Where the major says, major where
The general says, and the general he goes

Where the government says, and it—hang it!—
It's cooking up schemes all over the globe.
They'll drum and drum til the drumskins split!"
WALTER: Disgraceful!
EVE:                            "Well, then, God help me," say I.
  "But when on your list you wrote Ruprecht's name,
  You clearly stated his assignment."—
  "His assignment, ay!" says he. "Cheese for mice!
  Once they've got them all in Utrecht—*clap*—
  Down behind them falls the trap. Be wise,
  Eve. Have him deed you those hundred guilders."—
  "Is that certain?" I ask, "Your Honor Adam?
  Will they indeed be used to fight a war?"—
  "Will they be used to fight a war? you ask.
  Will you swear to keep a secret that none
  May share, a solemn secret?"—"Oh Lord," I say,
  "What is this now, Your Honor? Why look you
  So strange? Speak it out!"
WALTER:                            Well? Well? What then?
EVE: What then? Sir, he tells me now, as you
  Yourself must know, that the militia will
  This time be shipped to far Batavia,
  There to fight against the native princes
  Of, was it Bantam, Java, or Djakarta?—
  I've forgotten which. To loot the land
  To sate the greed of merchants in the Hague.
WALTER: What? To Batavia?
RUPRECHT:                      To Asia? Me?
WALTER: I never heard of this.
EVE:                            Your Grace is,
  I know, pledged to say so.
WALTER:                      On the honor
  Of my office!
EVE:            Yes, yes. On the honor
  Of your office. Which compels you to conceal
  The truth from us.
WALTER:            That will do. If I say . . .
EVE: Beg pardon, but I saw the letter you
  Sent out from Utrecht to the several courts.

WALTER: What letter?

EVE: The secret letter, Sir,
  Concerning the militia and how
  It should be mustered from the countryside.

WALTER: You have it?

EVE: Sir, I saw it.

WALTER: And it stated?

EVE: That the militia, deluded to believe
  It would be used for peaceful purposes
  At home, should be so tricked till March. In March,
  It would be shipped to Indonesia.

WALTER: Did you yourself read that in the letter?

EVE: Not I. I did not read it. I can't read.
  But he, the justice, read it out to me.

WALTER: So. He, the justice.

EVE: Yes. And word for word.

WALTER: Yes, yes. Go on.

EVE: "God in Heaven," I cry then.
  "Out young men, in their bloom—to Batavia!
  That ghastly island where one-half of each crew
  That nears its shores buries the other half.
  That is no open, honest draft of men,
  Your Grace; that is deceit. Robbed is our land
  Of its splendid young, and in exchange for what?
  Nutmeg and peppercorns. Now, guile for guile.
  Make out a certificate for Ruprecht
  And I, in gratitude, will give to you
  Whatever, within reason, you may ask."

WALTER: That you ought not have done.

EVE: Guile for guile.

WALTER: Whereat he . . . ?

EVE: "My charming Eve," he says,
  "It will be arranged. The thanks can wait;
  Now, the certificate. When must Ruprecht leave?"—
  "Now, any day."—"Good," he says. "The timing suits.
  Today the doctor is expected here.
  I'll see what luck I have with him. How late,
  Eve, do you leave your garden gate unlocked?"—
  "The garden gate?" I ask.—"Yes, the garden gate."—

"Till close on ten," I say. "Why, Your Honor?"—
"I just might bring you that certificate
Tonight."—"You, bring me? But why should you do that?
Tomorrow early I'll come by for it."—
"And that's fine, too," he says. "It's all the same.
You come for it. I rise at half-past eight."
WALTER: And then?
EVE:                 Then I go home to mother and,
   Filled with cares I cannot speak of, wait,
   Wait the whole day through within my room,
   My cell, and wait till ten that night for Ruprecht,
   Who does not come, and, sick at heart, at stroke
   Of ten, go down the stairs to lock the gate,
   And, opening it, see far off, in the gloom,
   This figure slinking out beneath the lindens,
   And I say: "Ruprecht!"—"Eve," it whispers back.—
   "Who's there?" I ask.—"Shh. Who else would it be?"—
   "It's you, Your Honor?"—"Old Adam, yes, indeed."—
RUPRECHT: God's bolts!
EVE:                 He himself . . .
RUPRECHT:                        God's thunder!
EVE:                              . . . it
                                    [is,
   And comes and jokes and, when he's pinched my cheeks,
   He asks, has Mother gone to bed?
RUPRECHT:                    The rat!
EVE: Then I: "Just what, Your Honor, brings you here
   At such an hour so late at night to me?"—
   "You silly girl," he says.—"Out with it," I say.—
   "What brings you here at ten o'clock at night?"—
   "What brings me here at ten o'clock at night?"—
   And I: "Keep your hands off me! What do you want?"—
   "You must be mad!" he says. "Did you not come,
   This morning at eleven, to the court
   And ask for a certificate for Ruprecht?"—
   "Did I . . . ? Well, yes."—"Well then. That is what I
                                    [bring."—
   "I thought I told you I would come for it."—
   "By my faith! A nippy filly, this one!"

I must be off at dawn tomorrow and,
Uncertain when I shall return, I bring
Tonight the document to her, and she—
No thank you and good night—shows me the door.
She'll come for the certificate tomorrow."—
"You must leave at dawn tomorrow, yet
This morning at eleven, you had no
Inkling you would go?"—"You *have* gone mad,"
Says he. "The order only came this noon."—
"That is different. That I didn't know."—
"Well, now you do," says he.—"Well then, Your Honor,
I thank you kindly for your pains. Forgive me.
Where is the certificate?"

WALTER:                         This order,
  Did you know of it?

LINK:                   Not a word, Your Grace.
  Rather he received another order
  Bidding him not to be absent from his post.
  And thus you found him here at home today.

WALTER: Well then?

EVE:                   If he lied, Sirs, I could not prove it.
  I had to trust his word.

WALTER:                   Quite right.
  You could not prove it. Go on. You asked him
  Where is the certificate?

EVE:                         "Here, Eve,"
  He says, and takes it out. "But first," he says,
  "Upon my soul, you'll have to tell me first
  Your Ruprecht's surname. Ruprecht Muddle, is it?"—
  "Who, Ruprecht?"—"Yes. Or Fuddle? Huddle,
  Fuddle?"—"Nonsense. Puddle is his name."—
  "God's bolts, of course!" he says. "Ruprecht Puddle.
  What a fuddled tongue I have, may God
  Destroy me, muddling all those blasted names!"—
  I say: "Your Honor Adam, don't you know . . . ?"—
  "Devil take me, no!" he says.—"You mean
  That the certificate still lacks his name?"—
  "Ruprecht's name?"—"Yes, on that paper here."—
  "I don't know what has gotten into you,"

He says. "God knows I tried to find his name
This afternoon when, with the doctor, I
Sat down to fabricate his injuries,
But I could not find it."—"Then that," I say,
"Is no certificate. It is, if I
May say so, nothing but a scrap of paper.
I need a proper document, Your Honor."—
"Upon my soul, the girl is mad," he says.
"The document is all prepared and signed,
And sealed and dated, too, and in the middle
I have left a space that Puddle will just fill.
Once I've filled it in with ink, it will
Become the proper document you need."—
But I: "How, Your Honor, at this hour,
Beneath this pear tree, will you fill that space?"—
"Why, silly girl," he says, "there's a candle
In your room, and ink and quill I carry
In my pocket. Quick! Two minutes and it's done!"

RUPRECHT: Oh, what a blasted rascal. Damn!

WALTER: And then you went with him up to your room?

EVE: I say: "Your Honor, what you propose to do
   Is strange. I now should go with you, now while
   My mother sleeps, up to my room? Surely
   You know there will be none of that."—"Fine,"
   He says. "As you please. I am content.
   We'll take the matter up another time.
   I should be back in three days or in eight."—
   "Good Lord," I say, "eight days! That long?
   And Ruprecht goes in three . . ."

WALTER: Now, Eve, be brief . . .

EVE:                     Brief, Sir . . .

WALTER:                             You
                                 [went . . .

EVE:                                 I went.
   I led him to my room, and in.

MRS. MARTHA:                Eve! Eve!

EVE: Don't be angry!

WALTER:           Now then. And what then?

EVE: Now that we are in the room—and ten times

I cursed my folly before we had arrived—
And I had closed the door with care, he sets
Certificate and quill and ink upon
The table there, draws up a chair as if
To write, and I think: now he'll sit; but he,
He goes and draws the bolt across the door,
And clears his throat, and doffs his vest,
And carefully removes his wig and, since
He finds no rack to hang it on, he puts
It on that pitcher there, which I had set
Upon the shelf to scour. And when I ask
What this should mean, he sits him down upon
The chair and grasps me so, with both hands,
So, and looks at me.

MRS. MARTHA:        And looks . . . ?

RUPRECHT:                And looks at
                         [you . . . ?

EVE: Two endless minutes staring at my face.

MRS. MARTHA: And says . . . ?

RUPRECHT:              Says nothing . . . ?

EVE:                        "You vile
                      [wretch," I say,
When he does speak. "What do you take me for?"
And push him back, so that he tumbles over . . .
And, "Jesus Christ!" I cry. "Ruprecht comes!"—
For I could hear him pounding on the door.

RUPRECHT: You see! The nick of time.

EVE:                    "Blast!" he says.
"I've been betrayed!"—and leaps, clutching paper,
Ink, and quill, to gain the windowsill.
"You," he says. "Be wise!"—and, opening
The window, cries: "Tomorrow morning, girl,
You come to me for this certificate.
Say just one word and I will rip it and,
With it, your whole life's happiness in two."

RUPRECHT: The monster!

EVE:             And steps first on the footstool,
Then the chair, and, mounting the windowsill,
Looks about to see if he can leap,

And turns, and reaches toward the shelf where he
Had hung his wig, which he had forgot,
And grabs and pulls it from the pitcher, and pulls
From off its shelf the pitcher, too. It falls;
He leaps; and Ruprecht crashes through the door.
RUPRECHT: God's bolts and thunder!
EVE:                                   And now I want, I want—
God the omnipotent knows I want to speak!
But this one—he flies snorting through the room
And pushes . . .
RUPRECHT:        Damn! Damn!
EVE:                          . . . Strikes my breast . . .
RUPRECHT:                                   Darling Eve!
EVE: And I fall fainting back upon the bed.
VEIT: You damned hothead, you!
EVE:                          When I stand up,
Gold-green, like flames, swims all about me and
I stagger, leaning on the bed; then he
Falls, crashing backward from the window;
I think: in this life, he'll not rise again.
I cry: "Oh, Savior of the World!" and run,
Bend over him and hold him in my arms,
And say: "Ruprecht! Dear man! What is wrong?"
But he . . .
RUPRECHT:   Damn me!
EVE:                  He kicks out . . .
RUPRECHT:                          Did I hit you?
EVE: Horrified, I dodge the blow.
MRS. MARTHA: That ruffian!
RUPRECHT:                  May my foot be paralyzed!
MRS. MARTHA: To kick the girl!
EVE:                          And now Mother, she
Now appears and gasps and lifts the lamp and,
Looking about, she sees the broken pitcher, and,
Sure that Ruprecht is the culprit, storms
At him. He—he stands there fuming, speechless—would
Protest his innocence, but Neighbor Rolph,
Deceived by what appears so clear, and Henk,
They start in on him, and Aunty Nell and Bess,

And Mistress Bridget, drawn by all that din,
They all, deaf, revile and heap abuse on him
And stare, big-eyed, at me, while he, with streams
Of curses, protests it was not he, but someone
Else, who just escaped, who smashed that pitcher.

RUPRECHT: Oh, damn. Why could I not just hold my tongue!
Someone else. My dear, dear Eve!

EVE:                                   Mother
Stands before me, pale, lips trembling, arms
Akimbo. "Was it, then," she asks, "another?"
And "Joseph," I say, "and Maria, Mother,
What would you think?"—"And what more need you ask?"
Scream Aunty Nell and Bess: "It was Ruprecht!"
And then all shout: "The wretch. The villain! Liar!"
And I—I kept silent, Sirs; I lied, I know,
But only lied, I swear, by keeping silent.

RUPRECHT: My soul, that's true. She didn't say a word.

MRS. MARTHA: She said nothing, no; but only nodded
With her head when asked if it was Ruprecht.

RUPRECHT: Yes. Nodded. Right.

EVE:                                   I nodded? Mother!

MRS. MARTHA:                                   No?

RUPRECHT: And that's right, too.

EVE:                                   When did I . . . ?

MRS. MARTHA:                                   No? Did
                                            [you not,
When Aunty Nell came up close and asked:
"It was Ruprecht, no?" did you not nod yes?

EVE: What? Mother? Truly? I nodded, did I?

RUPRECHT: Snuffling. When you snuffled, Eve. Admit it.
You held your handkerchief and blew your nose.
By my soul, it seemed you sort of nodded.

EVE *(bewildered)*: It must have been too slight to notice then.

MRS. MARTHA: Or just enough to notice.

WALTER:                                   Will you conclude?

EVE: This morning early still my first thought was,
I will confide in Ruprecht, tell him all,
For if he knew the true ground for the lie,
All's well, I think, and he will lie as well

And say, Yes, I broke that earthen pitcher—
And the certificate I still could have
If so. But Mother, when I walked into
Her room, once again brings up the pitcher,
Makes me come with her to Father Puddle,
And there she orders Ruprecht to appear
In court. In vain I try to speak to him.
When I approach, he scolds and turns away
And will have nothing more to do with me.

RUPRECHT: Forgive me.

WALTER: Now learn from this, dear child,
How many steps, each reprehensible,
Reprehensible, I say, and yet
Deserving pardon, a gross deception leads to.

EVE: Oh? Really?

WALTER: The militia will not
Be sent off to Batavia. It will remain,
It does in fact remain, here in Holland.

EVE: Good. Good. Good. For the justice lied. That's so?
Lied often. And *therefore* yesterday
He lied to me. The letter was a fraud.
Those words he read, he simply made them up.

WALTER: I assure you—yes.

EVE: Oh, Sir! O God.
How can you do a thing like this to me?

WALTER: Clerk Link! Tell us what the letter said.
You must know.

LINK: Utterly innocuous.
As is common knowledge, the militia
Stays within the land. Hence, *land* militia.

EVE: Oh, Ruprecht! Oh, my life. It's all over now.

RUPRECHT: Eve! Is that the way it read? You're sure?
Think!

EVE: If I . . . ? You will find out.

RUPRECHT: That was
Really what it said?

EVE: You've heard it. Everything.
And this as well, my friend. That they would trick us.

WALTER: And if I give my word . . . ?

EVE:                                        Oh, good Sir!
RUPRECHT:                                        It's true.
  It wouldn't be the first time, either.
EVE:                              Be still.
  It does no good.
WALTER:            What's this? Not the first time?
RUPRECHT: Seven years ago something like this
  Happened, too, they say . . .
WALTER:                        If the government
  Deceived him, it would be the first and only time.
  Each time the government's sent troops to Asia,
  It still has dared to tell them where they go.
  He goes . . .
EVE:            You go. Come.
WALTER:                        . . . where he is assigned.
  In Utrecht he will see that he will stay.
EVE: You go to Utrecht. Come. There you'll see.
  Come. Follow me. These are the final hours
  Of farewell the government allows for tears.
  This gentleman would not spoil them for us.
WALTER: How? Is your bosom so devoid of trust?
EVE: Oh God! God! That I did not hold my tongue.
WALTER: What you told me, I believed it word for word.
  I fear almost that I have acted rashly.
EVE: And I believe you, too, as you intend.—
  Come now.
WALTER:      Stay. I will make good my promise.
  You have made manifest those qualities
  Your countenance reveals; I will prove mine
  To you, although I must employ another
  Means of proof than you. Here. Take this purse.
EVE: You ask . . .
WALTER:            Here. This purse. With twenty guilders!
  With this sum you can buy your Ruprecht free.
EVE: What? With this . . . ?
WALTER:                    Yes, you free him from all service.
  But hold. Should the militia sail for Asia,
  The purse is then a gift, is yours. But should
  It stay at home, as I assured you, you

    Must pay the penalty for your mistrust,
    And pay, as is but fair, purse, plus interest
    At four percent, at stated times, back to me.
EVE: What, good Sir? If the . . .
WALTER:                    The terms are clear.
EVE: If the militia sails to Asia, the purse
  Is then a gift, is mine. But if it stays
  At home, as you assured me, then I must
  Endure the penalty for my mistrust
  And pay back purse, as is but fair, plus . . .
              *(She looks at Ruprecht.)*
RUPRECHT: Fooey. It isn't true. Not a word is true.
WALTER: What is not true?
EVE:                There. Take it. Take it. Take it.
WALTER: What?
EVE:         Take, I beg you, take it, Sir!
WALTER:                   The purse?
EVE: O Lord God!
WALTER:         The money? But why? The coins
  Are full-weight, newly minted guilders. Look.
  Here is the visage of the Spanish king.
  You think the king himself would cheat you?
EVE: Oh, dear, good, noble Sir, forgive me.
  Oh, that vile justice.
RUPRECHT:         Ay, the blasted rogue!
WALTER: So now do you believe I spoke the truth?
EVE: You spoke the truth? Oh, sharply printed
  And shining face of God thereon! O Jesus!
  That I no longer recognize such coin!
WALTER: Come. I give you now a kiss. May I?
RUPRECHT: A hefty one! So. That's the way.
WALTER:                    So now,
  Will you go to Utrecht?
RUPRECHT:         I'll go to Utrecht,
  And stand guard bravely on the walls.
EVE:                   And I
  Will go each Sunday and look for him
  Upon the walls and bring him fresh-churned butter

In a cool pot, until the time when I
Can bring him home with me.
WALTER:                          I shall commend
Him to my brother, the captain there, and, if
You will, bid him take you in his company.
EVE: You would do that?
WALTER:                          I will look after it
At once.
EVE:        Oh, good Sir, you give us so much joy!
WALTER: And when his year of service has sped by,
I'll come at Whitsun, not this year, but the next,
And present myself as wedding guest: for surely
You won't let that Whitsunday slip by.
EVE: No, our joy will blossom with that next spring.
WALTER: That meets with your approval, Mistress Martha?
RUPRECHT: You're not still mad at me, are you, Mother?
MRS. MARTHA: Why should I be mad at you, dumb boy?
Toppled you that pitcher from its shelf?
WALTER: Well then.—And, Father, you—?
VEIT:                          With all my heart.
WALTER: —I wonder now, where has the justice gone?
LINK: The justice? Hm. I do not know, Your Grace.
I've stood awhile at the window here
And see a fleeing man, in black array,
Stomping across the furrowed winter fields,
As if in flight from gallows and the rack.
WALTER: Where?
LINK:           If you would care to step this way . . .
*(They all go to the window.)*
WALTER: That is Justice Adam?
LINK:                          Yes. If my eyes . . .
RUPRECHT: Hang it!
LINK:           Is that he?
RUPRECHT:                          As I live and breathe!
Look, Eve. Please?
EVE:           That is he.
RUPRECHT:                          It's him, all right.
That limping gallop makes it Justice Adam.

VEIT: That fellow trotting down there to the pines,
  The justice?
MRS. MARTHA: As I'm an honest woman.
  Look you how his wig lashes at his back!
WALTER: Quick, Clerk. Away. Fetch the justice back,
  Lest he make what is bad enough, worse yet.
  I shall, of course, suspend him from his office,
  Which you shall occupy in the interim.
  Yet if his funds are found to be in order,
  As I hope they will, I will not force him
  Into exile. Do, I beg you, fetch him.
                    *(Link exits.)*
MRS. MARTHA: Now then, Your Worship, tell me this: where will
  I find this government of ours in Utrecht?
WALTER: Why so, Mistress Martha?
MRS. MARTHA *(touchily):*          Hm! Why so? Well,
  But shall justice not be done my pitcher?
WALTER: Forgive me. So it should. The Great Square.
  On Tuesday and on Friday the court convenes.
MRS. MARTHA: Good! Today a week, I will be there.
                    *(All exit.)*

*Translated by Jon Swan*

*Translator's Note:* I would not have dared to translate this wonderfully fluent, pun-filled comedy without the assistance of Carl Weber, who has directed *Der zerbrochne Krug* in Europe and who directed the first production of this translation in New York City in the fall of 1981. I should note that I have translated the Court Clerk's name, Licht, as Link, not Light. I have done so because Carl Weber and I believe that Link—an old word for a torch—has more bite than the exact English equivalent for Licht, which is Light—a word that would sound weak and rather sweet when spoken in stage producions.

# AMPHITRYON

*A Comedy after Molière*

# Act I

## SCENE 1

*It is night. Enter Sosia with a lantern.*

SOSIA: Hey! Who's that sneaking by there? Ho!—If day
  Would break, I wouldn't mind; the night is . . . What?
  I'm friendly, gentlemen! We share one road. . . .
  You've come across the truest fellow, by
  My faith, the sun has ever shone upon—
  Or rather I should say right now: the moon. . . .
  They're either rascals, arrant coward knaves
  That haven't got the stomach to attack me,
  Or else the wind was rustling through the leaves.
  Each sound is shrieking noise here in these hills.—
  Go easy! Take it slow!—But if I don't
  Soon bump my head against the gate of Thebes,
  I'll travel down into the dark of Orcus.
  Oh! Devil take it! Testing me to see
  If I have courage, if I'm a man of spirit,
  My master could have tried a different way.
  Fame crowns him, so the whole world says, and honor,
  But sending me out in the dead of night
  Was what I'd call a pretty low-down trick.
  A bit of feeling, love of fellow-man,
  Would suit me better than the wedge of virtues
  He drives to split the ranks of enemies.
  "Sosia," said he, "bestir yourself, my servant;
  You shall proclaim my victory in Thebes
  And make announcement to my tender lady
  Of my arrival, which will follow soon."

But if that couldn't wait until tomorrow
I'll be a horse—a saddled horse at that!
But look! There stands, I do believe, our house!
Hurrah! You're at your destination, Sosia,
And to all enemies shall be forgiveness.
Now, friend, you must be thinking of your errand.
You will be solemnly brought to the princess,
Alcmena, and to her you then will owe
A full report composed with rhetoric
Of the engagement that Amphitryon
Has fought to victory for the fatherland.
—But how the devil can I do that when
I wasn't present? Damn! I do wish I
Had peeped out of the tent from time to time
While both the armies were in combat there.
Oh, well! I'll talk away of hacks and thrusts
And won't come off one bit worse than some others
Who never heard a whizzing arrow either.
It wouldn't hurt, though, to rehearse the part.
A good idea, Sosia! Try it out.
Let this spot be the audience hall, and let
This lantern be Alcmena waiting on her throne.
                  *(He sets the lantern on the ground.)*
Serenest Highness! From Amphitryon,
My gracious master and your noble spouse,
I come to bring you joyous tidings of
His triumph over the Athenians.
—(A good beginning!)—*"Truly, dearest Sosia,
I cannot moderate my joy, now that
I see you once again."*—Most excellent lady,
Your kindness shames me, though it surely would
Cause any other man to swell with pride.
—(See! That's not too bad either!)—*"And the dearly
Beloved of my soul Amphitryon,
How is he?"*—Gracious lady, I'll be brief:
Like any man of spirit on the field of glory!
—(O clever fellow!)—*"When will he be coming?"*
No later than his duties will allow,
Though not so soon as he perhaps might like.
—(Damnation take me!)—*"Was there nothing else*

*He bade you tell me, Sosia?"*—He says little,
Does much, and all earth trembles when his name is heard.
—(By damn! Where am I getting all this wit?)
*"They're in retreat, you say, the Athenians?"*
—They are; and Labdacus is dead, their leader;
Pharissa's fallen; and wherever there
Are hills, they echo with our shout of triumph.—
*"O dearest Sosia, you must tell me all
About it to the very last detail."*
—My gracious lady, I am at your service.
About this victory I can, I flatter
Myself, provide you with a full report.
Imagine, then, if you will be so kind,
Pharissa standing over on this side—
            *(He indicates the places on his hand.)*
That is a city, you must realize,
In area as large as, *praeter propter,*
With no exaggeration, if not larger,
Than Thebes. Here runs the river. Our men are
In battle order here upon a hill;
And thronging in the valley are the foe.
And now when they have offered up their vows to heaven
So that the region of the clouds resounded,
And all appropriate orders being issued,
They pour forth toward us like the streams in flood.
But we, no whit less brave than they, showed them
The road for home—and you shall see just how.
First they came up against our vanguard here;
It broke. Then they came up against our archers there;
They yielded ground. Emboldened now, they moved against
The body of our slingers; these ceded them the field.
Now as they recklessly approached our main contingent,
The latter plunged—Wait! Something's wrong with that.
I think I hear a noise from over there.

## SCENE 2

*Mercury, in Sosia's form, steps out of
Amphitryon's house.*

MERCURY *(aside):* If I don't get that uninvited rascal

Out there away from this house pretty soon,
Then, by the Styx, endangered stands the pleasure
Of the embraces in Alcmena's arms
For which Zeus the Olympian today
Took on Amphitryon's form and came to earth.

SOSIA (*without seeing Mercury*):
I guess it's nothing, and my fear is gone.
But just in order to avoid adventures,
I think I'll now complete the journey home
And there acquit myself of my commission.

MERCURY (*aside*): You'll have to outwit me, my friend, or else
I'll find some method of preventing that.

SOSIA: But this night surely is of endless length.
If I have not been five hours on the road,
Five hours by the sundial there in Thebes,
I'll shoot that sundial piecemeal off the tower.
Either my master, in the drunkenness
Of victory, mistook the evening for the morning,
Or else the wanton Phoebus slumbers on
From last night's too deep gazing into bottles.

MERCURY: The disrespect with which that rascal there
Speaks of the gods! But have a little patience:
This arm will soon be teaching him respect.

SOSIA (*catching sight of Mercury*):
Oh! By the gods of night, now I am lost!
Around the house there stalks a prowling thief
That soon or late I'll see upon the gallows.
—I must be bold about it, self-assured.
                    (*He whistles.*)

MERCURY (*aloud*): Who might that lout be over there, that takes
The liberty, as if he were at home,
Of dinning in my ears with whistling now?
Is my stick maybe meant to dance the tune?

SOSIA: He doesn't seem to be a friend to music.

MERCURY: It is a week now since I've found a man
Whose bones I've had a chance of smashing up.
My arm is getting stiff, I feel, from resting,
And some back just about the breadth of yours
Is what I'm looking for to get in practice.

SOSIA: Now who the devil sired that fellow yonder?

I feel a deathly pallor seizing me
That stops the breath inside of me.
If hell itself had spewed him up,
The sight of him could not so rob me of my wits.
—But maybe this clown feels the way I feel
And he's just trying out the role of fire-eater
To scare the living daylights out of me.
Hold on, lout! I can do that too. What's more,
I'm here alone; so's he; I've got two fists;
He's got the same; and if good luck's against me,
I've got a sure retreat right there. So: forward!
        *(Mercury blocks his way.)*
MERCURY: Halt there! Who goes there?
SOSIA:                        Me.
MERCURY:                        What kind of me?
SOSIA: My own, so please you. And I think my me
   Goes toll-free like another. Courage, Sosia!
MERCURY: Halt! You won't get away so easily.
   What kind of standing have you?
SOSIA:                     Kind of standing?
   Why, I stand on two feet, as you can see.
MERCURY: I mean, are you a master or a servant?
SOSIA: That all depends on how you look at me.
   I may be master or I may be man.
MERCURY: Good. I don't like you.
SOSIA:                   Well, now, that's too bad.
MERCURY: In one word, traitor, I am asking you,
   You good-for-nothing street-and-corner-lounger,
   Who you may be, where you are coming from
   And going to, and why you're loitering here?
SOSIA: To all these questions I can give no answer
   But this: I am a man, I come from that way,
   I'm going this way, and I have before me
   Something that is beginning to annoy me.
MERCURY: I see that you are witty, and that you
   Are of a mind to shrug me off. But still
   I feel a hankering to prolong acquaintance.
   And so, to start off our involvement, I
   Now lift this hand of mine to box your ears.
SOSIA: Who? Me?

MERCURY:     Yes, you. And now you know for sure.
  Now what conclusion do you draw?
SOSIA:                    Damnation!
  You deal a mighty blow there, my good man.
MERCURY: A blow of medium-gauge. Sometimes I hit
  Still harder.
SOSIA:     If I were in the same mood,
  We could start in and have a lovely fight.
MERCURY: I'd like that. I enjoy that sort of thing.
SOSIA: But business forces me to take my leave.
                    *(He starts to go.*
                    *Mercury blocks his way.)*
MERCURY: Where?
SOSIA:         What the devil's that to you?
MERCURY:                        I want to know.
  Where are you off to?
SOSIA:           Through that gate there, which
  I'm going to have them open. Let me pass.
MERCURY: If you are impudent enough to go
  Up to that castle gate there, on your head
  A tempest and a storm of blows will pour.
SOSIA: What? I am not to enter my own house?
MERCURY: Your house? Say that again.
SOSIA:                    Why, yes; my house.
MERCURY: You mean to say that you are of this household?
SOSIA: Why not? Is it Amphitryon's house or not?
MERCURY: Is this Amphitryon's house? Of course it is,
  You dolt. Of course this is Amphitryon's house.
  The mansion of the Captain of the Thebans.
  So what do you conclude?
SOSIA:             What I conclude
  Is that I'm going in. I am his servant.
MERCURY: His serv . . .
SOSIA:         His servant.
MERCURY:             You?
SOSIA:                 Yes, me.
MERCURY:                    Amphitryon's
                                [servant?
SOSIA: Amphitryon's servant, the Theban Captain's servant.

MERCURY: Your name is . . . ?
SOSIA:                          Sosia.
MERCURY:                                      Sos . . .
SOSIA:                                                      My name is
                                                                    [Sosia.

MERCURY: Listen, I'm going to smash your every bone.
SOSIA: What? Are you crazy?
MERCURY:                          Who gave you the right,
   You shameless wretch, of taking Sosia's name?
SOSIA: I didn't take it, it was given to me.
   My father can account to you for it.
MERCURY: Who ever heard of impudence like this?
   You dare to tell me, rascal, to my face
   That you are Sosia?
SOSIA:                          Yes, of course I do.
   And on the very best of grounds: because
   The great gods will it so; because it is
   Not in my power to contend against them
   And claim to be some other than I am;
   Because I must be me, Amphitryon's servant,
   Though I might ten times rather be Amphitryon
   Himself, his cousin, or his brother-in-law.
MERCURY: Just wait! I'll try to change you into something.
SOSIA: Help, citizens! Help, Thebans! Murder! Thieves!
MERCURY: What, good-for-nothing, you cry out yet?
SOSIA:                                                      What?
   You beat me, and I'm not supposed to shout?
MERCURY: Don't you know it is night-time, sleeping-time,
   And that inside this castle here Alcmena,
   Amphitryon's spouse, is sleeping?
SOSIA:                                      Devil take you now!
   I have to come off worst because you see
   I have no stick at hand the way you do.
   But dealing blows without sustaining any,
   That's no heroic act. I'm telling you:
   It's wrong to flaunt your courage against people
   Who are compelled by Fate to hide their own.
MERCURY: So, to the point: who are you?
SOSIA *(aside)*:                          If I do

Escape this man, I'll offer half a bottle
Of wine and pour it out upon the ground.
MERCURY: Are you still Sosia?
SOSIA:                         Oh, please let me go.
  Your stick will make me cease to be at all,
  But not cease to be me, because I am.
  The only difference is that I now feel
  That I'm the Sosia who has had a beating.
MERCURY: Look here, you cur, I'm going to knock you cold.
                    *(He threatens him.)*
SOSIA: Stop your molesting me!
MERCURY:                    No, I won't stop
  Until you stop . . .
SOSIA:              All right, then I will stop.
  Not one word will I say. You shall be right,
  Whatever you propose, I'll say "Yes!" to it.
MERCURY: Are you still Sosia now, you traitor?
SOSIA:                                    Ah!
  I'm what you say I am. Command what I
  Must do; your stick makes you the master of my life.
MERCURY: You did say Sosia used to be the name you had?
SOSIA: It's true that up until the present moment I
  Believed that that was how the matter stood.
  But stress has now convinced me of your reasons,
  And now I see that I was in the wrong.
MERCURY: I am the one whose name is Sosia.
SOSIA:                                Sosia. . . . ?
  You?
MERCURY: Sosia, yes. And anyone who adds
  A gloss to that should watch out for this stick.
SOSIA *(aside):* O ye eternal gods up there! Must I
  Renounce my very self now, let myself
  Be robbed of my own name by an imposter?
MERCURY: You're muttering between your teeth, I hear?
SOSIA: Oh, nothing that has much to do with you.
  But I implore you though, by all the gods
  In Greece that hold sway over you and me,
  Allow me for a single moment's time
  To speak with you in frank and open discourse.

MERCURY: Speak.
SOSIA:        But your stick will play a silent role?
  Not take part in the conversation? Promise
  Me now that we shall make a truce.
MERCURY:               So be it.
  This point I will allow.
SOSIA:        Well, tell me then:
  How did you ever get this unheard-of
  Idea: making off thus with my name?
  Now, if it were my cloak, or if it were
  My supper . . . But my name! Why, can you wear it?
  Or can you eat it? Drink it? Mortgage it?
  How can this act of thievery profit you?
MERCURY: What! You—presume—
SOSIA:             Now stop, now stop, I say!
  We did conclude a truce.
MERCURY:        What impudence!
  You good-for-nothing!
SOSIA:        There I won't protest.
  Abuse I can put up with. Bargaining
  Can still go on.
MERCURY:    You say your name is Sosia?
SOSIA: Yes, I admit, an unconfirmed
  Report did reach my ears. . . .
MERCURY:               Enough. The truce
  Is off, and here I take the floor again.
SOSIA: To hell with you! I can't annihilate
  Myself, transform myself, slough off my skin
  And hang my skin around your shoulders. Since
  The world began, was there the likes of this?
  Can I be dreaming? Did I overdo
  My morning dram of fortifying tonic?
  Or can it be that I'm not fully conscious?
  And did Amphitryon not send me here
  To bring the princess news of his return?
  Am I not charged with telling her how he
  Gained victory and how Pharissa fell?
  And didn't I just recently arrive?
  Do I not hold this lantern? Did I not

Find you hanging around here by this gate,
And when I started to come near this entrance
Did you not take your stick and thrash my back
Inhumanly till it was black and blue,
Maintaining to my face it was not I
But rather you who was Amphitryon's servant?
All this, I feel, alas! is but too true;
Would that the gods had rather deigned to have me mad!

MERCURY: Look, dolt! My anger will come pouring down
On you again like hail at any moment.
All you have just been saying, point for point,
Applies to me—except, of course, the beating.

SOSIA: To you?—Now by the gods, this lantern here
Is witness . . .

MERCURY:         That's a lie, I say, you traitor.
I was the one Amphitryon sent here.
And yesterday the Captain of the Thebans,
When covered with the dust of battle still
He left Mars' shrine where he had sacrificed,
Charged me to tell his victory in Thebes
And how the foe's commander, Labdacus,
Had perished at his hands in the engagement:
Because, I tell you, I am Sosia,
His servant, son of doughty shepherd Davus,
Born here, and brother to that Harpagon
Who died abroad, and husband of that Charis
Who drives me frantic with her moods and whims;
The Sosia who was recently in jail
And who got fifty counted on his rear
For having carried honesty too far.

SOSIA *(aside):* He's right! And short of being Sosia
Himself, there's no one who could be aware
Of all the things he seems to know about.
You can't help but believe in him a bit.
Besides, now that I look him in the eye,
He has my shape and size, he has my bearing,
And my own rascally expression too.
—I'll put a couple of good questions to him

To get this matter straight. *(aloud)* About the booty
That was discovered in the enemy camp,
Will you tell me what was Amphitryon's
Intention and what share of it was his?

MERCURY: His share was Labdacus's jeweled head-band
Which was discovered in that monarch's tent.

SOSIA: And what was done then to that jeweled head-band?

MERCURY: Amphitryon's monogram was then engraved
In gleaming strokes upon its golden brow.

SOSIA: Presumably he wears it now himself?

MERCURY: It's destined for Alcmena. She will wear
Its jewel at her breast in memory of
The victory.

SOSIA:          And from the camp this gift
Will be sent to her . . . ?

MERCURY:                    In a golden casket
On which Amphitryon's coat of arms is stamped.

SOSIA *(aside):* Why, he knows all about it.—Thunderation!
I really now begin to doubt myself.
By impudence he was already Sosia,
And by his stick; and now—that's all I need—
He's getting to be so by valid reasons.
Yet when I pinch myself I still would swear
This body's Sosia's body yet.
—How will I get out of this labyrinth?
The things I did when I was all alone,
The things that no one saw, no one can know,
Unless *he's* really me, as well as *I* am.
—Good! Here's a question that will shed some light.
Why not? We'll see now if this catches him.
                    *(aloud)*
When both the armies there were locked in combat,
What were you doing in among the tents,
I ask you, where you hid so cleverly?

MERCURY: There was a ham—

SOSIA *(aside):*                Can this man be possessed?

MERCURY: —that I found in a corner of the tent;
I sliced myself a juicy center cut,

And then I neatly broached a case of bottles
To get a bit of cheer and spirit for
The battle that was being fought outside.

SOSIA *(aside):* I'm done for now. It would make no difference
If earth were to engulf me on the spot,
For no one drinks out of a bottle-case
Unless he accidentally found the key
That fits it, in the sack, the way I did.

*(aloud)*

I see, old friend, quite clearly now that you
Embody all the share of Sosia that
Could ever be of use upon this earth.
Beyond this I find all superfluous.
And far be it from me to importune;
I gladly yield precedence to you. But do have
The kindness, if you please, to make it clear,
As long as I'm not Sosia, *who* I am.
Because, you will admit, I must be *something*.

MERCURY: When I get through with being Sosia, you
Have my permission to be he; I grant this.
But just as long as I am he, you risk
Your neck by taking up that shameless notion.

SOSIA: All right, all right. My head begins to swim.
I see now, by my soul, how matters stand,
Though I can't say I fully understand it.
But somehow this thing must come to an end.
The wisest thing, to bring it to conclusion,
Would be for me to go my way.—Farewell.

*(He starts toward the house. Mercury
thrusts him back.)*

MERCURY: What's this, you gallows-bird! Must I be forced
To smash your every bone?

*(He beats him.)*

SOSIA:                              Just gods above!
Where is your care of me? My back won't heal
In weeks, not even if Amphitryon
Withholds *his* stick. All right! I'll just get out
Of this fiend's way and go back down to camp
For all this hellish night may blackly stare.

Some glorious embassy I've made of it!
But what reception will your master give you, Sosia?
(Exit.)

SCENE 3

MERCURY: Well, finally! Couldn't you have scampered sooner?
    You might have spared yourself some nasty blows.
    This clown has no idea of the honor
    Of having had a thrashing from a god;
    I hit him like the best of jailers, too.
    But that's no matter. He has sinned enough
    And merits beating—maybe not today,
    But if not, then he's part-paid in advance.
    I only hope the rascal with his yelling
    As if he had been skewered for the grill
    Did not wake up the lovers!—But, as I live!
    Here comes Zeus now, the father of the gods,
    And tenderly Alcmena gives him escort
    As if he were her dear Amphitryon.

SCENE 4

*Enter Jupiter in Amphitryon's shape, accompanied by Alcmena,*
*Charis, Mercury. Torches.*

JUPITER: Command the torches, dear Alcmena, to
    Withdraw. They cast a radiance, to be sure,
    Upon the loveliest charm that blooms on earth
    And no Olympian has seen one more fair.
    And yet—how shall I say it? They betray
    Him who was lured here by that charm, beloved.
    And it had best remain our little secret
    That your Amphitryon has been in Thebes.
    They have been stolen from the war, these moments
    That I have spent in sacrifice to love;
    The world might misconstrue this act of theft,
    And I would gladly do without all other
    Witness than the one who thanks me for it.

ALCMENA: Amphitryon! Oh, must you go? Oh, what
    A burden so much glory is, my dearest!
    How gladly would I change the head-band
    That you have won, for a bouquet of violets
    That had been gathered by a lowly cottage.
    What do we need besides ourselves? Why must
    So many alien things be forced upon you,
    A crown and the commanding general's staff,
    For, when the people cheer you and their rapture
    Expends itself in every glorious name,
    The thought is very sweet that you belong to me;
    But can that fleeting charm make up for what
    I feel whenever in the thick of combat
    An arrow is aimed at this cherished breast?
    How empty is this house when you are gone!
    How dull without you is the merry dance
    Of hours that should escort me up the day!
    Ah! What the country robs me of, I did
    Not feel, Amphitryon, until today
    When I possessed you for two rapid hours.
JUPITER: How you delight me, my beloved! But
    You do cause me concern on one count, which,
    As trivial as it is, I still must mention.
    You know there is a law of marriage, and
    A duty, and that anyone denied
    In love can yet before a judge demand it.
    This law upsets my fairest happiness.
    To *you*, my dearest, to your heart, I long
    To owe all favors, and I would not like
    Compliance with a mere formality,
    Which you may look on as an obligation.
    How soon you could dispel this trifling doubt!
    Disclose your inmost heart and tell me whether
    It was your legal spouse whom you received
    Today or whether it was your beloved.
ALCMENA: My spouse and my beloved! What are you saying?
    Is it not that most sacred bond alone
    That justifies receiving you at all?
    How can a social law distress you so,

Which, far from operating for restriction,
Most fortunately rather opens wide
All barriers opposed to bold desires?
JUPITER: Alcmena dearest, what I feel for you
    Outsoars, you see, as far as to the sun,
    What any husband owes you. Disaccustom
    Yourself, beloved, to your spouse,
    Make a distinction between me and him.
    It pains me so, this odious confusion;
    I find the thought intolerable that you
    Have merely granted access to a puppy
    That coldly fancies he has rights on you.
    My own desire, my sweetest light,
    Is to have seemed a being quite unique,
    Your conqueror because the mighty gods
    Taught me the art of conquest over you.
    But why drag in the vain Commander of
    The Thebans who for his exalted house
    Wooed recently and won a wealthy princess?
    What do you say? I would so like to leave
    Your virtue all to him, that public coxcomb,
    And keep your love entirely for myself.
ALCMENA: Amphitryon! You jest. If the people here
    Should hear you thus revile Amphitryon,
    They could not help but think you someone else,
    I don't know whom. It was not I who dropped
    Remarks this cheerful night about distinctions
    That can be made between husband and lover.
    But since the gods conjoined one and the other
    In you for my sake, I forgive the latter
    For any wrong the former may have done.
JUPITER: Then promise me that this glad festival
    That we have celebrated in reunion
    Shall never fade out of your memory,
    And that the godlike day that we have spent,
    My best beloved, shall not be confused
    With humdrum days of further married life.
    O promise me that you will think of me
    When once Amphitryon returns from war . . .

ALCMENA: Why, surely. What else should I say?
JUPITER:                                        Oh, thank you!
  It has more sense and meaning than you think.
  Farewell. My duty calls me.
ALCMENA:                      Must you go?
  And not, beloved, finish this brief night
  With me as it flees on ten thousand pinions?
JUPITER: Have you found this night shorter than the others?
ALCMENA: Ah!
JUPITER:       But, sweet child, Aurora could not do
  More for our happiness than she has done.
  Farewell. I shall see to it that the others
  Shall last no longer than the earth requires.
ALCMENA: He's drunk, I do believe. And so am I.
                    *(Exeunt.)*


## SCENE 5

*Mercury. Charis.*
CHARIS *(aside):* I call that tenderness! And loyalty!
  A pretty festival, when married people
  Meet once again after long separation!
  But that oaf over there who's wed to me—
  A log would have the tenderness that he has.
MERCURY *(aside):* Now I must hurry and remind Dame Night
  So that the universe does not become disordered.
  That good matchmaking goddess now has tarried
  For more than seventeen hours over Thebes.
  She may proceed now in her way and cast
  Her veil upon still other fine adventures.
CHARIS *(aloud):* See that unfeeling creature! Off he goes.
MERCURY: Well, mustn't I go with Amphitryon?
  If he is going to bed, should I not also
  Go and stretch out upon my bearskin too?
CHARIS: You could say something.
MERCURY:                          Time enough for that.
  What you were asking, you already know,
  And that's enough. On that score I'm laconic.

CHARIS: You're just a blockhead. You should say: "Dear wife,
  Be fond of me, don't cry," and other things.
MERCURY: Now, what the devil's getting into you?
  Should I spend time here making faces for you?
  Eleven married years kill conversation,
  And it's a dog's age since I was talked out.
CHARIS: Look at Amphitryon, you traitor, how
  He can be tender, like the simplest people.
  And stand in shame that in submission to
  His wife and in his matrimonial love
  A lord in the great world surpasses you.
MERCURY: Why, child, he still is on his honeymoon.
  There is an age at which all things are charming.
  What's right for that young couple, I would want
  To watch from far away, if we should do it.
  But two old donkeys like ourselves would look
  Quite silly tossing sweet nothings around.
CHARIS: Unfeeling boor! What kind of talk is that?
  Am I no longer able . . . ?
MERCURY:                          I didn't say that.
  Your obvious decline can be ignored,
  And when it's dark, you look quite grey. But out
  Here in the open it would cause a riot
  If I should start to fool around with you.
CHARIS: Did I not go and wash as soon as you
  Arrived? Did I not comb my hair, you traitor?
  And did I not put on fresh change of clothes?
  And all for nothing but to be abused?
MERCURY: What is the use of changing clothes? If you
  Could doff the garb bestowed on you by Nature,
  I'd find your dirty apron good enough.
CHARIS: When you were courting me you seemed to like it.
  I should have put it on while in the kitchen,
  While washing, and while helping with the hay.
  Can I help things if time has left its mark?
MERCURY: No, dearest wife. But I can't mend them either.
CHARIS: You rascal, you just don't deserve a wife
  Of upright character and conduct such as mine.

MERCURY: I wish you were a trifle less the wife
  Of character and didn't wear my ears
  Out with your everlasting bickering.
CHARIS: Oho! So you mislike my having always
  Maintained my honor and my good repute?
MERCURY: Heaven forfend I should! Maintain your virtue.
  But just don't drive it jingling through the streets
  And to the market like a horse with sleighbells.
CHARIS: You ought to have a wife, the kind they have
  In Thebes: deceitful, full of sly intrigue.
  A wife who'd drown you in her honeyed words
  To make you swallow your own cuckolding.
MERCURY: As far as that's concerned, I'll tell you frankly:
  Imagined evils torment none but fools.
  And I feel sorry for the man whose friend
  Advances his connubial pay: that man
  Grows old and lives up all his children's lives.*
CHARIS: Are you so shameless as to egg me on?
  So impudent as to incite me outright
  To take up with the friendly Theban who
  Lurks in the evenings on my every path?
MERCURY: The devil take me, yes! Provided only
  That you will spare me the reports of it.
  Complaisant sin, I find, is worth as much
  As tedious virtue; and my motto is:
  Not so much honor and more peace in Thebes.
  Farewell, now, Charis darling. I must go.
  Amphitryon must be in camp by now.
               *(Exit.)*
CHARIS: Oh, why must I lack the determination
  To punish this contemptible poltroon
  By clear and overt action, O ye gods!
  How I regret the fact now that the world
  Takes me as being such an upright woman!

---

* The "friend's" advance spares him the expenditure of vital strength in begetting his own children.

# Act II

## SCENE 1

*It is daylight. Amphitryon. Sosia.*

AMPHITRYON: Answer me, you thieving vagabond,
    You cursed clown! Do you know, good-for-nothing,
    Your chatter's going to bring you to the gallows?
    And that to deal with you as you deserve
    My anger needs no more than a good stick?

SOSIA: If that's the way you take it, I'll keep still.
    Command—and I was dreaming, or I'm drunk.

AMPHITRYON: To palm off such a fairy tale on me!
    The kind of stories that our nurses murmur
    Into the ears of children in the evening.—
    Do you imagine I'll believe such nonsense?

SOSIA: O never! You're the master, I'm the servant,
    And you will do or not do, as you choose.

AMPHITRYON: So be it. I shall now repress my wrath.
    Constrain myself to patience, and once more
    Hear the entire occurrence told anew.
    —I must unsnarl this devil's riddle and
    I won't set foot in that house till I do.
    —Now gather all your wits together once
    And answer me on each and every point.

SOSIA: But, Sir, from fear—forgive me—of offending,
    If I request before we start this topic
    That you should set the tone of the discussion:
    Am I to speak from my sincere convictions,
    —An honest fellow, you may be assured—
    Or talk with you the way they do at court?
    Should I come straight out with the truth, or should I
    Comport myself like one of proper breeding?

AMPHITRYON: No nonsense now. What I require of you
    Is a report with nothing kept from me.

SOSIA: Good. Let me do that now. You shall be served.
    All you need do is toss the questions at me.

AMPHITRYON: With orders that I issued you . . .

SOSIA:            I went
   Through an infernal darkness, as if day
   Had been submerged ten thousand fathoms deep,
   Consigning to all devils you, the errand,
   The road to Thebes, and the whole royal palace.

AMPHITRYON:
   What's that you're saying, knave?

SOSIA:            Sir, that's the truth.

AMPHITRYON: Good. Further. As you made your way
   along . . .

SOSIA: I steadily put one foot down ahead of
   The other, and I left my tracks behind me.

AMPHITRYON: I'm asking whether anything occurred!

SOSIA: No, nothing, Sir, except that *salva venia*
   I did have fright and terror in my soul.

AMPHITRYON: And on arrival here . . . ?

SOSIA:            I did a bit
   Of practice on the speech I had to make
   And wittily pretended that the lantern
   Would represent for me your spouse the princess.

AMPHITRYON: That being done . . . ?

SOSIA:            I was disturbed. It came.

AMPHITRYON:
   Disturbed? By what? Who then disturbed you?

SOSIA:            Sosia.

AMPHITRYON:
   What do you mean by that?

SOSIA:            What do I mean by that?
   My goodness! There you're asking me too much.
   While practicing, I was disturbed by Sosia.

AMPHITRYON: By Sosia! What Sosia? What sort
   Of gallows-bird or lout then of a Sosia,
   Apart from you, that bears that name in Thebes
   Disturbed you while you're at your practicing?

SOSIA: What Sosia? Why, the one that's in your service,
   Whom yesterday you sent out from the camp
   To tell of your arrival at the palace.

AMPHITRYON: What? You?

SOSIA:                              Yes, me. A me that is informed
  Of all our secret acts and private matters,
  Who knows about the casket with the diamonds,
  Exactly like the me now talking with you.

AMPHITRYON: What fairy tales!

SOSIA:                              This fairy tale is real.
  I hope to die, Sir, if I'm telling lies.
  And that me had arrived ahead of me,
  So I was here, in that case, by my soul,
  Before I ever had arrived.

AMPHITRYON: Where are you getting all this crazy stuff?
  This mish-mash? Out of dreams? Or drunkenness?
  Your unhinged brain? Or could it be a joke?

SOSIA: I'm absolutely serious, Sir, and you
  Will grant me credence, on my word of honor,
  If you will be so kind. I swear to you
  That I, who set out single from the camp,
  Arrived at Thebes and destination double;
  That here I met myself and stared at me;
  That here the me that stands before you now,
  Exhausted then with weariness and hunger,
  Found the other one, who came from inside
  The house, all fresh, a devil of a fellow;
  And that that pair of rascals, each one jealous
  About the carrying out of your commission,
  Got straightway in an argument, and I
  Was forced to scamper back to camp again
  For having been unreasonable about it.

AMPHITRYON: I must be of a gentle disposition,
  And peaceable by nature, self-effacing,
  To stand for having any servant talk like this.

SOSIA: Sir, if you are annoyed, I will be silent
  And we will talk about some other topic.

AMPHITRYON: All right. Go on. I'll hold my temper down,
  You see, and hear your story out with patience.
  But tell me now upon your conscience whether
  The things that you propound to me as true
  Convey the faintest plausibility.
  Can anyone make sense of them? Or grasp it?

SOSIA: Far from it! But who's asking that of you?
  I'd send off to the madhouse any man
  Who claims he understands a bit of this.
  There simply is no rhyme or reason to it,
  It's wizardry, as in a fairy tale,
  And yet it's there, like sunlight, just the same.

AMPHITRYON: Yet how can one in his right mind believe it?

SOSIA: My goodness! It cost me the utmost pain,
  Just as with you, before I did believe it.
  I thought I was possessed when I discovered
  Myself ensconced and raving on the spot,
  And for some time I called myself a swindler.
  But finally I recognized, was forced
  To recognize both this me and the other.
  He stood, as if the air had formed a mirror,
  In front of me—appearance just like mine,
  Of just my bearing—see?—and just my figure;
  Two drops of water could not be more like.
  If he had only been more sociable,
  Not such a surly brute, I could, upon
  My honor, have been very pleased with him.

AMPHITRYON: O, to what self-restraint I am condemned!
  —But did you finally get in the house?

SOSIA: Get in the house! What! You're a good one! How?
  Would I permit it? Listen to reason? Did I
  Not stubbornly forbid myself the door?

AMPHITRYON: How, in the devil's name?

SOSIA:                        How? with a stick,
  The marks of which are still upon my back.

AMPHITRYON:
  So someone thrashed you?

SOSIA:              Soundly.

AMPHITRYON:              Who? Who thrashed you?
  Who dared to do that?

SOSIA:          Me.

AMPHITRYON:         You thrashed yourself?

SOSIA: Yes, I did. Not the me now standing here,
  But that accursed me outside the house
  That beats a man like five good oarsmen.

AMPHITRYON: Misfortune come to you for talking so to me!
SOSIA: Sir, I can prove it, if you want me to.
  My witness, and a most trustworthy one,
  Is my companion in bad luck: my back.
  —The me that chased me out of here had great
  Advantage over me: he had his courage
  And two trained arms, just like a gladiator's.
AMPHITRYON: Well, to conclude, then. Did you see my wife?
SOSIA: No.
AMPHITRYON: No? Why not?
SOSIA:                     Ah! For the best of reasons.
AMPHITRYON: And who, you traitor, was the cause of failure
  To do your duty? Good-for-nothing dog!
SOSIA: Must I repeat it ten and ten times over?
  Me, as I told you, me, that devil-me
  That had acquired possession of the entrance,
  The me that claims to be the only me,
  The me there in the house, the me that has
  The stick, the me that beat me half to death.
AMPHITRYON: This animal must have been drinking and
  Completely lost what little brains he had.
SOSIA: The devil take me if I've had a drop
  To drink today above my proper portion.
  You can believe me on my oath, my goodness.
AMPHITRYON: —Well, maybe you have overdone the matter
  Of sleeping?—Maybe you had some bad dream
  In which you saw this crazy happening
  That you are telling me as actual fact . . . ?
SOSIA: No, it's not that. I did not sleep last night
  And didn't feel like sleeping in the woods there;
  And I was wide awake when I arrived here;
  The other Sosia too was wide awake
  And lively when he cudgeled me so soundly.
AMPHITRYON: Stop. Why should I exhaust my brain? I will
  Myself go crazy listening to such drivel.
  Useless, spineless, rattle-headed creature
  With no sense in you, no intelligence.
  Come on.
SOSIA *(aside):* That's how it is. Because it's my mouth says it,

It's silly stuff and not worth listening to.
But let a great man thrash himself that way,
And everyone cries: Miracle!

AMPHITRYON: Go, have them open up the gate for me.
—But what is this I see? Here comes Alcmena.
She'll be surprised; she's not expecting me.


## SCENE 2

*Enter Alcmena and Charis.*

ALCMENA: Come, my Charis. Let us gratefully
Lay offering on the altar for the gods.
Let me implore their sacred, high protection
To be continued for the best of husbands.
                    *(catching sight of Amphitryon)*
O heaven! Amphitryon!

AMPHITRYON:                    May heaven grant
My wife may not be frightened by me now!
I shall not fear that after our brief parting
Alcmena will receive less tenderly
Than her Amphitryon returns to her.

ALCMENA: What? Back so soon?

AMPHITRYON:                    This exclamation
I find to be a really dubious omen
Of whether the gods will fulfill that wish.
This "Back so soon?" does not sound like the greeting—
By heaven, no!—of true and ardent love.
Fool that I was! I fancied that the war
Had kept me all too long away from here;
Too late, as I had reckoned, I returned.
But you inform me that I was in error,
And with surprise I now perceive that I
Have dropped inopportunely from the clear sky.

ALCMENA: I don't know . . .

AMPHITRYON:                    No, Alcmena,
Forgive me. With those words you cast cold water
Upon the flames of my impassioned love.
Since I have been away, you have not cast

A single fleeting glance upon the sundial.
Here not a single throbbing of Time's wings
Was heard, and in this palace five whole months
Have all been whiled away in raucous pleasures
As if they merely were as many minutes.

ALCMENA: I find it difficult, dear friend, to grasp
What grounds you have for making this reproach.
If coldness on my part is your complaint,
Then you behold me at a loss to know
How I could satisfy you. Yesterday
When you appeared around the hour of twilight,
I did discharge the debt that you remind
Me of, and amply, from my ardent heart.
But if you want still more, expect still more,
I must confess my insufficiency,
Because I really gave you all I had.

AMPHITRYON: What's this?

ALCMENA:                      Can you still ask? Last evening, when
You pressed that stealthy kiss upon my neck—
You stole into the room, and I was spinning,
Lost to the world—did I not fly to you?
Can one rejoice more deeply in a lover?

AMPHITRYON: What are you saying to me?

ALCMENA:                                 Oh, what questions!
You were yourself full of unbounded joy
To find yourself so loved; and as I laughed
And as my intermittent tears flowed down.
You swore an oddly solemn oath that Hera
Had never so delighted Jupiter.

AMPHITRYON: Eternal gods!

ALCMENA:                   And then, as day was dawning,
No plea of mine could hold you any longer.
You would not so much as wait for the sun.
You left; I threw myself down on the bed;
The morning was too warm, I could not sleep;
I got up to make offerings to the gods,
And here I come upon you in the forecourt!
I think you owe me, faith!, some explanation
If your return now takes me by surprise,

Or, if you will, throws me in consternation;
But reason there is none for your reproaches.

AMPHITRYON: Can it be that a dream foreshowed me to you,
Alcmena? Could you have received me in
Your sleep, so you imagine that you have
Already paid the debt that love demands?

ALCMENA: Can you have been robbed of your memory,
Amphitryon, by evil demons? Can
A god have made your cheerful mind confused
So you now mock the chaste love of your wife
And seek to strip it of morality?

AMPHITRYON: What? Do you dare to tell me that I stole
In here around the twilight hour last evening?
And kissed you on the neck in jest . . . Damnation!

ALCMENA: What? Do you dare deny that yesterday
You did steal in here round the hour of twilight?
Permitting yourself every liberty
That can be at a husband's disposition?

AMPHITRYON: You're jesting. Let's return to seriousness,
For jesting of this kind is out of place.

ALCMENA: You're jesting. Let's return to seriousness,
For jesting of this kind is coarse, unseemly.

AMPHITRYON: —Permitted myself every liberty
That can be at a husband's disposition?—
Were those your words?

ALCMENA:                    Leave me, ignoble creature!

AMPHITRYON: O heaven! What a blow has struck me! Sosia!
My friend!

SOSIA:        She needs five grains of hellebore;
She's not quite level in her upper story.

AMPHITRYON: Alcmena! By the gods, you do not weigh
The consequences that such talk can lead to.
Reflect a minute. Gather up your wits.
And then say what you will and I'll believe you.

ALCMENA: Come what come may, Amphitryon, I want
You to believe me; you must not consider
Me capable of such unseemly jesting.
You see how calm I am about the outcome.
If you can seriously deny the fact

That you were at the palace yesterday
Without the gods' most direly striking you,
All other baser motives do not matter.
My inner peace you cannot trouble, nor,
I trust, the world's opinion of me either;
My heart alone will feel the laceration
Of having my beloved seek to hurt me.

AMPHITRYON: Unhappy woman! What a thing to say!
 Have you already got your testimony?

ALCMENA: Who ever heard the like? The entire corps
 Of servants in this palace bears me witness.
 The very stones you trod upon, the trees,
 The dogs that wagged their tails about your knees
 Would testify about you if they could.

AMPHITRYON: The entire corps of servants? Impossible!

ALCMENA: Must I, incomprehensible man, present
 You now with finally decisive proof?
 From whom did I receive this belt I'm wearing?

AMPHITRYON: What's this? A belt? To you? From me? Already?

ALCMENA: The head-band, you told me, of Labdacus,
 Whom you had killed amid the final battle.

AMPHITRYON: You traitor there! Now what am I to think?

SOSIA: Let me step in here. These are sorry dodges.
 I hold that head-band right here in my hands.

AMPHITRYON: Where?

SOSIA: Here. *(He draws a casket from his pocket.)*

AMPHITRYON: The seal has not been broken yet.
 *(He observes the girdle at Alcmena's bosom.)*
 And yet—if all my senses don't deceive me . . .
 *(to Sosia)*
 Quick, break the lock.

SOSIA: My goodness! Why, it's empty.
 The devil has made off with it; there is
 No head-band of King Labdacus inside it.

AMPHITRYON: O ye almighty gods who rule this earth!
 What destiny have you ordained for me?

SOSIA: What destiny's ordained for you? You're double,
 Amphitryon with the stick was here before you,
 And I would say you're lucky . . .

AMPHITRYON: Quiet, rascal!

ALCMENA *(to Charis)*: What in the world can he find so
[upsetting?
  And why should shock and consternation grip him
  When he looks at this jewel that he knows?

AMPHITRYON: I have heard tell of marvels in my time,
  And of unnatural phenomena, of objects
  Which had strayed down here from another world;
  But this cord from beyond has looped itself
  Around my honor and is strangling it.

ALCMENA *(to Amphitryon)*: After this testimony, my odd friend,
  Will you go on denying that you came
  And that I paid my obligation to you?

AMPHITRYON: No. But you will recount how matters went.

ALCMENA: Amphitryon!

AMPHITRYON: You hear? I do not doubt you.
  The jeweled head-band can't be disallowed.
  But certain reasons merely make me want
  To have you tell the story in detail
  Of what went on while I was in the palace.

ALCMENA: My friend, you are not ill, then?

AMPHITRYON: No—not ill.

ALCMENA: Perhaps your head is heavy with some worry
  About the war that presses hard upon you
  And deadens your mind's cheerful competence . . . ?

AMPHITRYON: That much is true. My head does feel all numb.

ALCMENA: Come in and rest a little.

AMPHITRYON: Let it be.
  It isn't urgent. As I said, it is
  My wish, before I go inside the house,
  To hear the tale of yesterday's arrival.

ALCMENA: It is soon told. Twilight was coming on.
  I sat there spinning in my room and dreaming,
  Amid the spindle's hum, dreams of myself
  Out on the field among the warriors' weapons,
  When I heard the glad cries by the outer gate.

AMPHITRYON: Glad cries from whom?

ALCMENA: Our servants.

AMPHITRYON: Well?

ALCMENA:                                                                                  It
                                                                                          [passed

Out of my thoughts again. Not even in
My dream did I consider what a joy
The gods had destined for me, and I was
Just taking up the thread again, when through
My every limb there passed a sudden shock.

AMPHITRYON: I know.

ALCMENA:                      You know of that.

AMPHITRYON:                                           And then?

ALCMENA:                                                      And then

There followed lots of talking, lots of jesting,
And questions overlapped in quick exchange.
Then we sat down—and then in warrior's language
You told me all about what happened at
Pharissa, and about King Labdacus,
And how he went down to eternal night,
—And all the gory episodes of battle.
And then you gave the splendid head-band to
Me as a gift, and that cost me a kiss.
We long examined it by candle-light
—And I arranged it like a sash around me,
Which your own hand then tied across my breast.

AMPHITRYON *(aside):* Can daggers be more keenly felt than this?

ALCMENA: Then supper was brought in, but neither you
Nor I paid very much attention to
The partridge pasty waiting there before us,
Nor to the bottle. You said playfully
That you lived on the nectar of my love,
You were a god, and other things besides,
As your gay sportiveness would prompt you to them.

AMPHITRYON:
—As my gay sportiveness would prompt me to them!

ALCMENA: Yes, as you thought of them. Then, after that . . .
But why so somber, friend?

AMPHITRYON:                      Then, after that . . . ?

ALCMENA: We got up from the table, and . . .

AMPHITRYON:                                           And then?

ALCMENA: And after we had got up from the table . . .

AMPHITRYON: And after you had got up from the table . . . ?
ALCMENA: We went . . .
AMPHITRYON:　　　　　You went . . . ?
ALCMENA:　　　　　　　　　　Why, then we
　　　　　　　　　　　　[went . . . of course!
　　Why do such blushes mount into your cheeks?
AMPHITRYON: This dagger cuts me to the very heart!
　　No, no, deceiving wife, it was not I.
　　Whoever stole in here last evening at
　　The twilight hour as Amphitryon
　　Was the most dastardly of vagabonds!
ALCMENA: Revolting husband!
AMPHITRYON:　　　　　Faithless, thankless wife!—
　　Farewell now to restraint, and to love also,
　　Which up till now has paralyzed my honor,
　　Farewell to memory, hope, and happiness,
　　Henceforth I'll revel in revenge and fury.
ALCMENA: Farewell to you as well, ignoble spouse,
　　From you my bleeding heart I wrench away.
　　Your guile is loathsome, it outrages me.
　　If your affections have turned to another,
　　Compelled to do so by Love's dart, your wish,
　　Confided properly to me, would have
　　As soon succeeded as this coward's ruse.
　　You now see me determined to dissolve
　　The bond that galls your vacillating soul;
　　Before the present day has seen its evening
　　You shall be free of every tie that binds you.
AMPHITRYON: Considering the ignominy of this
　　Offense that has been done to me, that is
　　The least my wounded honor can demand.
　　That a deception has been perpetrated
　　Is clear, although my mind does not yet grasp
　　The whole nefarious web. But I shall now
　　Call witnesses who'll rip it all apart.
　　I shall call on your brother, the commander,
　　And on the entire army of the Thebans,
　　Out of whose midst I had not stirred until
　　The first ray of this morning's dawning light.

Then I shall probe down to this riddle's root,
And woe! I say to him who has deceived me!
SOSIA: Sir, shall I . . . ?
AMPHITRYON:                Silence! I don't want to listen
To anything. Stay here and wait for me.
*(Exit.)*

CHARIS: My lady . . . ?
ALCMENA:                Silence! I don't want to listen
To anything. I want to be alone.
*(Exit.)*


SCENE 3

*Charis. Sosia.*

CHARIS: Well, that was what I'd call a scene! But he
Is crazy, thinking he can claim that he
Had spent last night asleep down there in camp.—
But once her brother comes, we'll clear this up.
SOSIA: This is a nasty blow my master's had.
—I wonder if I've had somewhat the same?
I think I'll beat the bushes for a bit.
CHARIS *(aside)*: What's this? He has the gall to stand right there
And sulk away and turn his back on me.
SOSIA: I feel a cold chill running down my back
Now that I'm coming to the ticklish point.
I'm almost tempted to forgo the asking,
But it won't make much difference, though,
As long as it's not scrutinized too closely.—
So come, let's take a chance, I have to know!
—Greetings to you, Charis!
CHARIS:                    What? You dare come near me,
Deceiver? You still have the impudence
To speak up boldly to me while I'm angry?
SOSIA: Ye righteous gods, what is the matter with you?
When people meet again, they greet each other.
The way you get so ruffled over nothing!
CHARIS: And what do you call "over nothing"? What
Do you call "nothing"? Tell me that, you wretch!

SOSIA: To speak the honest truth, what I call "nothing"
    Means simply "nothing," both in verse and prose,
    And "nothing," as you know, means just about
    Plain nothing, or at least, not very much.
CHARIS: Oh, if I only knew what holds my hands
    As if tied down. They itch so I can hardly
    Restrain myself from scratching out your eyes
    To show you what a raging woman is.
SOSIA: Now heaven shield me! What a wild attack is here!
CHARIS: So I suppose you call it "nothing," then,
    The shameless way that you behaved to me?
SOSIA: How was it I behaved to you? What happened?
CHARIS: What happened? Oh, just see the innocence!
    The next thing, he'll be claiming, like his master,
    That he did not come here to Thebes at all.
SOSIA: My goodness, as to that, I'll tell you now
    That I'm not playing any mystery-man.
    What happened was: we drank some devil's wine
    That washed the thoughts clean out of our poor heads.
CHARIS: Do you think you'll escape me with that dodge?
SOSIA: No, Charis. On my word. Call me a rascal
    If I did not arrive here yesterday.
    But I don't know a thing of what went on.
    To me the world seemed nothing but a bagpipe.
CHARIS: Would you be claiming you don't know the way
    You treated me when you arrived last evening?
SOSIA: The devil take it! Just as good as nothing.
    So tell me. I'm a good sort, as you know,
    And I'll condemn myself if I've done wrong.
CHARIS: You good-for-nothing! It was well past midnight,
    And the young couple had been long at rest,
    And there you were up in Amphitryon's
    Apartments still, without so much as showing
    Your face in your own quarters. Finally
    It was your wife that had to go and start
    The hunt for you. What was it that I found?
    Where did I find you then, you duty-shirker?
    I found you all stretched out upon a cushion,

As if you were at home where you belonged.
And at my tenderly concerned complaint
You said it was Amphitryon's command
Lest you should oversleep the hour of parting,
Because he wanted to leave Thebes quite early,
And more unlikely stories of the sort.
Not one kind word did I get out of you.
And then when I bent down in loving fashion
To kiss you, over to the wall you turned,
You lout, and said that I should let you sleep.

SOSIA: O good old Sosia, full of honor!

CHARIS:                                        What!
I do believe you're glad about it. Are you?

SOSIA: My goodness, you should thank your stars I did.
I had been eating some horseradish, Charis,
And rightly turned my breath away from you.

CHARIS: Nonsense! I noticed nothing of the sort.
At dinner time we had horseradish too.

SOSIA: I didn't know. But no one smells it then.

CHARIS: You won't worm your way out of it like this.
Sooner or later the contempt with which
You treated me last night will be avenged.
I can't get over all those things that I
Was forced to listen to at dawn today;
That liberty you gave me I will put
To some use yet, as sure as I am honest.

SOSIA: What was the liberty that I gave you?

CHARIS: You said, and well you knew what you were saying,
You wouldn't mind a pair of cuckold's horns,
In fact, you'd even be quite satisfied
If I took up with that Young Theban who,
As you well know, has lurked about my path.
So, very well, my friend: your will be done.

SOSIA: It was some donkey told you that; I didn't.
Joking aside: I won't take blame for that.
And on that score you will be reasonable.

CHARIS: But can I help myself, in any case?

SOSIA: Be quiet now! Here comes Alcmena.

## SCENE 4

*Enter Alcmena.*

ALCMENA:                                          Charis,
  What has befallen your unhappy mistress?
  O tell me what has happened! See this jewel.
CHARIS: What jewel is this, may I ask, my lady?
ALCMENA: It is King Labdacus's head-band jewel,
  The splendid present from Amphitryon,
  And has his monogram engraved upon it.
CHARIS: This? This King Labdacus's head-band jewel?
  Why, this is not Amphitryon's monogram.
ALCMENA: Unhappy woman, have you lost your senses?
  It's not, so one can read it, with one's finger,
  Engraved in gold, and clearly, capital A?
CHARIS: Indeed it's not, my lady. What odd fancy?
  Here is a different and quite strange initial.
  This is a "J."
ALCMENA:        A "J"?
CHARIS:                          A "J." There's no
  Mistaking it.
ALCMENA:        Alas, then, I am lost.
CHARIS: What is it, tell me, that upsets you so?
ALCMENA: How shall I find the words, dear Charis, to
  Explain to you the unexplainable?
  As I regained my room bewildered and
  Uncertain if I was awake or dreaming,
  Still baffled by the crazy notion that
  Some other man had spent the night with me,
  Yet thinking of Amphitryon's impassioned
  Grief and of his final words to me
  That he was going to summon my own brother—
  Just think of it!—to testify against me;
  And as I asked myself: "Can I be wrong?"—
  For error must be mocking one of us,
  Since neither he nor I could be deceitful;
  And as that jest of double meaning darted
  Through my memory, when my beloved,
  Amphitryon—I don't know if you heard it—

Was slandering Amphitryon, my husband;
And as I shuddered and was gripped with horror
And all my faithless senses fled from me—
Then, dearest Charis, I seized up this jewel,
This dear, this priceless token which alone
Can serve as evidence without deception.
I clutched it and was just about to press
Its precious monogram, my cherished liar's
Own refuter, to my delighted lips,
When I perceived a strange and different letter—
And stood there as though thunderstruck—a "J"!
CHARIS: O horrible! Could you have been mistaken?
ALCMENA: Mistaken!
CHARIS:            In the monogram, I mean.
ALCMENA: As to the monogram . . . It almost seems so.
CHARIS: And therefore . . . ?
ALCMENA:           What: "and therefore . . . ?"
CHARIS:                                          Calm
[yourself.
Everything still will turn out for the best.
ALCMENA: O Charis!—I'd sooner be mistaken in
    Myself! I'd sooner take this firm conviction
    That I drank in while at my mother's breast
    And which assures me that I am Alcmena,
    And say I was a Parthian or Persian.
    Is this hand mine? And is this bosom mine?
    Is my reflection in the mirror mine?
    Would he be stranger to me than myself?
    Remove my eyes and I will hear him still;
    My ears, I'll feel him still; my touch, I'll breathe him;
    Take eyes and ears and touch and sense of smell
    And all my senses, and but leave my heart,
    And you will leave me with the bell I need
    To find him anywhere in this wide world.*
CHARIS: Of course! Could I have doubted it, my lady?
    How could a woman err in such a case?
    Wrong clothes, wrong household items one might take,

* The heart emits a bell-tone.

But husbands are known in the dark.
And didn't he appear before us all?
And did the entire staff of grooms not greet
Him at the gate with joy when he appeared?
It still was daylight, and a thousand eyes
Would have to have been cloaked in midnight here.

ALCMENA: But still there is this curious initial.
Yet why did such an alien symbol, which
No sense impaired could possibly mistake,
Not catch my eye then from the very first?
If I could not distinguish, dearest Charis,
Between two names like that, could they belong
To two men—is that possible?—between
Whom I could not distinguish any better?

CHARIS: But you are sure of this, I hope, my lady?

ALCMENA: As of my own pure soul and innocence!
Else you would misconstrue my exaltation
In finding him more beautiful than ever
Last night. I could have thought him his own picture,
A painting of him by an artist's hand,
Quite true to life, yet heightened to the godlike.
He stood before me as if in a dream,
And an ineffable awareness of
My happiness, such as I never knew,
Came over me, when in a shining glory
The victor of Pharissa came to me.
It was Amphitryon, the son of gods!
He seemed to be one of the glorified
Himself; I would have liked to ask him whether
He had descended to me from the stars.

CHARIS: Imagination, Princess. Love's conception.

ALCMENA: Ah, Charis, that ambiguous jest of his
That kept recurring, making a distinction
Between him and Amphitryon. If it
Was he to whom I gave myself, why did he
Keep saying he was only the beloved,
The thief, who merely stole a dainty morsel?
To think I took the jest so smilingly
If it did not come from my husband's lips!

CHARIS: Let no such over-hasty doubts torment you.
  Did not Amphitryon acknowledge the initial
  When you showed him the head-band jewel today?
  There surely is some error here, my lady.
  If this strange letter did not puzzle him,
  It must be in the nature of the stone,
  And *yesterday* illusion blinded us,
  While all *today* is as it should be.
ALCMENA: What if he only hurriedly observed it,
  And now comes back with all the field commanders
  And frantically repeats his former claim
  That he did not set foot across this house's threshold!
  Not only would *all* evidence be forfeit,
  This jewel would be evidence *against* me.
  Confounded then, what answer could I make?
  Where shall I flee from pain and from destruction
  Once these suspicious men examine it?
  Must I not then confess that this initial
  Simply does not start Amphitryon's name?
  And further that a present with a different
  Initial could not be a gift from him?
  And if I swear upon the altar that
  He gave me this gem yesterday himself,
  Can I be sure that yesterday I did
  Receive from him *this* token now before us?
CHARIS: Be calm! He's coming. All will be resolved.


SCENE 5


*Enter Jupiter.*
ALCMENA: My husband and my lord, permit me, on
  My knees, to proffer you this jewel here.
  My life I loyally lay at your feet;
  If you gave me this stone, observe it well,
  With the initial of a strange name on it,
  I'll kiss it for sheer joy and weep upon it;
  If you did not, if you disclaim it to me
  And disavow it, let death be my lot
  And everlasting darkness hide my shame.

JUPITER: My lovely wife! Shall I take up this jewel
  When such great worth lies in the dust before me?
  Arise. What do you wish? Compose yourself.
ALCMENA: My over-confidence offended you,
  I then felt sure of innocence and strength.
  But since observing this strange monogram
  I mistrust my most intimate emotion.
  I now think . . . someone else . . . appeared before me,
  If your lips will assure me of that fact.
JUPITER: My noble wife! How you put me to shame.
  What falsehood is this that has crossed your lips?
  How could another have appeared before you?
  Who can come near you, you, before whose soul
  Are one and only one man's features ever?
  You are, my saint, encinctured with a zone
  Of diamond against all other comers.
  Even the lucky man whom you receive
  Leaves you still pure and guiltless, for all who
  Approach you turn into Amphitryon.
ALCMENA: But O my husband! Will you kindly tell
  Me: was it you? Or not? O say it was!
JUPITER: It was. No matter who it was. Be calm.
  All that you saw and touched and thought and felt
  Was I. Who else, besides me, could there be,
  Beloved? For, whoever crossed your threshold,
  You still received, my dearest, none but me,
  And for whatever favors you bestowed
  I am your debtor, and I thank you for them.
ALCMENA: No, no, Amphitryon, that is not right.
  So now farewell forever, my beloved,
  I was prepared for that event.
JUPITER:                  Alcmena!
ALCMENA: Farewell! Farewell!
JUPITER:                How can you?
ALCMENA:                        Go, go, go . . .
JUPITER: Star of my eyes!
ALCMENA:             Go, go, I say.
JUPITER:                  But hear me!

ALCMENA: I will not hear. I do not want to live
    Unless my heart is irreproachable.
JUPITER: My wife whom I adore, what are you saying?
    What law, my holy one, could you transgress?
    No matter if a devil came to you
    And spat the slime of sin and slaver from
    The depths of hell itself upon you, still
    He would not spoil the splendor of my wife's
    Breast with a single blemish! This is madness!
ALCMENA: Oh, I was shamefully deceived!
JUPITER:                    He was
    The one who was deceived, my idol! *He*
    Was cheated by his wicked craftiness,
    Not you, not your unfailing sense! If he
    Imagined he had you in his embrace,
    You lay upon Amphitryon's dear breast,
    And if he dreamed of kisses, you were pressing
    Your lips upon Amphitryon's dear mouth.
    He has a sting in him, you may be sure,
    Which all the skill of all the gods can not
    Extract from his enflamed, love-smitten heart.
ALCMENA: If only Zeus would hurl him at my feet!
    O God! The two of us must part forever.
JUPITER: The kiss that you bestowed on him has linked
    Me far more firmly to you now than all
    The love for me that ever fired your heart.
    And if out of the rushing dance of days
    I could, my dearest wife, shoot yesterday
    And drop it like a jackdaw from the air,
    Not for the bliss of all Olympus, not
    For Zeus' immortal life, would I do it.
ALCMENA: And I would deal my heart ten deaths. Now go!
    You'll never see me in your house again,
    Nor show me to a woman in all Hellas.
JUPITER: To all the host of the Olympians,
    Alcmena!—I will introduce you into
    The radiance-darting host of all the gods.
    And were I Zeus, once you approached their ranks,

Eternal Hera could not other than
Rise up, and Artemis the strict, to greet you.
ALCMENA: Your favor crushes me. Go! Let me flee.
JUPITER: Alcmena!
ALCMENA:          Let me flee!
JUPITER:                         Wife of my soul!
ALCMENA: Amphitryon, I want to leave at once.
JUPITER: You think you can escape out of these arms?
ALCMENA: Amphitryon, I want to leave. Release me.
JUPITER: And if you fled across far lands among
    The hideous races of the wilderness,
    As far as to the ocean's strand, I would
    Pursue you, overtake you, kiss you, weep,
    And lift you in my arms, and carry you
    In triumph home again and to my bed.
ALCMENA: If you will have it so, I swear to you,
    And summon all the host of gods, the dread
    Avengers of false oaths, to be my witness:
    While I have breath, I'll sooner take this heart
    Down to my grave than back into your bed.
JUPITER: By power innate in me I will shatter
    That oath and strew its fragments on the winds.
    It was no mortal man that came to you
    Last night, but Zeus himself, the god of thunder.
ALCMENA: Who?
JUPITER:          Jupiter.
ALCMENA:                    Who, madman, did you say?
JUPITER: He, Jupiter, I said.
ALCMENA:                    He, Jupiter?
    Wretch, do you venture . . . ?
JUPITER:                              Jupiter, I said,
    And I repeat it. No one less than he
    Appeared before you in the night just past.
ALCMENA: You dare blame the Olympians, you godless
    Man, for the sacrilege that was committed?
JUPITER: Blame the Olympians for sacrilege?
    Rash woman, never let me hear your lips
    Pronounce a thing like that again.
ALCMENA: Not let my lips . . . ? Is it not sacrilege . . . ?

JUPITER: Silence, I say! I so command.
ALCMENA:                                        Doomed man!
JUPITER: If you care nothing for the honor of
   Ascending up the ladder-rungs to the immortals,
   I do! And you'll permit me to be so.
   If you do not feel envy for Callisto
   The glorious, nor for Leda and Europa,
   So be it; but I envy Tyndarus
   And long for sons like the Tyndarides.*
ALCMENA: Feel envy for Callisto? For Europa?
   Those women venerated throughout Hellas?
   The high elect of Jupiter himself?
   Who dwell in the eternal realms of aether?
JUPITER: Most certainly! Why should you envy them?
   Contented as you are completely with
   The fame of seeing one lone mortal at your feet.
ALCMENA: O, the unheard-of things that you suggest!
   Dare I so much as think of such a thing?
   Would I not perish in such radiance?
   If he had been the one, would I still feel
   Life coursing joyously through this warm heart?
   I, all unworthy of such grace! A sinner!
JUPITER: Whether you are worthy of such grace
   Or not, is not for you to judge. As he
   Deems you to be, you will submit in patience.
   Would you presume, short-sighted woman, to
   Judge him who knows the human heart?
ALCMENA: Good, good, Amphitryon. I understand you,
   Your magnanimity moves me to tears.
   You threw out that remark, I realize,
   In order to distract me . . . But my soul
   Returns to take up once again its painful thought.
   Go, my own darling, you who are my all,
   Go find yourself another wife, be happy,
   And let me weep out all my days to think
   Of how I cannot make you happy.

* The sons of Tyndarus—the "Tyndarides"—were the heroic brothers Castor and
Pollux.

JUPITER: My dear wife, how you touch my heart!
  Look at the jewel now that you are holding.
ALCMENA: Celestials, save me from illusion!
JUPITER: It *is* his name? Where *mine* was yesterday?
  Are all these things that happen here not marvels?
  Did I not hold this head-band gem today
  Inside its casket under lock and key?
  And opening it to give the gem to you,
  Did I not find a mere dent in the cotton?
  And see it glittering at your breast already?
ALCMENA: Is that how I should see it? Jupiter?
  The sire of men and of eternal gods?
JUPITER: Who else could ever have deceived you in
  The instantaneous gold-scales of your feelings?
  Who else could so elude your woman's soul
  That so acutely senses all around it
  On those fine chimes of bells within your heart
  That quiver into sound at a whispered breath?
ALCMENA: His very self!
JUPITER:                 Almighty ones alone
  Dare come to you as boldly as that stranger,
  And over such a rival I prevail!
  I willingly see those omniscient ones
  Seek out and find the way into your heart
  And watch those omnipresent ones approach you,
  For are they not themselves obliged, beloved,
  To be Amphitryon, and steal his features,
  If your soul is to grant them access to you?
ALCMENA: That's true.

                    *(She kisses him.)*

JUPITER:          My goddess!
ALCMENA:                        Oh, I am so happy!
  And oh! how glad I am to be so happy!
  How glad I will be to have borne the pain
  That Jupiter has given me
  If only all is well, as once it was.
JUPITER: So, shall I tell you what I'm thinking?
ALCMENA:                                        Well?
JUPITER: And what, short of a revelation to us,
  I even feel inclined now to believe?

ALCMENA: Well? Well? You frighten me . . .
JUPITER:                                   . . . What if you
                                                        [have
  Provoked—Do not be frightened—his displeasure?
ALCMENA: I? His displeasure?
JUPITER:                          Do you believe in him?
  Do you perceive the world, his handiwork?
  Do you behold him in the sunset's glow
  As it slants through the silent greenery?
  And hear him in the rippling of the waters,
  In the song of the sumptuous nightingale?
  Does not the mountain towering to the sky
  In vain proclaim him to you, not in vain
  The cataracts that cliffs dash into spray?
  And when the sun aloft lights up his temple
  And, rung in on the throbbing pulse of joy,
  All races of created things sing praise
  To him, do you not go down in your heart's
  Abyss and there adore your idol?
ALCMENA: What are you saying? Can he be adored
  In any way more reverent or more childlike?
  Has any day burned out to darkness but
  That I knelt at his altar giving thanks
  For life, for this heart, and for you, beloved?
  And did I not just now, by starry night,
  Bow down before him, fervently adoring,
  And send my ardent prayer like incense up
  To heaven from the seething depths of feeling?
JUPITER: Why did you bow before him?—Was it not
  Because amid the lightning's jagged script
  You recognized a certain well-known letter?
ALCMENA: O dreadful! But how do you know of that?
JUPITER: Who is it that you pray to at his altar?
  Is it to him up there above the clouds?
  Can your engrossed mind ever comprehend him?
  Or can your feelings, in their wonted nest
  Dare spread their pinions in such flight? And is
  It not Amphitryon, your beloved, always,
  Before whom you bow to the dust?
ALCMENA: Unhappy woman! How confused you make me.

Can even our involuntary actions
Be blamed? Must I pray to white marble walls?
To think of him, I need some form and features.

JUPITER:
You see? That's what I said. And don't you think that such
Idolatry offends him? Does he enjoy
Not having your fair heart? Does he not also
Yearn to feel your fervent adoration?

ALCMENA: Ah yes, of course he does. Where is the sinner
Whose homage is not pleasing to the gods?

JUPITER: Of course! So, *if* he came to you, he came
Down only to *compel* your thoughts toward him,
To take revenge on you for your neglect.

ALCMENA: O horror!

JUPITER:                     Have no fear. He will not punish
You more than you deserve. But in the future
When at his altar, you must think of none
But him who came to you by night, not me.

ALCMENA: That I swear holily to do. I know,
Down to the last detail, just how he looked,
And I will not confuse him with you.

JUPITER: Do that. Else you will risk his coming back.
As often as you see his monogram
Engraved upon that head-band gem, you are
To think most fervently of his appearance,
Recalling each detail of that occurrence,
Recalling how, in that immortal presence,
The shock went through you at your distaff, how
You then received the jewel from him, and who
Helped you adjust the sash, and what took place
Around the partridge pasty. If your husband
Should intervene as a distraction, ask him
To leave you for an hour to yourself.

ALCMENA: Good, good, you will be satisfied with me.
For the first hour every morning I
Shall not so much as think one thought of you,
And then no longer think of Jupiter.

JUPITER: But if the everlasting Thunderer of
The clouds, touched by such great improvement,

Were now to come to you in all his glory,
   Beloved, how would you comport yourself?
ALCMENA: How dread a moment that would be! If only,
   When at his altar, I had thought of him,
   As long as he so slightly differs from you.
JUPITER: You have not yet seen his immortal face,
   Alcmena. Ah, beholding it, your heart
   Will leap up in delight a thousandfold.
   What you will feel for him will seem like fire,
   And ice what you feel for Amphitryon.
   Yes, if he were to touch your soul this moment
   And then depart and go back to Olympus,
   You would experience the incredible
   And weep that you could never follow him.
ALCMENA: No, no, Amphitryon, do not believe that.
   If I could just live backwards one day's time,
   And shut myself away inside my room
   From gods and heroes, under lock and key,
   I would be willing . . .
JUPITER:                          Really? Would you do that?
ALCMENA: With all my heart I would be willing to.
JUPITER *(aside):* Curse the illusion that enticed me here!
ALCMENA: What is it? Are you angry? Have I hurt you?
JUPITER: Ah, would you then, my worthy child,
   Not sweeten his atrocious life for him?
   Would deny your breast when his head seeks it,
   His head that orders all the worlds,
   To rest upon its downy softness? Oh, Alcmena,
   Olympus too is empty without love.
   What good are nations prostrate in the dust
   With adoration, to a heart athirst?
   He wants their love, not their illusion of him.
   Enshrouded in eternal veils,
   He craves to mirror himself in a soul
   And be reflected in a tear of rapture.
   Beloved, see! Twixt earth and heaven he
   Pours forth such vast infinities of joys,
   If you were chosen now by fate
   To pay the gratitude of many millions

Of creatures and to pay back all his claims
Upon creation with a single smile,
Would you, perhaps . . . Oh! I cannot believe that . . .
Oh, do not let me think . . .

ALCMENA:                          From me far be it
To oppose the high decree of gods.
If I was chosen for such sacred duty,
May my creator rule and govern me!
And yet . . .

JUPITER:          Well?

ALCMENA:                     If the choice were mine . . .

JUPITER:                                                    The
                                                         [choice . . .

ALCMENA: . . . were mine, my reverence would go to him,
And all my love to you, Amphitryon.

JUPITER: But if to you I were this god . . . ?

ALCMENA:                                   If you . . .
—What strange sensation . . . If you were this god
To me . . . I don't know whether to fall on
My knees, or not, before you . . . Are you? Are you?

JUPITER: Yours the decision. I am Amphitryon.

ALCMENA: Amphitryon . . .

JUPITER:                     Amphitryon—to you.
But still I ask you: if I were this god
To you, in love descending to you from
Olympus, how would you comport yourself?

ALCMENA: If you, beloved, were this god to me—
I would not know where my Amphitryon was,
And I would follow you no matter where,
Yes, even like Eurydice, to Orcus.

JUPITER: If you did not know where Amphitryon was,
Yes. But what if Amphitryon appeared?

ALCMENA: If he appeared?—Oh, you are torturing me.
How can Amphitryon appear to me
When I now hold Amphitryon in my arms?

JUPITER: And yet you might well have the god in your embrace
Because you thought he was Amphitryon.
Why should your feelings then cause you surprise?
If I, the god, held you in my embrace

And your Amphitryon were to appear,
How would your heart declare itself?

ALCMENA: If you, the god, held me in your embrace
And now Amphitryon were to appear,
Yes—I would then be sad, and I would wish
That he were then the god, and that you would
Remain Amphitryon, as you surely are.

JUPITER: O my sweet creature whom I so adore,
In whom I call myself so blessèd, blessèd!
One truer to the ultimate divine
Conception, both in form and mould,
Has not in eons gone forth from my hands!

ALCMENA: Amphitryon!

JUPITER:            Be calm, be calm, be calm!
All will yet be resolved for your sheer triumph.
The god longs to reveal himself to you,
And yet, before the starry hosts have danced
Their way across the silent fields of night,
Your heart shall know for whom it burned in ardor.
Sosia!

SOSIA:    Sir!

JUPITER:       Up now, my faithful servant,
In order that this day may be made glorious!
Alcmena has, in love, made peace with me,
And you shall go and summon to a feast
All guests that you find anywhere in camp.

           (*Exeunt Jupiter and Alcmena.*)

## SCENE 6

### *Charis. Sosia.*

CHARIS (*aside*): What have you overheard, unhappy woman!
There may have been gods from Olympus here?
And that the one who passes here for Sosia
May also be one of the deathless ones—
Apollo, Hermes, maybe Ganymede?

SOSIA (*aside*): It may have been great Zeus, the god of lightning!

CHARIS (*aside*): O shame upon me for the way I acted.

SOSIA (*aside*): My goodness, he was not served badly.

The fellow stood up stoutly to his man
And like a panther battled for his lord.
CHARIS *(aside):*
  Who knows but what I'm wrong? I'm going to test him.
                    *(aloud)*
  Come, Sosia, let us also make our peace.
SOSIA: Another time. Right now I'm much too busy.
CHARIS: Where are you going?
SOSIA:                        I must invite the captains.
CHARIS: Grant me a word before you go, my husband.
SOSIA: Your husband . . . ? Oh, with pleasure.
CHARIS:                                        Did you hear
  How to my lady in the twilight yesterday,
  And to her faithful servant too,
  Two mighty gods descended from Olympus,
  How Zeus, the god that rules the clouds, was here,
  And Phoebus the magnificent was with him?
SOSIA: Yes, if it's true. I'm sorry to have heard it.
  I always did dislike that sort of union.
CHARIS: Dislike? Why so? I can't imagine why . . .
SOSIA: Well, if you want to know the honest truth,
  It's much like horse and donkey.
CHARIS:                            Horse and donkey!
  A princess and a god! *(aside)* Then he must not
  Come from Olympus . . . *(aloud)* You are pleased
  To make a jest with your unworthy servant.
  A triumph such as has befallen us
  Was never known in Thebes before.
SOSIA: As far as I'm concerned, it costs me dear.
  A proper measure of disgrace would be
  As welcome to me as these devilish trophies
  That gleam on both my shoulders now.
  But I must hurry.
CHARIS:            Yes, but I was saying—
  Who ever dreamed of having guests like that?
  Who thought that in those wretched human bodies
  Two of the high immortals would be hidden?
  There certainly was many a good trait
  Left deep inside from carelessness, that could

Have been turned outside much more than was done in this
[case.

SOSIA: My goodness, how I could have used it, Charis!
  For you were just about as tender with me
  As wildcats might have been. Do mend your ways.
CHARIS: I don't recall offending you exactly,
  Or doing more than . . .
SOSIA:               Not offending me!
  Call me a scoundrel if this morning you
  Did not deserve as sound a thrashing as
  Has ever rained down on a woman's back.
CHARIS: What ever did I do?
SOSIA:             What did you do,
  You silly creature! Didn't you say you
  Were going after that oaf of a Theban
  That I threw recently out of the house?
  You didn't promise me a pair of horns?
  You didn't call me cuckold to my face?
CHARIS: Oh, I was joking! Really!
SOSIA:               Joking! Try
  That joke on me again, and I will smack you,
  The devil take me . . . !
CHARIS:           Heavens! What's coming over me?
SOSIA: The dirty dog!
CHARIS:         Don't look at me so fiercely!
  I feel my heart is shattering within me!
SOSIA: You ought to be ashamed, blasphemous woman,
  For making mock of sacred marriage duty!
  Go and be party to this sin no more,
  That's my advice.—And when I get back, I'll
  Be wanting cabbage with fried sausages.
CHARIS: Just as you say. But why do I postpone
  And keep delaying? Is he? Isn't he?
SOSIA: Well, am I what?
CHARIS:          Behold me in the dust.
SOSIA: What's wrong?
CHARIS:       Behold me in the dust before you.
SOSIA: Are you out of your mind?
CHARIS:               You are! You are!

SOSIA: What am I?
CHARIS:                Why do you deny yourself?
SOSIA: Has everyone gone mad today?
CHARIS:                                    Did I
  Not see the flaming anger of your eyes,
  Far-darting and betokening Apollo?
SOSIA: Apollo? Is the devil in you?—One
  Calls me a dog and one calls me a god?—
  I'm no one but the old familiar donkey
  Sosia!

                              *(Exit.)*

CHARIS: Sosia! What? The old
  Familiar donkey Sosia, nothing more?
  Clown, it's a good thing that I know;
  There'll be no sausage fried for you today.
                              *(Exit.)*


# Act III

## SCENE 1

              [*Amphitryon alone before his house.*]
AMPHITRYON: Oh, how repugnant are the faces of
  These captains. Each one wants to offer me
  Congratulations on the victory won,
  And I must clasp each one in my embrace
  Right when I'm cursing all of them to hell.
  Not one of them would have the sort of heart
  That I could pour out my full heart to him.
    That jewels can be stolen from a sealed
  Receptacle and not disturb the seal:
  Agreed; a mountebank some distance off
  Can trick us out of things held in our hands.
  But taking over some man's shape and manner
  And making payment to his wife in full besides,
  That is a nasty trick of Satan's doing.
  In rooms where candlelight was shining fair
  No one who had five healthy senses has

Mistaken friends until today. Mere eyes
Wrenched from their sockets and laid on the table,
Mere limbs, ears, fingers, severed from the body
And packed in boxes, would have been enough
To recognize a husband by. But now they will
Be branding husbands of necessity
And hanging bells around their necks like rams.
   She is as capable of such deception
As her turtle-dove, and I will sooner
Believe in honesty of thieves escaped
From nooses than this woman's trickery.
—She is insane, and when dawn comes tomorrow
I'll surely have to send out for physicians.
—If only I could find a way to start.

## SCENE 2

*Enter Mercury on the balcony.*

MERCURY *(aside):* This following you, old father Jupiter,
  Upon this earthly love-adventure is
  True friendship on the part of Mercury.
  For, by the Styx, it bores me thoroughly!
  And playing husband, more deceptively
  Than need be, to that lady's maid, that Charis,
  Is something I can't say I'm eager for.
  —I'll pick out an adventure of my own
  And drive that jealous lout down there to madness.

AMPHITRYON:
Why should this house be all locked up this way in daytime?

MERCURY: Hey! Easy there! Who's knocking?

AMPHITRYON:                          Me.

MERCURY:                                 Who's me?

AMPHITRYON: Ah! Open up!

MERCURY:                  Why should I? Who are you
  To raise this racket and to talk that way?

AMPHITRYON: I guss you don' know me?

MERCURY:                         Oh, yes.
  Yes, I know everyone that pulls that latch.
  —Do I know him!

AMPHITRYON:          Has all Thebes eaten mad-wort
  Today and gone out of their senses too?—
  Hey, Sosia! Sosia!
MERCURY:             Yes, my name is Sosia.
  The rascal shouts my name into my ears
  As if he were afraid I might forget it.
AMPHITRYON: Just gods, man, don't you see me?
MERCURY:                              Perfectly.
  What's up?
AMPHITRYON: You clown! "What's up," he says.
MERCURY:                          What isn't up?
  Well, speak, if I'm supposed to talk with you.
AMPHITRYON: You rascal, just you wait! I'll bring a stick
  Up there and teach you how to speak with me.
MERCURY: Ho, ho! Down there's a rough and ready cus-
  tomer.*Don't be offended.
AMPHITRYON:             Devil!
MERCURY:                      Calm yourself.
AMPHITRYON: Hey! Isn't anybody home?
MERCURY: Hey! Philip! Charmion! Where are you all?
AMPHITRYON: You low-born rascal!
MERCURY:                         But you must be tended to.
  But if you don't wait patiently until
  They come, and if you lay hand on that knocker
  So much as one more time, I'll send you down
  A whizzing embassy from up above here.
AMPHITRYON: The shameless impudence of him! A fellow
  I've often kicked, whom, if I felt like it,
  I could send off and have him crucified.
MERCURY:
  Well? Are you through now? Have you looked me over?
  Have you surveyed me with those staring eyes
  Of yours? How wide, wide open he does stretch them!
  If looks could bite, he would have gotten to me
  By now and torn me limb apart from limb.
AMPHITRYON: I tremble, Sosia, myself to think
  Of what you're getting into by such talk.

* Reading *Rüpel*, not *Riegel*, in this uncertain line.

What monstrous blows you are accumulating!
—Come down and open up this door.

MERCURY:                   At last!

AMPHITRYON: Don't keep me waiting any longer, this
  Is urgent.

MERCURY: You'll declare your errand then.
  You say you want that door there opened?

AMPHITRYON:                     Yes.

MERCURY: All right. You could have said as much politely.
  Who is it that you're after?

AMPHITRYON:           That I'm after . . . ?

MERCURY: Yes. Are you deaf? Whom do you wish to see?

AMPHITRYON:
  . . . I wish to see? You cur, I'll kick your every bone in
  Once I get inside of that house.

MERCURY: Do you know something, friend? Take my advice
  And go along. You gall me. Go along.

AMPHITRYON: You low-born scoundrel, you will soon find out
  What kind of treatment comes to servants
  Who make fun of their masters.

MERCURY:                Of their masters?
  I make fun of my master? You're my master?

AMPHITRYON: Now I hear him deny it yet!

MERCURY:                 I know
  Of only one, and that's Amphitryon.

AMPHITRYON: Who else but me, then, is Amphitryon?
  You blear-eyed rascal taking day for night?

MERCURY: Amphitryon?

AMPHITRYON:           Amphitryon, I tell you.

MERCURY: Ha, ha! You Thebans, come on over here.

AMPHITRYON:
  Oh that the earth would swallow me What shame!

MERCURY: Good friend, do tell me which the tavern was
  Where you got such a jolly jag on.

AMPHITRYON:          Heaven!

MERCURY: And was the wine new wine or old?

AMPHITRYON:                Ye gods!

MERCURY: And why not just one snifter more? You could
  Have drunk yourself to be the king of Egypt.

AMPHITRYON: Now it's all up with me.

MERCURY:                                    Just go along,
  Dear lad. I'm sorry for you. Go sleep it off.
  Here dwells Amphitryon, the Theban captain.
  Just go, and don't disturb his rest.

AMPHITRYON: What's that? Amphitryon's inside this house?

MERCURY: Yes, he's inside this house, he and Alcmena.
  But once more: go along, and don't disturb
  The happiness of that enamored pair,
  Unless you want him to come out here now
  And punish you himself for your offense.

                         *(Exit.)*


## SCENE 3


AMPHITRYON [*alone*]:
  Oh, what a blow has struck you, luckless man!
  A crushing one, and all is up with me.
  I am already buried, and my widow
  Already wedded to another husband.
  What decision ought I now to make?
  Should I reveal the shame that has befallen
  My house to all the world, or should I hide it?
  Here's nothing that needs sparing! Nothing's heard
  Amid this meeting of the council but
  The fiery hot consensus of revenge;
  Be it my one and only care now that
  The traitor does not get away alive.


## SCENE 4


        *Enter Sosia with Commanders of the Army.*

SOSIA: Sir, these were all that I was able to
  Round up and bring you here to be your guests.
  My goodness, even if I don't dine at
  Your table, I deserve the meal.

AMPHITRYON: Ah! There you are.

SOSIA:                              Eh?

AMPHITRYON:                                    Dog! How you shall die!

SOSIA: Me? Die?

AMPHITRYON:    Now you'll find out just who I am.

SOSIA: The Devil! Don't I know?

AMPHITRYON:F                    You did know, then, you
                                                [traitor?

*(He puts his hand on his sword.)*

SOSIA: O gentlemen, protect me now, I beg you.

FIRST COMMANDER: Forgive me! *(He grabs his arm.)*

AMPHITRYON:                Let me go.

SOSIA:                                What have I done?

AMPHITRYON: You still ask that?—Away, I tell you. Let
    My righteous vengeance find its satisfaction.

SOSIA: When someone's hanged, at least they tell him why.

FIRST COMMANDER: Do be so kind.

SECOND COMMANDER:                And say what wrong he did.

SOSIA: Sirs, stand your ground, if you will be so good.

AMPHITRYON: What! Just a little while ago this scurvy
    Knave here shut that door right in my face
    And hurled down such abusive streams of insults,
    Each one enough to get him crucified . . .
    Die, cur!

SOSIA:    I'm dead already. *(He falls to his knees.)*

FIRST COMMANDER:        Calm yourself.

SOSIA: Commanders! Ah!

SECOND COMMANDER:    What?

SOSIA:                        Is he stabbing at me?

AMPHITRYON: Hands off, I tell you once again! He must
    Have payment, to the full, there for the shame
    That he has heaped on me within this hour.

SOSIA: But when can I have possibly done wrong
    When for the last nine hours, by the clock,
    I've been down there in camp and at your orders?

FIRST COMMANDER: That's true. He asked us to your dinner
                                                [table.
    It's two hours now that he has been in camp
    And never once out of our sight.

AMPHITRYON: Who gave that order?

SOSIA:                        Who? Why, you yourself!

AMPHITRYON: When? I?

SOSIA:                              Right after you had made up with
                                                                    [Alcmena.
　You were so happy and at once gave orders
　For festival throughout the palace.
AMPHITRYON: O heavens! Every hour, every step
　Just gets me deeper in the labyrinth.
　What am I now to make of this, my friends?
　Did you hear what he said has happened here?
FIRST COMMANDER: What this man here has told us is so poorly
　Designed for comprehension that right now
　Your prime concern must be to rip apart
　The riddle of this whole deceitful web.
AMPHITRYON: All right, so be it! I shall need your help.
　My lucky star has brought you here to me.
　I shall assay the fortune of my life.
　Oh, my heart is afire for clarification,
　And yet I dread it worse than death.


### SCENE 5

*Enter Jupiter.*
*He knocks.*

JUPITER: What noise obliges me to come down here?
　Who's knocking at the door? What! You, Commanders?
AMPHITRYON: Who are you? Ye almighty gods!
SECOND COMMANDER: What do I see? Gods! Two Amphitryons!
AMPHITRYON: My very soul is frozen numb with horror!
　Alas for me! The riddle has been solved.
FIRST COMMANDER: Which of you two then is Amphitryon?
SECOND COMMANDER:
　Indeed! Two creatures so exactly like each other,
　No human eye can make distinction of them.
SOSIA: Sirs, this one is Amphitryon. The other
　Is a wretch deserving punishment.
                    *(He goes and stands at Jupiter's side.)*
THIRD COMMANDER *(pointing to Amphitryon)*:
　Incredible! Is this one an impostor?
AMPHITRYON: Enough of this disgraceful witchery!
　I'm going to break this mystery open.
                    *(He puts his hand on his sword.)*

FIRST COMMANDER: Stop!
AMPHITRYON:                    Let me be!
SECOND COMMANDER:                    What now?
AMPHITRYON:                                        I'm going to
                                                  [punish
  This vilest of deceits. Hands off, I say.
JUPITER: Composure there! No zeal is needed here.
  A man so much concerned about his name
  Must have shaky grounds for bearing it.
SOSIA: That's just what I say. He has padded
  His belly out, and painted up his face,
  The cheat, to make himself look like the master.
AMPHITRYON: You traitor, your revolting babble will
  Be punished with three hundred blows of whips
  Administered by three arms alternating.
SOSIA: Ho, ho! My master is a man of spirit,
  And he'll teach you to beat his servants up.
AMPHITRYON: Don't keep me any longer now, I say,
  From washing out my shame in scoundrel's blood.
FIRST COMMANDER: Excuse us, Sir. We can't allow this fight:
  Amphitryon against Amphitryon.
AMPHITRYON: What? Can't allow . . . ?
FIRST COMMANDER:                    You must compose
                                        [yourself.
AMPHITRYON: Is this your friendship for me too, Commanders?
  This the support that you had vowed to lend me?
  Instead of taking vengeance for my honor,
  You back the vile deceiver's cause and block
  The righteous fall of the avenging sword?
FIRST COMMANDER: If you judged fairly, as you are not doing,
  You would give your approval to our steps.
  Which one of you two is Amphitryon?
  Why, you are. Very well—but so is he.
  Where is God's finger that could point out for us
  Inside which bosom, one just like the other,
  The traitor heart is lurking in concealment?
  Once it has been identified, doubt not
  But we'll have found the object of our vengeance.
  But since the sword-blade could do no more here
  Than rage with futile indiscrimination,

It surely would be better in its scabbard.
Let us investigate the matter calmly,
And if you feel you are Amphitryon,
As we in this odd situation truly
Hope that you are, but yet must feel some doubt,
It will be no more difficult for you,
Than it will be for him, to prove the point.

AMPHITRYON: To prove the point . . . . .?

FIRST COMMANDER:                                    With cogent evidence.
And till then, nothing will be done about this.

JUPITER: You're quite right, Photidas. And this resemblance
Prevailing here between the two of us
Excuses your suspended judgment for me.
Nor shall I feel resentment if between me
And him comparison is to be made.
Only, no coward's settlement by swords!
I mean to summon all of Thebes myself
And in the thronged assembly of the people
Establish of what blood I am descended.
My nobleness of line he shall himself
Acknowledge, and that I am lord in Thebes.
Before me, to the dust, he shall bow down.
All fertile fields of Thebes he shall call mine,
Mine all the herds that feed among the pastures,
Mine too this house, and mine its lady mistress
That quietly commands throughout its rooms.
The entire realm of earth shall be informed
That no shame has befallen Amphitryon.
As for suspicions that the fool has roused,
Here stands one who can set them all at naught.
Thebes presently will be assembled here.
Meanwhile come in and kindly grace the table
To which Sosia has invited you.

SOSIA: My goodness, this is just what I had thought.
Sirs, this announcement casts all further doubts
To the four winds. The real Amphitryon
's the one at whose house dinner is now served.

AMPHITRYON: Ye everlasting and ye righteous gods!
Can any man be so humiliated?

To be robbed of my wife, dominion, name,
And honor by so infamous a trickster!
And friends of mine should tie my hands?
FIRST COMMANDER: No matter who you are, you must be patient.
  A few hours yet, and we will know. And then
  Without delay revenge will be exacted.
  And woe, I say, on whom it falls.
AMPHITRYON: Faint-hearted lot! Go, honor the impostor!
  I still have other friends besides you two.
  There still are men in Thebes here who will come to me
  And share the suffering in my heart and not
  Refuse their arms to be avenged for it.
JUPITER: All right! You call them. I shall wait for them.
AMPHITRYON: You rascal mountebank! You in the meantime
  Will sneak out by the back way and be off.
  But you will not elude my vengeance!
JUPITER: You go and call and bring your friends to me,
  Then I shall say a word or two; not now.
AMPHITRYON: By Zeus, there you are right, the god of clouds!
  For if it is my lot to find you then,
  You won't say more than two words, filthy cur,
  Before my sword is hilt-deep down your throat.
JUPITER: Go call your friends. I won't say anything,
  I'll speak in glances only, if you wish.
AMPHITRYON: Come on, then, fast, before he slips away.
  You must, ye gods, grant me the joy of sending
  Him down this very day into your Orcus!
  Soon with a band of friends I shall return,
  Armed friends, who'll cast a net around this house,
  And like a wasp I'll jab my stinger through
  His breast and pluck it, sucking, out again
  So winds will whistle through his withered bones.
                  *(Exit.)*

## SCENE 6

*Jupiter. Sosia. The commanders.*
JUPITER: Come, Sirs, then, if you please, and by your entrance
  Do honor to this house.

FIRST COMMANDER:     Now, by my oath,
　My wits are all awry from this adventure.
SOSIA: Now call a truce to your astonishment.
　Go in to table and carouse till morning.
　　　　　*(Exeunt Jupiter and the Commanders.)*


## SCENE 7


SOSIA: And how I'm going to pull my chair up too!
　What tales I'll tell
　When they all get to talking of the war.
　I'm dying to report on how they cut
　Their way into Pharissa. And in all
　My life I've never been so wolfish-hungry.


## SCENE 8


*Enter Mercury.*

MERCURY:
　Where to? I'll bet you're sticking your nose in here too,
　You shameless sniffer-out of kitchens, you.
SOSIA: No!—By your leave.
MERCURY:　　　　　Away there! Off, I say!
　Or do I need to fix your wagon for you?
SOSIA: What's this? Magnanimous and noble me,
　Restrain yourself. Go just a wee bit easy
　On Sosia, Sosia. Who would always want
　To be dead set on beating up himself?
MERCURY: So you're back up to your old tricks again?
　You take my name away, you good-for-nothing?
　You rob me of the name of Sosia?
SOSIA: Oh, nonsense! God forbid, my doughty self,
　Now would I ever be that stingy with you?
　So jealous of you? Take half of this name,
　It's trash. Or if you like, take all of it.
　If Castor were the name, or Pollux, what
　Would I not gladly share with you, my brother?
　I tolerate you in my master's house,
　So tolerate fraternal love in me,

And while those two Amphitryons go breaking
Each other's necks in jealous rivalry,
Why should the Sosias not sit down together
In mutual understanding and clink glasses
And drink to wish each other good long lives?

MERCURY: No, none of that!—Now, what a silly notion.
Should I sit meanwhile gnawing Hunger's paw?
The table's only set for one.

SOSIA: What difference does that make? One mother's womb
Gave birth to us, one cottage gave us shelter,
We both have slept together in one bed,
We've shared one set of clothes fraternally,
One fate, so why not eat out of one dish?

MERCURY: I know of no such life in common. From
My childhood I have been all on my own,
And never have I shared a bed, a set
Of clothes, or any bite of food.

SOSIA: Reflect a minute. We are two twin brothers.
You are the elder; I'll take second place,
You'll take precedence over me completely.
You'll take the first and all odd-numbered spoonfuls,
I'll take the second and all even-numbered.

MERCURY: No, none of that. I want my own full serving,
And anything that's left, I'll save for later.
And anyone that reaches toward my plate
I'll show a thing or two, by the high gods.

SOSIA: Well, then at least let me become your shadow
That falls behind your chair while you are eating.

MERCURY: Not so much as my footprint in the sand!

SOSIA: O you barbaric heart! You man of iron,
Forged like a thunderbolt upon an anvil!

MERCURY: Do you think I should sleep outside the gates
On grass, as if I were a journeyman,
And live by breathing the blue air of heaven?
No horse has earned a good square meal today,
By God, as thoroughly as I have earned one.
Did I not come up here by night from camp?
And didn't I walk back down there this morning
To round up guests to come up for this dinner?

And on those devilish trips have I not just
About run these old busy legs of mine
Right off and worn them out up to the thighs?
We're having sausages and warmed-up cabbage,
Just what I need to get my spirits back.

SOSIA: You're right there. Going over all those damned
Pine-root gnarls all that way is just about
Enough to break your legs—and break your neck.

MERCURY: Well, then!

SOSIA:                    Poor me, deserted by the gods.
So Charis has fixed sausages . . . ?

MERCURY:                              Yes, fresh ones.
But not for you. There was a pig to slaughter.
And I have patched my quarrel up with Charis.

SOSIA: Ah, good. I'll just lie down and die. And cabbage?

MERCURY: Yes, cabbage. Warmed-up, yes. And anyone
That might find his mouth watering at the thought
Should not start anything with me and Charis.

SOSIA: For all I care, eat cabbage till you choke.
What need do I have of your sausages?
The god that feeds the birds of heaven won't,
I think, neglect to feed old honest Sosia.

MERCURY: You still dare call yourself by that name, traitor?
You dare, you scurvy cur . . . ?

SOSIA:                          Go on! I didn't mean
                                                        [myself.
I meant a former relative of mine
Named Sosia. Long ago he used to work here—
And used to beat the other servants up—
Till someone dropped out of the sky one day
And turned him out of doors at dinner time.

MERCURY: Watch out, I say, and no more now about it.
Just watch your step, I'm telling you, if you
Still want to count yourself among the living.

SOSIA (*to himself*):
How I would like to knock you, if I had the courage,
You whoreson, bastard rascal that you are,
Puffed up with arrogance.

MERCURY:                    What's that you're saying?

SOSIA:                                                      What?

MERCURY: You said some words . . . ?
SOSIA:                          Me?
MERCURY:                              You.
SOSIA:                                      I never
                                   [made a sound.
MERCURY: I heard you mention "knocking," if I'm not
   Mistaken; also "whoreson bastard rascal."
SOSIA: There must have been a parrot talking somewhere.
   They chatter when the weather's nice.
MERCURY:                          So be it.
   For now, farewell. But if your back gets itchy,
   I'm always to be found here at this house.
(Exit.)


SCENE 9


SOSIA: You overbearing devil! I just hope
   That slaughtered pig will be the death of you!
   "He'd show the man that reached out toward his plate!"
   I'd sooner have a shepherd's dog to share
   A dinner-dish with, than I would with him.
   He'd let his father starve before his eyes
   Before he'd let him have as much as he
   Has sticking in between his middle teeth.
   —Go on! You have been rightly served, deserter.
   If I now held a sausage in each hand
   I wouldn't take a bite of either one.
   Leaving my poor good master in the lurch
   When greater force turned him out of his house!
   —There he approaches with his sturdy friends.
   —Here crowds are coming this way too! What is this?


SCENE 10


Enter Amphitryon with Colonels from one<br>side and citizenry from the other.

AMPHITRYON: Welcome, my friends! But who has summoned you?
ONE OF THE CITIZENS: All through the city heralds are
                                   [proclaiming
   That we're to gather here before your palace.

AMPHITRYON: Heralds! But to what purpose? Why?

THE CITIZEN: They told us that we would be witnesses
  To a decisive statement from your lips
  That would clear up the riddle that has thrown
  The whole town in dismay.

AMPHITRYON (*to the Colonels*): The gall of him!
  Can impudence be carried any further?

SECOND COLONEL: Then he'll appear at last.

AMPHITRYON:                                    What if he does?

FIRST COLONEL: Don't worry. Here's Argatiphontidas.
  Just let me get to look him in the eye
  And his life will be dancing here upon this sword-point.

AMPHITRYON (*to the citizenry*):
  You citizens of Thebes, listen to me!
  *I* was not the one who summoned you,
  Although the surging tide of your assemblage
  Is very welcome to me. It was he,
  That lying spirit up from hell, who wants
  Me out of Thebes, and out of my wife's heart,
  Out of the world's remembrance, if he could,
  Out of the fortress of my consciousness.
  So muster all your senses now, and even
  If every man of you, like Argus, had
  A thousand eyes and could at midnight's hour
  Tell crickets from their footprints in the sand,
  Do not spare any effort now, but open
  Your eyes up wide the way that moles will do
  When they are looking for the sun at noon;
  Direct your glances in a single mirror,
  Then turn that full and total ray on me,
  Survey me head to foot and up and down,
    And then pronounce and speak and answer me:
  Who am I?

THE CITIZENRY: Who are you? Amphitryon!

AMPHITRYON: All right. Amphitryon. So much for that.
  Now when that son of Darkness comes in sight,
  That monster of a man upon whose head
  Each individual hair curls just like mine,
  And when your dazzled senses presently
  Discover no more marks than mothers need

When they identify their youngest babes,
And when you are obliged to choose between us
As though between two drops of water, one
All sweet, pure, genuine, and silvery,
The other poison, guile, deceit, and death—
Be sure then to remember *I*'m Amphitryon,
You citizens of Thebes,
The one that bent his helmet crest like this.
THE CITIZENRY: What are you doing? Don't break off the crest
  As long as you stand in your prime before us.
SECOND COLONEL: Do you think we would . . . ?
AMPHITRYON:                        Friends,
                              [don't interfere.
  My wits are clear and I know what I'm doing.
FIRST COLONEL: Do as you like. Meanwhile I trust that you
  Have not done such a silly thing for my sake.
  If your Commanders hesitated when
  That ape appeared, it does not follow that
  Argatiphontidas would do the same.
  If some friend needs us in a matter of
  His honor, down we pull our helmets over
  Our eyes and close in on the adversary.
  To stand and listen to opponents' bragging
  Is something for old women. As for me,
  I'm always for the shortest course of action;
  In cases of this sort the only way
  To start is: run the adversary through
  Straight off—not stand on any ceremonies.
  So, short and sweet, Argatiphontidas
  Will show you all a thing or two today,
  And not at any other's hand than mine,
  By Ares, shall this rascal bite the dust.
AMPHITRYON: Come on, then!
SOSIA:                 Here I kneel before your feet,
  My true, my noble, persecuted master.
  I now am in a state of full repentance
  To take the wages of my impudence.
  So hit me, box my ears, beat, push, and kick me,
  Yes, kill me, and I won't so much as whimper.
AMPHITRYON: Get up. What's happened now?

SOSIA:                                  Not so much as a
                                                 [smell
Of dinner would they let me have in there.
The other me, that serves the other you,
The very devil was in him again,
And in a word, I've been de-Sosia-ized
The way that you are dis-Amphitryon-ated.
AMPHITRYON: Hear, citizens!
SOSIA:                        Yes, citizens of Thebes!
Here stands the actual Amphitryon.
The one inside at table there
Deserves to have the ravens eat him up.
Go storm the house, if you will be so kind,
The cabbage may just still be warm.
AMPHITRYON: So follow me.
SOSIA:                        Look! There he comes now. He and
                                                 [she.


## SCENE 11

*Enter Jupiter, Alcmena, Mercury, Charis,
and the Commanders.*

ALCMENA: Appalling! A mortal man, you say, and you
   Would shamefully expose me to his sight?
THE CITIZENRY: Ye everlasting gods! What's this we see?
JUPITER: The entire world, Beloved, must be shown
   That *no one* else came near your soul
   Save your own husband, save Amphitryon.
AMPHITRYON: Lord of my life! The poor unlucky woman!
ALCMENA: What? No one! Can you alter lots once cast?
THE COLONELS: All ye Olympians! Amphitryon there.
JUPITER: You owe it, Dearest, to yourself and me,
   You *must,* you will, my life, bring yourself to it.
   Come, pluck your courage up: a triumph waits you.
AMPHITRYON: Lightning, hell, and devils! This to me?
JUPITER: I bid you welcome, citizens of Thebes.
AMPHITRYON: You dirty dog, they're here to bring you death.
   Come on!
                       *(He draws his sword.)*

SECOND COMMANDER *(blocking his way):*
        Stop there!
AMPHITRYON:       Come on, I say, you Thebans!
FIRST COMMANDER *(pointing to Amphitryon):*
    Thebans, seize him, I cry. There's the impostor!
AMPHITRYON: Argatiphontidas!
FIRST COLONEL:        Am I bewitched?
THE CITIZENRY: Can any human eye here tell the difference?
AMPHITRYON: Death! Devil! Rage and no revenge!
    Annihilation! *(He collapses in Sosia's arms.)*
JUPITER: Fool, listen to a word or two from me.
SOSIA: My goodness! He can't hear you. He is dead.
FIRST COLONEL: What good now is the bent-down helmet crest?
    "Open your eyes up wide the way that moles do . . ."
    The one his wife accepts must be the real one.
FIRST COMMANDER: Commanders, here's the real Amphitryon.
AMPHITRYON *(reviving):*
    Which one does his own wife accept?
FIRST COLONEL:          The other,
    The one with whom she issued from the house.
    Around whom would she, vine-like, wreathe her tendrils
    If it is not her tree, Amphitryon?
AMPHITRYON: To think I do not have enough strength left
    To crush in dust the tongue that said that!
    Accept him she does not.
              *(He gets to his feet again.)*
FIRST COMMANDER:     Ah, that's a lie!
    Do you think you'll becloud the people's judgment
    When they can see with their own eyes?
AMPHITRYON: I say again that she does not accept him!
    —If she can recognize her husband in him,
    I will inquire no further who I *am,*
    But I will hail him as Amphitryon.
FIRST COMMANDER: Agreed. Pronounce.
SECOND COMMANDER:              Declare yourself now,
                           [Princess.

AMPHITRYON: Alcmena! My young wife! Declare yourself,
    Grant me once more the light of your dear eyes!
    Say you accept that man there as your husband,

And faster than that lightning-thought can flash
This sword will rid you of the sight of me.

FIRST COMMANDER: That sentence will be carried out at once.

SECOND COMMANDER: You know that man?

FIRST COMMANDER: You know that
[stranger there?

AMPHITRYON: Can it be that you should not know this heart,
Of which your listening ear so often told you
How many loving beats it throbbed for you?
Or could you fail to recognize my voice
Which you so often stole with glances from
My lips before it could attain to sound?

ALCMENA: Could I but sink into eternal darkness!

AMPHITRYON: I knew it. Citizens of Thebes, you see
The swift Peneus will reverse its streams,
The Bosporus will make its bed on Ida,
The dromedary will traverse the ocean,
Before she will accept that stranger there.

THE CITIZENRY: What? He, Amphitryon? She hesitates.

FIRST COMMANDER: Pronounce!

SECOND COMMANDER: Speak!

THIRD COMMANDER: Tell us!

SECOND COMMANDER: Princess, speak
[one word!

FIRST COMMANDER: We're lost if she is silent any longer.

JUPITER: Lend, lend your voice unto the truth, my child.

ALCMENA: Amphitryon, my friends, is here beside me.

AMPHITRYON: That is Amphitryon! Almighty gods!

FIRST COMMANDER: So be it, then. Your lot is cast. Withdraw.

AMPHITRYON: Alcmena!

SECOND COMMANDER: Go, impostor, go, unless
You'd have us carry out that sentence for you.

AMPHITRYON: Beloved!

ALCMENA: Worthless, shameless wretch!
Do you still dare address me by that term?
Before my husband's awe-inspiring face
Can I not be secure from your affront?
You monster! More abhorrent to me
Than any bloated things that nest in swamps!

What did I do, that you should come to me
Beneath the hellish cloak of darkness
And spew your venom out upon my pinions?
What more, O evil man, than having gleamed
In silence like a glowworm in your sight?
I now see what delusion blinded me.
I needed the bright splendor of the sunlight
To tell the venal body of a lout
From the high glory of these regal limbs,
To tell the bullock from the royal stag!
A curse upon the senses that fall prey
To such a gross deception, and upon
The heart that uttered such false sounds!
A curse upon the soul that could not even
Remember and identify her own beloved!
Oh, let me flee up to the mountain tops,
To dead waste regions where not even owls
Will visit me unless some guardian
Attends me and preserves my heart in blamelessness!—
Go! You succeeded in your vile deceit,
And all my peace of soul is broken down.

AMPHITRYON: Unhappy woman that you are! Was I
The one that came to you in this past night?

ALCMENA: Enough of this! Release me now, my husband.
You will now kindly charm away somewhat
This bitterest hour of my life.
Let me escape these thousand stares that beat me,
Like cudgels intercrossing, to the ground.

JUPITER: Divine one! Yet more radiant than the sun!
For you a triumph waits, the like of which
Befell no princess ever yet in Thebes.
And you must tarry for a moment yet.
                         *(to Amphitryon)*
Do you believe now *I'm* Amphitryon?

AMPHITRYON: Do I believe not *you're* Amphitryon?
You creature . . . horrible
Beyond what breath has power to convey!

FIRST COMMANDER: Impostor! You refuse?

SECOND COMMANDER:                          You still deny it?

FIRST COMMANDER: You would not be about to try to prove
  The Princess has played false with us?
AMPHITRYON: Oh, every single word of hers is true—
  And gold ten times refined is not more true.
  Not if I read what lightnings write upon
  The night, not if I summoned up the voice
  Of thunder, would I trust those oracles
  As I trust what her faithful lips have said.
  I now take oath upon the very altar
  And straightway go to die death sevenfold
  In the unshakeable conviction that
  He is Amphitryon to her.
JUPITER: Good, then.—You are Amphitryon.
AMPHITRYON:                          I am!
  —And who are you, dread spirit, then?
JUPITER: Amphitryon. I would have thought you knew that.
AMPHITRYON: Amphitryon! No mortal man can grasp this.
  Speak so we understand.
ALCMENA:                  What talk is this?
JUPITER: Amphitryon! You fool! And still you doubt?
  Argatiphontidas and Photidas,
  The citadel of Cadmus, Greece itself,
  Light, aether, and the element of water,
  All things that were, and are, and ever shall be.
AMPHITRYON: Come gather, friends, around me now, and let us
  See how this riddle is to be resolved.
ALCMENA: Oh, monstrous!
THE COMMANDERS:         What are we to make of this?
JUPITER *(to Alcmena):* You think Amphitryon appeared to you?
ALCMENA: Leave me forever in my error, if
  Your light is not to shade my soul forever.
JUPITER: A curse upon this bliss you gave me, if
  I must not be forevermore beside you!
AMPHITRYON:
  Then out with your pronouncement now: Who are you?
          *(A flash of lightning and a peal of thunder.*
          *The stage is enveloped in clouds. An eagle with*
          *the thunderbolt swoops down out of the clouds.)*

JUPITER: You seek to know?
> *(He seizes hold of the thunderbolt.*
> *The eagle flies off.)*

THE CITIZENRY:              Ye gods above!

JUPITER:                         Who am I?

THE COMMANDERS AND THE COLONELS:
   It is the dread god Jupiter himself!

ALCMENA: Protect me, ye celestials!
> *(She falls into Amphitryon's arms.)*

AMPHITRYON:               Worship to you
   From here in dust. You are the mighty thunderer!
   And yours is all that I possess.

THE CITIZENRY: The god! To dust, to dust bow down your faces!
> *(All prostrate themselves, except Amphitryon.)*

JUPITER: Amid your household Zeus has been well pleased,
   Amphitryon, and of his divine favor
   A sign shall be made manifest to you.
   Let your black woe and care be now dispelled,
   And open up your heart to triumph.
   What you, in me, did to yourself, will not
   Harm you before my everlasting nature.
   If you find your reward amid my fault,
   Then I hail you in friendly words, and leave you.
   Your fame shall henceforth find, as my world finds,
   Its boundaries and limits in the stars.
   But if you are not satisfied with thanks,
   Then you shall have your fondest wish fulfilled.
   And I permit it voice before me now.

AMPHITRYON: No, father Zeus, I am not satisfied!
   And now my tongue grows unto my heart's wish.
   What you once did for Tyndarus, do likewise
   Now for Amphitryon: grant him a son,
   Great like the sons of Tyndarus.

JUPITER: So be it. To you will be born a son
   And "Hercules" shall be his name; no hero
   Of former ages shall match his renown,
   Not even my eternal Dioscuri.
   Twelve mighty labors shall he raise aloft,

A monument beyond comparison.
And when the pyramid has been completed
And lifts its brow up to the hems of clouds,
He shall ascend its steps as far as heaven
And I shall greet his godhead in Olympus.

AMPHITRYON:
My thanks—You will not take this woman from me?
She is not breathing.

JUPITER:                    She shall be left with you.
But let her rest, if she is to remain.—
Hermes!

> *(He disappears amid the clouds which
> in the meantime have opened at their top
> to reveal the summit of Olympus where
> the Olympians are assembled.)*

ALCMENA: Amphitryon!

MERCURY: I follow you at once, divine one!—
As soon as I have told that oaf down there
About how sick and tired I am of wearing
His ugly face, and how I'll take ambrosia now
And wash it off of my Olympian cheeks,
And how his beatings may make lofty poems,
And how I am no more nor less than Hermes,
The wing-foot messenger of the high gods.

> *(Exit.)*

SOSIA: If only you had left me unfit for
Those lofty poems! Never in my life
Did I see such a devil in his thrashings!

FIRST COMMANDER:
Well! Here is such a triumph . . .

SECOND COMMANDER:                    Such high fame . . .

FIRST COLONEL: You see, we're overwhelmed . . .

AMPHITRYON:                                        Alcmena!

ALCMENA:                                                        Ah!

> *(Curtain.)*

*Translated by Charles E. Passage*

# PENTHESILEA

*A Tragedy*

## CHARACTERS

PENTHESILEA, *Queen of the Amazons*
PROTHOE ⎫
MEROE  ⎬ *Amazon Princesses*
ASTERIA ⎭
THE HIGH PRIESTESS OF DIANA
ACHILLES   ⎫
ODYSSEUS  ⎪
DIOMEDE   ⎬ *Grecian Kings*
ANTILOCHUS ⎭
GREEKS AND AMAZONS

SCENE: *A battlefield near Troy.*

# Scene 1

*Enter Odysseus and Diomede from one side, Antilochus from the other, with attendant soldiers.*

ANTILOCHUS: Greetings, mighty kings! Tell me how things go
    Since last we met before the walls of Troy?

ODYSSEUS: Badly, Antilochus. You see upon this field
    The armies of the Greeks and Amazons
    Locked in dread conflict like two rav'ning wolves.
    And, by the gods, neither can tell the cause!
    If Mars in anger, or our lord Apollo,
    Do not restrain them, or the Thunderer
    With levin-bolts do not divide the hosts,
    They die, in hate inseparable,
    The fangs of either deep in other's throat.
                 *(to a soldier)*
    Bring me a helmet full of water, friend!

ANTILOCHUS: These Amazons—what do they want of us?

ODYSSEUS: At Agamemnon's word we started out
    With the whole company of the Myrmidons,
    I and Achilles; for 'twas said that she,
    Penthesilea, from her Scythian forests
    Had broken out as leader of a host
    Of Amazons, in scaly snakeskins clad,
    All hot with battle-lust, and fast approaching
    Through mountain tracks to raise the siege of Troy.
    Scamander's bank scarce reached, we hear yet more:
    Deiphobus, old Priam's son, with an arm'd power
    Has left the Trojan stronghold with intent
    To seek the Queen in friendship and to greet
    Her who brings help. We, hearing this, devour

The dusty miles in hope to plant ourselves
Between the dread alliance of such foes;
All night we march, hasting o'er winding tracks.
Yet as the dawn comes creeping up the sky
Amazement seizes us, Antilochus;
For there in the wide valley at our feet
Fiercely engaged with all the Trojan force
We see the Amazons! Penthesilea,
As storm winds sweep and rend the scudding wrack,
Tumbles the fleeing Trojans down the vale
As though her only thought across the Hellespont,
Ay, off earth's orb itself, to scatter them.

ANTILOCHUS: Strange, by my soul!

ODYSSEUS:                    We quickly close our ranks
To meet the Trojan rout which falls upon us
Thund'ring, a torrent, and to hurl it back;
Our spear points make a wall against the foe.
At sight of this Deiphobus stops short,
And we in panting council soon decide
To greet the Amazon queen as our ally;
The while she too halts her triumphant course.
Could there be better or more obvious counsel?
Pallas herself, if I had asked her mind,
Could she have spoke more sensibly and well?
By Mars, she must, this virgin Queen, she must—
Falling from heav'n thus sudden, fully armed,
Plump in the middle of our quarrel—she
Must seek her friends on this side or on that;
And we may well believe her friend to us
Since to the Trojans she is patent foe.

ANTILOCHUS: What else? She has no other choice.

ODYSSEUS:                                Very well!
Great Peleus' son and I—we find her there
The Scythian queen, in war's rich panoply,
Short-kilted, at the head of all her host
Immobile; from her crest the plume waves free;
And still her palfrey, tossing with eager head
His gold and crimson tassels, stamps the ground.
A moment long with blank, unseeing eye,

Expressionless, she looks into our ranks
As though mere blocks of stone we stood before her.
My bare palm here, this flat unseeing hand
Has more expression than her face then had.
Till suddenly her eye falls on Achilles,
And in a trice her brow, her cheeks, her throat
Are flushed with gules, as though the whole world round
At sight of him had sunk in leaping flame.
Then with a sudden spasm swings herself
—The while she darkly glances on Achilles—
Down from her horse, leaving with careless hand
Her reins to an attendant, and inquires
Why with such pomp and state we do approach her.
To which I then: that we were wondrous glad
To meet in arms so doughty a foe of Troy;
What hatred long burned in the Grecian's breast
Against the sons of Priam; how opportune
To her and us a sure alliance could be;
And what more in such strain the moment taught.
Yet with amazement, in mid flood of my speech,
I see she does not heed me, turns away,
Her face lit up with eager wonderment
(Like any silly girl, scarce yet sixteen,
Whose head is turned by some Olympic victor),
And to a friend who stands beside her, calls:
"Oh, such a man as this, dear Prothoe,
My mother, Otrere, never can have seen!"
Her friend, shamefaced, astonished, holds her peace,
While we exchange in wonder laughing glances.
And she herself, unconscious, infatuate,
Stands drinking in the Peleid's gleaming form;
Until her friend reminds her timidly
That she still owes an answer to my words.
She then, her mantling cheek, with rage or shame,
Ruddying her harness even to the waist,
Confus'dly, proudly, almost wildly, turns
To me and cries: "I am Penthesilea,
Queen of the Amazons, too soon ye shall
Have wingèd answer from our Scythian bows."

ANTILOCHUS: So word for word your messenger reported,
    Yet no one of us in the Grecian camp
    Could see what this—
ODYSSEUS:               We now still ignorant
    What from this strange retort we might expect,
    In shame and fury turn to regain our ranks,
    The while the Trojans, who with mocking glee
    Have marked all our discomfiture from far,
    Triumphant stand; and soon, mistakenly
    Deeming themselves the favor'd ones, and that
    Some error merely, soon to be put right,
    Had loosed on them the fury of this maid,
    Resolve through herald's voice to offer her
    Once more their heart and hand, which she had scorned.
    Yet e'er the herald, chosen to this task,
    Had shak'n the dust from armor and from arms,
    Crashes upon us both, Trojan and Greek,
    This centaur queen with all her reckless band,
    Like mountain torrent's headlong, swirling flood
    Sweeping both us and them to utter wrack.
ANTILOCHUS: Incredible, my friends!
ODYSSEUS:                     There then begins
    A struggle such as never yet was seen
    Since hate began, upon the fields of Earth.
    Each force in Nature, creates its opposite
    And fights with this; no room for any third.
    What quenches fire will not make water boil
    And turn to steam; likewise the opposite.
    Yet here appears a deadly foe of both,
    That makes fire doubt: should it not flow like water?
    And water: should it haply burn like fire?
    The hard-press'd Trojan, fleeing the Amazon
    Shelters behind a Grecian shield; the Greek
    Defends him from the maiden's blade, and both
    Trojan and Greek are almost forced, despite
    The rape of Helen, to hold each other friends
    And join to fight a common enemy.
                *(A Greek brings him water.)*
    Thanks, friend! A grateful draught.

DIOMEDE:                              From that day on
  The battle rolls unceasing on these plains,
  Its slack'ning rage ever again renew'd,
  Like to a grumbling thunderstorm hemm'd in
  By mountain peaks. But yesterday as I
  Brought rested pow'rs to stay the fainting Greeks,
  She was in act to cleave our wav'ring ranks
  As with intent to smite the whole Greek race
  And lay it, root and branch, forever low.
  The noblest boughs, Astyanax, Ariston,
  Lie scattered by the storm—Menander too—
  The grace and loveliness of their young limbs
  But dung about the roots of that high laurel
  That grows for her, the dreaded daughter of Mars.
  And prisoners she has victorious taken
  More than she leaves us eyes to mark their loss
  Or valiant arms to fight for their release.
ANTILOCHUS: But what she wants of us—is that still dark?
DIOMEDE: Quite dark—that is the strangest—cast where'er
  We will the lead line of our searching thought.
  Sometimes, to judge by that unnatural rage
  With which she seeks in every broil the son
  Of Thetis, we have deemed her heart was full
  Of some especial hatred for his person.
  Not more untiringly the rav'ning she-wolf
  Pursues through snow-lapped forests still her prey
  That she has marked her with gaunt, hungry eye,
  Than throughout all our battle she Achilles.
  Yet lately once, when for a moment's time
  She held his life within her bloodstained hand,
  Smiling she gave it him again; in truth
  He stood on Lethe bank, had she not held him.
ANTILOCHUS: What? Had not who? The Queen, you say?
DIOMEDE:                                              The
                                                     [Queen!

  For as at sundown yesterday those two,
  Penthesilea and Achilles met
  At point to fight, appears Deiphobus,
  Ranges him at the warrior-maiden's side

And strikes great Thetis' son, the Peleid,
An underhand blow, that all his harness rings,
And from the topmost elms the sound re-echoes.
The Queen, death-color, two whole minutes long
Hangs limp her arms: then shaking free her locks
Unschooled about her flaming cheeks, she stands
High in her gleaming stirrups towering up,
Then down as from the firmament itself
She drives her blade into the Trojan's neck,
That he—poor meddling fool—to earth down crashing
Rolls in his gore at our great Peleid's feet.
He then, Achilles, in his gratitude
Will serve her in like manner; but the Queen,
Pressed flat into her dappled charger's mane,
Who, straining at the bit, curvets and rears,
Avoids his murd'rous blow and shakes the reins
And, turning in the saddle, smiles and is gone.

ANTILOCHUS: Most strange indeed!

ODYSSEUS:                              What brings you here from
                                                    [Troy?

ANTILOCHUS: Our lord, great Agamemnon, sends me here
   To ask if 'twere not wiser, things so changed,
   That you should sound retreat; since our true purpose
   To raze the towers of Ilium, not interpose
   Ourselves between a wand'ring princess' host
   And her far aim, to us indifferent.
   If then you have acquired good certainty
   'Tis not to succour Troy she comes in arms,
   He is desirous you should straight return,
   Not weigh the cost, and shelter once again
   Behind the Argive ramparts by the shore.
   If she pursue you, he, great Atreus' son,
   Will sally forth in person with the host,
   To see with his own eyes upon which side
   This riddling sphinx will throw her battled power.

ODYSSEUS: By Jupiter, these orders like me well!
   Can you suppose Laertes' son is glad
   To fight where neither sense nor reason bid?
   But first get him away: him—him—Achilles!

For, as the hound unleashed with dreadful bay
Flings herself on the stag's wide-branching antlers,
The huntsman fears for her and calls her off,
But she, her teeth firm closed in the shaggy throat
Is dragged through streams, o'er mountains, clinging still,
Into the deepest forest's gloom; so he,
Infatuate since he's flushed such noble game
So strange, so lovely, from the coverts of war.
Though with an arrow you should pierce his thighs
To hobble him, yet never will he leave
The scent, he swears it, of this Amazon
Till he has dragged her by her silken hair
Off her pied tiger-steed into the dust.
Try it, Antilochus, try it yourself and see
What subtlest words can do against his madness.

DIOMEDE: Let us as one oppose an icy wedge
Of reason to his mad resolve and split it.
You, friend, of many wiles will doubtless find
The chink of weakness where we can break in.
If he is stubborn still, I'll pick him up
And, with two more Aetolians, on our backs
We'll carry him, a clod quite reft of sense,
And pitch him in the Argive camp.

ODYSSEUS:                            Lead on!

ANTILOCHUS: What now? Who is it hurries thus to us?

DIOMEDE: It is Adrastes, pale and all distraught.


# Scene 2

*Enter a Captain.*

ODYSSEUS: What bring'st thou?

DIOMEDE:              News?

CAPTAIN:                        For you the dismallest
That ever yet you heard.

DIOMEDE:             What news?

ODYSSEUS:                     Speak out!

CAPTAIN: Achilles—captive of the Amazons;
  So Ilium's walls will never now be razed.
DIOMEDE: Ye gods in heav'n, be kind!
ODYSSEUS:                       O hateful news!
ANTILOCHUS: When did this fearful thing, and where, take place?
CAPTAIN: A new onslaught of these daemoniac maids,
  This brood of Mars, like searing thunderbolt,
  Melted too fast the Aetolians' stalwart ranks
  And poured them down upon us Myrmidons,
  Till then unconquered, like a swirling flood.
  Vainly we strive, close-knit and firm, to stem
  Their fleeing hordes; in headlong inundation
  Swept from the field in welter and wrack we fly;
  And nowhere can we halt our swift career
  Till far from Peleus' son we stand aghast.
  At length he struggles, threaten'd on every side,
  Out of the battle's thickest gloom, and seeks
  His fearful course down a smooth-sloping hill.
  Towards us now he wings his way. Already
  Rejoicing, jubilant we call to him,
  But soon the grateful shout dies on our lips;
  For suddenly before his horses' hoofs
  A chasm gapes, and down from giddy height
  He gazes, frozen, into yawning depths.
  Vain now the skill in which he so excels,
  Deftly to guide the chariot to the goal:
  His team turn terrified their rearing heads
  Backwards against their driver's furious blows.
  And now in chaos of tangled harness lie
  Chariot and steeds, a sprawling, huddled mass,
  And with them in the wreck Achilles' self,
  Powerless as lion in the hunter's snare.
ANTILOCHUS: Insensate! Whither would he—?
CAPTAIN:                           Automedon
  His stalwart charioteer at once springs down
  And leaps to loose the tangle of steeds and harness;
  In little space indeed they stand again.
  Yet ere he can free every fettered leg
  From twisted trace or other hind'ring check,

The Queen herself, leading a jubilant swarm
Of Amazons, spurs into the ravine
And severs thus his only path to safety.
ANTILOCHUS:                               Ye gods!
CAPTAIN: She stops—dust billowing up and round her there—
In mid-career her charger's flight, and looks,
Her dazzling face thrown back to scan the height,
And measures with her eye the wall of rock.
Her nodding plume, as tho' himself appalled,
Seems to drag back and down her ardent head.
Then suddenly she lays her reins aside,
We see her quickly press her tiny hands,
As though herself now giddy, to her forehead,
O'er which all disarrayed her long locks fall.
Fill'd with dismay at such unwonted sight
Her maidens all press round imploring her
With eager, anxious gestures to hold back.
That one who seems her nearest friend, gently
Encircles her with tender arm; another,
Yet bolder, grasps her charger's hanging rein;
They seek with force to stay her mad resolve.
But she—
DIOMEDE: What? Does she dare?
ANTILOCHUS:                     Tell on!
CAPTAIN:                                She does.
Vain their beseeching, vain restraining hands;
With gentle majesty she puts aside
Those who would hold her and begins to trot
Restlessly up and down the sheer-walled cleft,
Seeking if there be nowhere some small path
Will help her longing to those wings it lacks.
And now in furious ardor she begins
To fling herself upon the beetling cliff
Now here, now there, in fierce desire to scale it,
Consumed with senseless hope that thus she may
Seize the rich prey that lies enmesh'd above.
Now she has tested ev'ry crack and cranny
Wash'd by the rains of many a winter storm;
She sees full well the cliff's unclimbable;

And yet, quite reft of judgment, she returns
And starts once more to seek and seek—in vain.
And swings herself indeed, no whit disheartened,
Up onto tracks that ev'n the he-goat shuns,
Swings herself up as much as by the height
Of a great elm. And as she perches there
Upon a jutting block of granite, where
No room would be ev'n for the chamois' hoof,
O'ertower'd on every hand by fearful cliffs,
Not forward and not back daring to move
While with shrill cries her maidens cleave the air,
Sudden to earth she tumbles, rider and steed,
With loosened boulders thund'ring down around,
As though to deepest Tartarus she were bent,
Right to the foot of that sheer cliff again
—And neither breaks her neck nor nothing learns,
But only girds herself again to climb.

ANTILOCHUS: A foaming-jawed hyena! 'Tis no woman!

ODYSSEUS: Automedon, the while?

CAPTAIN: At last he leaps—
For car and horses now stand in good order
(In all this time Hephaestos could have forged
Almost anew the whole great car of bronze),
He leaps into his place and grasps the reins:
Oh, what relief, what joy to all us Greeks!
But at this moment, as he turns his steeds,
At last the Amazons espy a path
That gently mounts the cliff. They call to her,
Filling the vale with shouts of exultation,
They call the Queen to come, who in her rage
Still hurls herself against the rock's sheer face.
But hearing them she reins her charger back,
Scans for one moment where the path ascends,
Then like a leopard leaping on his prey,
Follows her glance herself. He, great Achilles,
Fled at her coming, ever away from us;
Soon in the valleys he was lost to view,
And what became of him I cannot tell.

ANTILOCHUS: Lost without doubt!

DIOMEDE:                                Ah, friends! What should we
[do?

ODYSSEUS: Why, what our hearts all bid us! Mighty kings,
  Up, gird yourselves and wrest him from her grasp.
  What though for him we must face wounds and death,
  I'll face th' Atrides' wrath when he is safe.
            *(Odysseus, Diomede, Antilochus, off.)*

# Scene 3

*The Captain. A band of Greeks, who have been mounting a hill.*
A MYRMIDON *(looking out over the countryside):*
  Look! Look! Do you not see? Above that ridge
  A head appearing, plumed and helmeted?
  And now the neck—the massive neck beneath?
  The shoulders now, the arms, in flashing steel?
  Now! Now!—The mighty, deep-set chest; oh, see!
  Where gleams about his waist the belt of gold!
CAPTAIN: Whose? Whose? By the gods!
MYRMIDON:                          Whose? Still in doubt, ye
[Greeks?

  His horses now, their white-starred foreheads—See!
  His chariot's steeds; still but their legs—their hooves
  Are hidden by the summit of the ridge.
  Ah, now! Clear-cut against the sky behold
  The whole equipage, blazing like the sun
  That rises jubilant in his early spring.
GREEKS: Triumph! Achilles! Achilles! 'Tis he,
  'Tis he! Himself he drives his four-hors'd car.
  Rescued! He's safe!
CAPTAIN:          O all ye gods above!
  So then be yours the glory!—Where's Odysseus?
  Run, someone, bring the Argive chiefs this news.
            *(A Greek goes quickly off.)*
  Does he head this way, friends?
MYRMIDON:                        Oh, see! Oh, see!

CAPTAIN: What is it? Speak!
MYRMIDON: Oh, Captain! Past belief!
CAPTAIN: Tell us, then! Speak!
MYRMIDON: Oh, how he leans far out
  Over their flying backs and urges them!
  Oh, how he swings the lash around their heads,
  And they at the sound—immortal coursers!—they
  Devour in thund'ring flight the fleeting ground.
  Their throats' hot vapor, streaming out behind,
  Seems, by the god of life, to draw the car!
  The stag before the hounds is not more swift!
  Sight cannot penetrate the whirling wheels
  Whose spokes all mingle in a solid disc.
AN AETOLIAN: But, look! Behind him—!
CAPTAIN: What?
MYRMIDON: At the
                                [mountain's foot—
AETOLIAN: Dust—
MYRMIDON: Dust, uptowering like a thundercloud
  And like the lightning sweeping on—
AETOLIAN: Ye gods!
MYRMIDON: Penthesilea!
CAPTAIN: Who?
AETOLIAN: The Queen herself!
  Hard on Achilles' heels with all her band
  Of women she comes sweeping o'er the plain.
CAPTAIN: The raging fury!
GREEKS (*calling*): This way! Here to us!
  To us! To us, Achilles! This way, turn!
  This way your steeds!
AETOLIAN: Look, look! How with her thighs
  She clips her charger's tiger-stripéd flanks!
  Flat, all her length, upon the mane she stoops
  Greedily drinking down the impeding air.
  She flies as though sped headlong from the sun;
  Numidian arrows are not half so swift.
  The rest lag panting far behind, like curs
  When once the greyhound girds his strength to run.
  Her plume itself can scarcely follow her!

CAPTAIN: And does she gain?

A DOLOPIAN:                 She gains!

MYRMIDON:                            But not yet near!

DOLOPIAN: She gains! She gains! With ev'ry thund'ring hoofbeat
  She swallows down some portion of the space
  That still divides her from great Peleus' son—

MYRMIDON: O all ye gods! Protecting deities!
  Look! Now she is almost as large as he!
  The dust he raises in his headlong flight—
  She breathes it now, borne to her by the wind!
  The charger that she rides, in swift career
  Tears up whole clods of earth that now alight
  Beside him in the body of his car!

AETOLIAN: And now—Oh, insolence! Nay, madness! Look!
  In wide arc circling off he plays with her.
  But she will take the cord—she'll cut across.
  Look! Look! She intercepts him!

MYRMIDON:                        Help! O Zeus!
  Beside him now she rides. Her shadow, see,
  Vast as a giant in the morning sun,
  Now strikes him!

AETOLIAN:            But all unforeseen he wheels—

DOLOPIAN: Wrenches the team and chariot suddenly
  Aside.

AETOLIAN:    To us, to us he flies once more!

MYRMIDON: Oh, he is full of tricks! He cheated her!

DOLOPIAN: But look where she in headlong flight o'ershoots
  The chariot—

MYRMIDON:       Strikes, unseated now, now stumbles—

DOLOPIAN: And falls! She's down!

CAPTAIN:               What?

MYRMIDON:                    Down! The Queen
                              [herself.
  And over her one of her warrior-maids—

DOLOPIAN: Another now—

MYRMIDON:             A third—

DOLOPIAN:                 And yet another—

CAPTAIN: What? Down? They fall?

DOLOPIAN:                  They fall—

MYRMIDON:                                        Captain! They
                                                           [fall,
  Like iron molten in the furnace' maw,
  All in a heap together, steeds and riders.
CAPTAIN: Might they be all consumed!
DOLOPIAN:                              One great dust cloud,
  With flashes here and there of arms and armor:
  The eye is helpless, strain how it will to see.
  A struggling mass of maids—and horses too—
  All in a jumbled welter. Chaos' self,
  The aboriginal, had more of order.
AETOLIAN: But now—a breeze springs up and clears the dust.
  Now one that fell is on her feet again.
DOLOPIAN: Delightful how the heap struggles and heaves!
  Now some seek helmets, some their broken spears,
  That lie far scattered on the plain.
MYRMIDON:                          But look!
  Three horses still, and still one rider lies
  For dead upon the ground—
CAPTAIN:                        Is it the Queen?
AETOLIAN: Penthesilea?
MYRMIDON:          Can it be the Queen?
  Ah, no! Would that my eyes saw not so true!
  There she stands!
DOLOPIAN:          Where?
CAPTAIN:                  Quick, tell us!
MYRMIDON:                              There, by Zeus!
  Where first she fell, beside that shady oak,
  Supports herself upon her horse's neck,
  Bareheaded—there's her helmet on the ground—
  With feeble hand holds back her tangled hair
  And wipes her brow of dust—or is it blood?
DOLOPIAN: By God, 'tis she!
CAPTAIN:                    She's indestructible!
AETOLIAN: From such a fall a cat would die; not she!
CAPTAIN: And Peleus' son?
DOLOPIAN:              The gods protect him still.
  Three bowshots out, beyond her, he has flown.
  She scarce can reach him even with her eyes;

Her thought itself, that longs to catch him, seems
Too faint to leave the refuge of her breast.

MYRMIDON: Triumph! Look there! Odysseus marches forth,
The whole Greek army, flashing back the sun,
Comes marching out from yonder forest's gloom.

CAPTAIN: Odysseus? What! And Diomede as well?
How far is he still distant from their host?

DOLOPIAN: A stone's throw, Captain—hardly that. His team
Is skimming now the ridge above Scamander,
Where all our host is ordered in array.
E'en now he thunders down their ranks—

VOICES *(in the distance):*                    Hail! Hail!

DOLOPIAN: They call to him, the Argives—

VOICES:                              Hail to thee,
Achilles! Hail, great Peleid, goddess-born!
Hail to thee! Hail!

DOLOPIAN:              Now he has reined his steeds.
Before the Argive princes gathered there,
He reins his steeds. Odysseus steps to greet him.
Down from his car he springs, all gray with dust
Gives to Automedon his reins—now turns—
And they press round him, all the valiant kings.
The Grecian host itself, with jubilant shouts,
Bears him along, close thronging round his knees
The while Automedon with measured step
Leads at their master's side his smoking steeds.
This way they come! The whole triumphal throng
Bears down on us. Hail to thee, child of heaven!
Look all! Oh look this way! Look where he comes!

# Scene 4

*Enter Achilles, with Odysseus, Diomede, Antilochus following, and Automedon with the quadriga at his side, also the Grecian host.*

ODYSSEUS: Hail, lord of Phthia! With full heart we greet thee!
Thou victor even in the arts of flight!
By Jupiter! When thus behind thy back

Thy spirit's superior power can bring about
Such headlong ruin for thy tender foe,
What then will happen when at last she stands
At bay before thy dreadful countenance?
   *(Achilles holds his helmet in his hand and wipes the sweat*
   *from his brow. Two Greeks, unknown to him, take one of*
               *his arms and begin to bandage it.)*

ACHILLES: What's this? What are you doing?

ANTILOCHUS:                     Thou art victor
In such a contest of o'erleaping speed,
As never yet unleashed thunderstorms,
Sweeping resistless over heaven's vault,
Themselves have shown to the astonished world.
Nay, by the Fates! What tho' with grinding wheel
I had crashed through the wonted ruts of life
And heaped upon my hollow breast all sins,
Ev'ry iniquity of Priam's burg,
Had I thy wingèd car, I'd 'scape remorse.

ACHILLES *(to the two Greeks, whose activity seems to annoy him):*
                           Fools!

A GREEK PRINCE: Who?

ACHILLES:         Why bother me?

FIRST GREEK:                Keep still! You're
                              [bleeding!

ACHILLES: I know that!

SECOND GREEK:     Keep still, then!

FIRST GREEK:              Let us bandage you!

SECOND GREEK. We're nearly finished—

DIOMEDE:              Here at first 'twas said
The forced withdrawal of my troops had caused
Thee thus to flee; occupied as I was
Here with Odysseus and Antilochus,
Who had brought messages from Agamemnon,
I was not present when this thing befell.
Yet all that I have seen convinces me
That thy so masterly retreat was not constrained
But of free choice. One might indeed suppose
That with the crack of dawn, when we were girding
Our harness on against the day's alarms,

Already thou had'st marked that lucky stone
O'er which the Queen should stumble and crash to earth:
With such sure course, by the eternal gods,
Didst thou entice her to this very stone.

ODYSSEUS: But now, great Phthian hero, you will oblige,
Unless you have in mind some better scheme,
By falling back with us to the Greek camp.
The sons of Atreus bid us all withdraw.
Feigning retreat we are to be the bait
Which shall entice her to Scamander's banks,
Where, falling on her unawares, the King
Will seek to engage her in a general broil.
By Zeus the Thund'rer! There, there or nowhere
Thou'lt cool the heat that tingles in thy blood
And makes thee insatiate as a yearling buck:
And to this task I wish thee good success.
For to me too she's hateful even to death,
A Fury ranging over all these plains
And crossing all our work. Gladly I'd see,
I do confess, the mark of thy mail'd heel
Scarring the tender roses of her flesh.

ACHILLES (*his eye falling on his horses*):
They sweat.

ANTILOCHUS: Who?

AUTOMEDON (*feeling their necks with his hand*):
Ay, like lead.

ACHILLES:        Good. Take them off
And, when the air has cooled them thoroughly,
Wash their deep chests, their thighs, and hocks with wine.

AUTOMEDON: The wine will soon be here.

DIOMEDE:                                My excellent friend,
We fight at senseless odds against them here.
The hills are covered, far as sight can reach,
With rank on serried rank of women in arms;
Locusts that settle on the ripened crop
Fall not so thick nor half so numerous.
Was ever battle won just as we plan?
Who besides thee in all the host can boast
He has so much as seen the centaur Queen?

Vainly, in armor crusted o'er with gold,
We thrust ourselves before her, with loud blare
Of trumpets making known our princely state:
She will not budge from out the rearward ranks.
And if from far off, blown upon the wind,
We hear the silver fluting of her voice,
We first must hack through riffraff soldiery,
Who guard her like ten thousand hounds of hell,
A path of doubtful outcome, void of honor.

ACHILLES: *(looking into the distance):* Is she still there?

DIOMEDE:   Whom do you mean?

ANTILOCHUS:                    The Queen?

CAPTAIN: They cannot see! These plumes!— Out of the way!

THE GREEK *(who is binding Achilles' arm):*
    Wait! Just one moment!

A GREEK PRINCE:          Yes! Look! There she is!

DIOMEDE: Where? Show me!

GREEK PRINCE:             By the oak there, where she fell.
    Once more the wanton plume waves from her head.
    Her late misfortune seems forgotten—

FIRST GREEK:                          There!

SECOND GREEK: Now you can use your arm any way you like.

FIRST GREEK: There, off you go!

        *(The Greeks tie one last knot and drop his arm.)*

ODYSSEUS:                 Achilles! Did you hear
    The arguments we put forward?

ACHILLES:                    The arguments?
    Not one. What was it? What do you want?

ODYSSEUS:                              What want?
    Extraordinary! We told you of the orders
    From the Atridae. Agamemnon bids
    Us straight withdraw into the Grecian camp.
    He sent Antilochus—look on him here!—
    To bring this fiat of the supreme command.
    This is the stratagem—to entice the Queen
    With all her Amazons to the plains of Troy,
    Where she, caught between two such hosts in arms,
    Confined, press'd, squeez'd from every side at once

Must show us clearly if she is our friend;
And we, at least, choose she which side she will,
Will no more be in doubt what's to be done.
I know, Achilles, I can trust your sense
To follow the wisdom of these clear commands.
For madness were it, sheerest lunacy,
When the war calls us urgently to Troy,
To let these warrior-maids embroil us here,
Before we know what thing they want of us,
—If indeed there is anything they want.

ACHILLES *(as he puts on his helmet again):*
Fight then like eunuchs, if it pleases you.
A man I feel myself and to these women,
Though alone of all the host, I'll stand my ground.
Whether you all here, under cooling pines,
Range round them from afar, full of impotent lust,
Shunning the bed of battle in which they sport,
All's one to me; by heav'n you have my blessing,
If you would creep away to Troy again.
What that divine maid wants of me, I know it:
Love's messengers she sends, wings tipp'd with steel,
That bear me all her wishes through the air
And whisper in my ear with death's soft voice.
I never yet was coy with any girl.
You know yourselves, since first my beard began
To show, gladly I've stood at each one's service.
And if from this one I have still refrained,
By Zeus! there's but one cause: I've not yet found
That bush-girt spot where, as her heart desires,
Unhindered I can enjoy her, bedding her
On the hard pillows of our mailèd suits.
In short, go off. I'll follow you to Troy;
I'll soon have had my way with her. But though
I had to woo her many long months through—
Ay, years—I will not guide my chariot there
Back to my friends, I swear't by Zeus himself,
Nor once again see Ilium's tower'd heights,
Until I first have had my sport with her,

And then, her brow adorned with bleeding gashes,
Shall drag her by the feet behind my car.
Follow me!

*(Enter a Greek.)*

THE GREEK:   Penthesilea seeks thee, Prince.

ACHILLES: And I her. Is she mounted once again?

THE GREEK: Not yet. She comes afoot with lofty grace.
But at her side her charger proudly steps.

ACHILLES: 'Tis good so. Get me too a horse, my friends!
And you, my trusty Myrmidons, follow me all!

ANTILOCHUS: This is stark madness!

ODYSSEUS:                         Well, you try to move him
With all your orator's skill, Antilochus!

ANTILOCHUS: We must seize him by force—

DIOMEDE:                         Too late! He's
                                                    [gone!

ODYSSEUS: Curse on these women and their crazy war!

*(All off.)*

# Scene 5

*Enter Penthesilea, Prothoe, Meroe, Asteria, and Amazon soldiery.*

AMAZONS: Hail to thee, victorious! Unconquerable!
Queen of the Feast of Roses! Hail! All hail!

PENTHESILEA: Silence! No Rose Feast yet! No victory!
Once more the battle calls me to the field.
That young, defiant war-god—I will tame him.
My friends, ten thousand suns melted in one
Vast heat-ball seem not half so bright to me,
So glorious, as victory over him.

PROTHOE: Dearest, I beg thee—

PENTHESILEA:                         Leave me, Prothoe!
Thou'st heard my will. Much sooner couldst thou stem
The torrent leaping down the mountainside,
Than rule the thund'rous ruin of my soul.
I long to see him grov'lling at my feet,
This haughty man, who in this glorious

And gentle field of arms, as no man yet,
Sows strange confusion in my warlike heart.
Is that the conquering Queen, the fearful one,
Proud leader of the warrior Amazons,
Whose form's reflected in his burnished steel,
When I approach him? Oh, can that be she?
Do I not feel—ah! too accursèd I—
While all around the Argive army flees,
When I look on this man, on him alone,
That I am smitten, lamed in my inmost being,
Conquered and overcome—I! Only I!
Where can this passion which thus tramples me,
Harbor in me, who have no breast for love?
Into the battle will I fling myself;
There with his haughty smile he waits me, there
I'll see him at my feet or no more live!

PROTHOE: Will you not lay your head a little while—
My Queen! My dearest!—here upon my heart?
That fall—that blow that shook thy tender breast,
It has enflamed thy blood, confused thy mind.
See how thou tremblest—all thy delicate limbs.
We all implore thee make no rash decision
Until thy mind returns in clear, full strength.
Come rest—refresh thyself here in my arms.

PENTHESILEA: Why? What has happened? What have I been
[saying?
Have I?— What have I?—

PROTHOE:                       For a victory
That tempts thy fancy as a passing whim
Wilt thou begin again the chance of battle?
Because one wish, I know not what, lies still
Unsatisfied within thy heart, wilt thou
Like a spoil'd child thus wanton cast away
The gain that crowns with joy thy people's prayers?

PENTHESILEA: Hark ye! Accursèd be this day's success!
Ah, see how even my friends, my dearest friends,
League themselves with this fickle fate today,
To hurt, frustrate, and thwart me every way!
Where'er my itching hand stirs but to snatch

Renown that thunders by in pelting haste,
And seize him by his flowing yellow locks,
There interposes still some mocking power—
And still my heart is hatred and defiance!
Begone!

PROTHOE *(to herself):* Ye heavenly powers of good protect her!

PENTHESILEA: Am I so selfish? Is it *my* desires
Alone that call me back into the field?
Is it not my people, threatened by the fate
That even in the maniac flush of victory
With audible wingbeat hastens from afar?
What is achieved, that we to evening prayer
Should go, as though the long day's work were done?
'Tis true, the crop is reaped, tied well in sheaves,
Ay, stacked in fat abundance in the barns,
That bursting tower to heaven. Yet balefully
The livid storm cloud overshadows it,
Poised with its levin from on high to strike
These captive youths that you have taken in fight.
You'll never lead them to the fragrant vales
Of our homeland, crown'd all with flowers, with music
Joyous of cymbals and of shrilling pipes.
Lurking in ambush, crafty, insatiate,
I see him everywhere—Achilles, ready to spring
Upon your happy train and scatter it.
He'll follow you and all your captive band
Right to the circling walls of Themiscyra.
Ay, in the holy temple of Artemis
He'll tear from off their limbs the tender chains,
Plaited of roses, and will load our own
With harsh shackles of stithy-forgèd brass.
Should I—'twere madness but to think of it—
Cease now to dog him? I who still for five
Long days of toil and sweat have sought his fall?
Now, when the lightest breath of Fortune's wind
Will shake him like a ripe pomegranate down
To lie vanquished beneath my horse's hoof?
What! Am I not so greatly to complete
What is so fair begun? May I not seize

The laurel wreath that flutters o'er my head?
Not lead, as once I swore, the daughters of Mars
Triumphant to the very top of bliss?
If not, if not—Then let Mars' pyramid
Crash upon me and them in ruin down!
Cursed be the heart that knows not wise restraint!

PROTHOE: Dread lady! In thine eye is awful fire
  To me unknowable, and awful thoughts,
  Dark as though children of eternal Night,
  Do turn and jostle in my fearful breast.
  The hostile band thy mind so strangely fears,
  Has fled before thee like the winnow'd chaff;
  Hardly one spear can anywhere be seen.
  And for Achilles—as our army lies,
  He is cut off, he cannot reach Scamander.
  But tempt him not again; avoid his sight.
  His only thought will be, I promise thee,
  To throw himself behind the Grecian wall.
  I, only I, will guard the army's rear;
  I swear to thee by Zeus, no prisoner,
  No one, shall he snatch from thee! Not a glint
  Of arms of his, though distant many miles,
  Shall fright the host, nor far-off hoofbeats' sound,
  Borne on the wind, trouble thy maidens' joy.
  My head be warranty to thee for this!

PENTHESILEA *(turning suddenly to Asteria)*:
  Can this thing be, Asteria? Speak!

ASTERIA:                    My Queen—

PENTHESILEA: Can I, as Prothoe demands, lead back
  The army thus to Themiscyra?

ASTERIA:                    Queen!—
  Forgive, dread lady, if in my poor sight—

PENTHESILEA: Speak boldly out, I say.

PROTHOE *(timidly)*:            If you would call
  To council all Princesses and inquire
  Of them—

PENTHESILEA: Her counsel will I have, no other!
  What am I since these few hours past, by heaven!
        *(pause in which she controls herself)*

Asteria, can I lead back the host?
Speak out, can I yet lead it to our home?
ASTERIA: With your good leave, dread lady, I must own
Astonishment consumes me at the sight
That here has met my unbelieving eyes.
With all my people I left the Caucasus,
Thou knowest, one day behind the eager host;
Nor could I catch them in their swift career,
So recklessly they sped, like a torrent in spate.
Not till this day had just begun to dawn
Did we ride in, ready to join the fight;
And then with joyful shout from myriad throats
I hear the news: the victory is won,
The war is over, all our needs fulfilled.
Glad, I assure thee, that the people's prayer
Without my help has been so quickly granted.
I order everything against return;
Yet curious still to see the captive band
Of heroes, booty of our valiant arms,
I find a handful of slaves, hang-dog, cringing,
The very dregs of all the Argive host,
Picked up by our baggage train on some foray
And carried home on shields they'd thrown away.
Before the lordly walls of Troy still stands
The whole Hellenic host; there's Agamemnon,
There's Menelaus, Ajax, Palamede;
Odysseus, Diomede, Antilochus—
They still are free to taunt thee to thy face.
Ay, and that youth, son of the sea-nymph Nereid,
Dares to oppose thee still, o'erweening man.
His foot he will—declares it openly—
His foot he'll set upon thy queenly neck.
Great daughter of Ares, canst thou ask me still
If we may yet return in triumph home?
PROTHOE (*passionately*):
To the Queen's sword, base woman, heroes have fall'n
As brave and noble ev'ry whit—
PENTHESILEA:                              Silence!
Hateful one! She—Asteria—feels as I:

There is but one here worthy of my sword,
And he still strides the field, defiant, free!

PROTHOE: My Queen! Surely thou wilt not let thyself
By passion—

PENTHESILEA:    Viper! Bind they venom'd tongue!
Out of my sight—or feel thy Queen's full wrath!
Begone!

PROTHOE: Then I will dare my Queen's full wrath!
Much rather will I never see thy face
Again, than at this moment basely stand
In treacherous silence, worse than flattery.
Thou art not fit, thus all aflame, consumed
With amorous fire, to lead the virgins' war;
As little fit as is the lion to face
The hunter's spear when he has drunk too deep
Of poison craftily set out for him.
Achilles?—Ah! In this unhappy state,
By all the gods, him thou wilt never win;
Much rather ere the day is done, I tell thee,
Thou'lt lose us in thy madness all these youths
Whom in hard fight we won, the cherished prize
Of infinite toils and dangers palpable.

PENTHESILEA: Now this is past believing strange! What makes
You suddenly so chicken-hearted?

PROTHOE:                    Me?

PENTHESILEA: Tell me! Who is your prisoner?

PROTHOE:                       Lykaon,
The young prince of the Arcadian host. I think
You saw him yesterday.

PENTHESILEA:             Ah, yes! 'Twas he
That stood with drooping plume and trembling glance
When I surveyed the captives?

PROTHOE:                Trembling! He!
He stood as resolute as e'er Achilles!
My sure-sped arrows crippled him and there
He sank before me; proudly I will lead
Lykaon, proud as any, at the Feast
Of Roses to the holy temple's shrine.

PENTHESILEA: In truth? See, at the thought she's all aflame.

Good, then. Thou shalt not lose him. Be content!
Bring him before us from the band of captives,
Lykaon, the Arcadian, bring him here!
Take him, thou too unwarlike virgin, then!
Flee with him lest thou lose him here, flee far,
Far from the din of battle, hide yourselves
In thickets deep of fragrant-smelling elder,
In the wild mountains' steepest-sided glen
Where nightingales pour forth their amorous notes
And celebrate it now, thou wanton girl,
That rite thy heart cannot await in patience.
But from our countenance be banished
And from our capital forever. All
Thy comfort be thy lover and his kisses
When all—when fame, when honor, country, love,
Thy Queen, ay, and thy friend are lost to thee.
Go, spare me now—go, not a word to me!—
The pain to look upon thee more!

MEROE:                                    Oh, Queen!

ANOTHER PRINCESS *( from among her followers)*:
Oh! What a word of doom!

PENTHESILEA:                         Silence, I say!
My vengeance falls on whoso speaks for her!

AN AMAZON *(entering)*: Most gracious Queen, Achilles comes.

PENTHESILEA:                                    [He comes!
Up then, my virgins, up! Once more to the fight!
Bring me the spear that deals the mortallest wounds,
The sword that strikes most like the thunderbolt!
This bliss, ye gods, oh, grant it me today—
To smite with blade invincible this one
So hot-pursuèd youth down to the dust.
All other joy that to my life is fated,
I do renounce it here, grant me but this.
Asteria! You will lead out the companies.
Keep the Greek host engaged and see to it
The general broil thwart not my special aim.
Not one of you, no matter who she be,
May strike Achilles! She shall taste the sharp,
Swift shaft of death, who touches but his head—
Nay, but one lock—with overweening hand.

'Tis I alone know how to fell this man.
These mailèd arms, dear friends, shall draw him down
(Since thus in suits of mail it must be done!)
Into the tenderest of love's embraces
And press him all unscath'd against my breast.
Grow up to meet his fall, ye flowers of spring,
That none of his dear limbs take injury.
My own heart's blood rather than his, I'd spill.
No more will I now rest, till I have hailed
Him down out of the sky, like a gay bird,
Bright-feathered; yet when once he lies before me
With broken wing, but still with ev'ry speck
Of shimmering purple dust unblemished, then,
Then, ye virgins, then may all the gods
Sweep down from heav'n to celebrate our triumph.
Then homeward wends the joyous march, and I,
Queen of the Feast of Roses to you all!
And now—
(*As she goes off, she sees Prothoe weeping and turns, distressed.
Then suddenly, falling upon her neck—*)
      My Prothoe! My heart's own sister!
Wilt follow me?
PROTHOE (*in a broken voice*): Into death and beyond!
Could I without thee meet the Blessèd Ones?
PENTHESILEA: Ah, noble heart, nobler than all! Thou wilt?
Come, then, we'll fight and conquer side by side.
We two or none, and our watchword shall be:
Roses to crown our heroes' temples, or
For ours the cypress!
           (*Exeunt omnes.*)

# Scene 6

*Enter the High Priestess of Diana with Priestesses, followed by a
band of young girls with baskets of roses on their heads; also the
prisoners led by armed Amazons.*
HIGH PRIESTESS: Now, little ones! My dearest rose-maidens!
  Show me the fruit of all this morning's labors.

Here by the rocky stream's crystalline falls,
Shaded by this tall pine, here we are safe.
Pour out your harvest here before my feet.

A GIRL (*emptying her basket on the ground*):
Look, holy mother, this is what I picked!

SECOND GIRL: This apronful is mine!

THIRD GIRL:                                    And here is mine!

FOURTH GIRL: Look, I have gathered all the wanton spring!
                    (*The other girls follow suit.*)

HIGH PRIESTESS: Such sweet profusion grows not on Hymettus!
In truth a day so rich in every bounty
Never yet dawned, Diana, on thy folk.
The mothers bring me gifts, not less the daughters.
By all this double splendor blinded, I
Know not to which I should give warmer thanks.
But children, tell me! Is this all your store?

FIRST GIRL: More than we have here could we nowhere find.

HIGH PRIESTESS: Then were your mothers more industrious.

SECOND GIRL: Most holy dame, 'tis harder far to win
Roses upon these fields than prisoners.
Though on the hills around the bounteous harvest
Of Argive youths stand rank on rank and wait
Only for reaping by the eager scythe,
Yet in these vales so sparingly, believe me,
And so well-fortified the roses bloom,
That it is lighter work to hew through lances
Than break a way through their entwinèd thorns.
—Look here at these poor fingers, gracious lady!

THIRD GIRL: I ventured on a sharply jutting rock
To pick thee one rose, lovelier than all:
Pale still through the embracing, dark green cup,
A scarcely opened bud its beauty gleamed,
Not yet expanded to the kiss of love.
But still I grasp it—then slip, reel, and fall
Down into the abyss and think myself
Lost to the world of day in death's dark womb.
And yet it brought me luck, for there I found
Such myriad splendor of wanton-blooming roses
As would deck out ten feasts of victory.

FOURTH GIRL: I plucked thee, holy priestess of Diana,
  I plucked for thee a rose—one rose—no more.
  Yet such a rose it is—look, this one here!
  Fit for the wreath a captive king must wear.
  Penthesilea could not wish a fairer
  For great Achilles, when she has laid him low.
HIGH PRIESTESS: Ay, *when* she has laid Achilles low, thou may'st
  Thyself hand her this more than kingly rose.
  So keep it safe for her, until she comes.
FIRST GIRL: Another time when all the Amazon host
  Marches to war with cymbals and with drums,
  We will go too, and not—oh, promise us!—
  Only to grace the mothers' victory
  With rose-plucking and winding toilsome wreaths!
  My arm here—look!—can hurl the javelin,
  And from my sling the stone flies swift and true.
  Why not? Why not? I am no more a child;
  And he for whom these sinews here grow strong
  Already he fights boldly in the fray.
HIGH PRIESTESS: Well, is that so? And who should know but thou?
  Hast thou already chosen the roses for him?
  Next spring, when they are all abloom once more,
  Thou shalt seek out thy man on the field of battle.
  —But come! The exultant mothers bid us haste:
  Quick! Lace these roses into wreaths of love!
THE GIRL: Yes, quick to work! How do we best begin?
FIRST GIRL *(to the second):* Come here, Glaucothoe!
THIRD GIRL *(to the fourth):*                          Come,
                                                    [ Charmion!
            *(They sit down in pairs.)*
FIRST GIRL: We—for Ornythia do we wind this wreath,
  Who overcame the nodding-plumed Alcestes.
THIRD GIRL: And we—'tis for Parthenion. Athenaeus
  Her prisoner is, he with the Gorgon shield.
HIGH PRIESTESS *(to the armed Amazons):*
  Have you no thought to entertain your guests?
  How awkwardly you stand, like senseless logs!
  Is it for me to teach the game of love?
  Will you not even dare a friendly word?

Not ask what all these battle-weary men
Perchance desire or need? What wants they have?
FIRST AMAZON: They say they have no needs, most holy dame.
SECOND AMAZON: They're angry with us—
THIRD AMAZON:                                    When we would be
                                                        [kind,
    Defiantly they turn their backs on us.
HIGH PRIESTESS: Why, silly girls! If they are angry now,
    Speak to them! Make them kind! Why in the fray
    Did you deal down on them such pitiless blows?
    Tell them what pleasures are in store for them;
    Soon their unfriendliness will melt away.
FIRST AMAZON *(to a prisoner)*:
    Thou handsome youth, wilt thou on deep-piled rugs
    Rest thy cramp'd limbs? Shall I make ready a couch—
    For thou seemst weary—of tender flowers of spring
    In the deep shade of yonder dark-leaved laurel?
SECOND AMAZON *(also to a prisoner)*:
    Shall I some fragrant-scented oil of Persia
    Mix with the spring-drawn water, clear and cool,
    To lave the dust from thy hot, aching feet?
THIRD AMAZON: Surely the juice of golden oranges,
    Prepared with love for thee—thou wilt not scorn it?
ALL THREE: Tell us! What can we offer you?
A GREEK:                                              Nothing!
FIRST AMAZON:
    Strange-mooded men! What gnaws thus at your hearts?
    Now that our arrows sleep within the quiver,
    How can the sight of us affright you still?
    Thou with the rich-wrought belt, what is it you fear?
THE GREEK *(looking at her keenly)*:
    For whom are these wreaths wound? Come, tell me that!
FIRST AMAZON: For whom? For you!
THE GREEK:                                    For us! Have you no shame,
    Inhuman girl? So you would lead us decked
    With flowers like bulls of sacrifice to our death?
FIRST AMAZON: Strange misconception! Nay, to Dian's fane,
    To her deep-shaded oak grove, where sweet orgies
    Without constraint or measure wait on you!

THE GREEK *(in astonishment, under his breath to the prisoners):*
  Was ever dream so crazed as this reality?

# Scene 7

*Enter an Amazon Captain.*

CAPTAIN: What make you in this place, most reverend dame,
  While scarce a stone's throw hence our armèd host
  Girds once again its loins for bloody war?
HIGH PRIESTESS: The host! Impossible! Where?—
CAPTAIN:                                    In yonder vale
  Licked out by old Scamander. Wilt thou but hark
  To the sweet mountain wind that hither blows,
  Full well thou'lt hear our great Queen's thund'ring shout,
  The clash of naked steel, neighing of steeds,
  With bugles, trumpets, horns, and cymbals' clang—
  The iron voice of brazen-armèd war.
A PRIESTESS: Quick! Who will spy from yonder hill?
THE GIRLS:                                    I! I!
                    *(They climb up the hill.)*
HIGH PRIESTESS: The Queen's voice? Not the Queen's! It cannot
                                                    [be!
  Why—if the battle still must rage—did she
  Bid me at once prepare the Feast of Roses?
CAPTAIN: The Feast of Roses!—Whom did she thus command?
HIGH PRIESTESS: Me! Me myself!
CAPTAIN:                    Where? When?
HIGH PRIESTESS:                                    A moment
                                                    [since,
  I stood within the shadow of yon obelisk
  When great Achilles, and she upon his heels,
  Swept by me swifter than the wind. I cried:
  "What news? What news?" as she flew by, and she:
  "To the Feast of Roses! Look! Canst thou not see?"
  With that was gone, but, going, call'd to me:
  "Let us not lack for flowers, thou holy one!"

FIRST PRIESTESS *(to the girls):*
  Can you not see her?
FIRST GIRL *(on the hill):*
                    Nothing can we see!
  Not even a plume can we distinguish there.
  Deep gloom of livid thunderclouds blots out
  The whole wide field; nought but the surge
  Confused of armèd hosts can we descry,
  That seek each other on the field of death.
SECOND PRIESTESS: She fights to cover the army's safe retreat.
FIRST PRIESTESS: It must be so.
CAPTAIN:                    She stands, I tell you, arm'd
  In matchless mail facing great Peleus' son,
  Herself, the Queen, fresh as her Persian steed
  That rears on high for very wantonness.
  Her lowering eye shoots fire as ne'er before;
  She draws the air freely, exultantly,
  As though her youthful, warlike bosom now
  For the first time drank in the breath of battle.
HIGH PRIESTESS: What—by the gods!—What can her purpose be?
  What can it be, when all around in thousands
  Our prisoners lie thick in every wood?
  What can remain that she would win by war?
CAPTAIN: You ask what still remains to win by war?
GIRLS *(on the hill):* Ye gods!
FIRST PRIESTESS:         What is it? Tell! Can you see more?
FIRST GIRL: O reverend ladies! Come yourselves!
SECOND PRIESTESS:                    Nay! Tell us!
CAPTAIN: What still remains for her to win by war?
FIRST GIRL: See! See! How from a cleft in the black cloud
  The sun as with a pillar of sheerest light
  Falls on the glorious head of Peleus' son!
HIGH PRIESTESS: On whose?
FIRST GIRL:            On his! On his! Whose else could it
                                      [be?
  Radiant he stands upon the rising ground,
  Cased all in steel his steed and he; sapphire
  Nor chrysolite cannot throw back such rays!
  The earth herself, the gay, flower-sprinkled earth,

Wrapped now in thunder vapors' blackest gloom,
Lies but a dark background, a murky foil,
To make his flashing glory brighter yet!

HIGH PRIESTESS: What should our girls know of this Peleus' son?
Does it befit a daughter of Mars, a Queen
To stake her all in battle on one name?

*(To an Amazon.)*

Run quick, Arsinoe, stand before her face
And tell her in the name of my dread goddess:
Mars has this day appeared unto his brides;
I now demand, on pain of the goddess' wrath,
That she do seemly crown the god and lead him
Back to our home, there straightway make for him
The Feast of Roses in Diana's shrine.

*(Exit the Amazon.)*

Was ever yet such madness heard or seen?

FIRST PRIESTESS: Children! Have you no sight yet of the Queen?

FIRST GIRL *(on the hill):*
Yes, there she is! The whole field now is clear.

FIRST PRIESTESS: Where can you see her?

GIRL: Leading all the host.
See how she dances forth to meet him, all
Flashing in golden armor, breathing war!
Is't not as though, in jealous emulation,
She longed to o'erleap the sun-goddess, who now
Kisses Achilles' youthful locks? Oh, look!
What though she wished to vault into the heav'ns
To match her flaming rival on equal terms,
Her stallion could not better do her wish,
So light, so wingèd is his dancing gait.

HIGH PRIESTESS *(to Captain):*
Did not one of her virgins then attempt
To hold her back, to warn her against this thing?

CAPTAIN: All her great vassals of the royal blood
Opposed her going; here upon this spot
Did Prothoe attempt her uttermost.
Not one of all persuasion's subtlest arts
Could move her to return to Themiscyra.
Deaf she appeared, stone deaf to reason's voice.

The most envenom'd of all love's shafts, they say,
Has pierced her tender heart to make her mad.

HIGH PRIESTESS: What word is this?

GIRLS *(on the hill):* Oh, see! Oh, now they meet!
Ye gods! Let not Earth shudder at the shock!
Now, even now, even as I speak, they crash
Together like two hurtling stars in heav'n!

HIGH PRIESTESS: The Queen, you say? Impossible, my friend!
Pierced by love's shaft? How can that be? When? Where?
She who doth wear the girdle of diamonds?
The daughter of Mars, who lacks even the breast
Where Cupid's poison'd shafts may strike and lodge?

CAPTAIN: So it is rumored in the ranks at least,
And now from Meroe I learned the same.

HIGH PRIESTESS: 'Tis fearful!

*(The Amazon returns.)*

FIRST PRIESTESS: Well, what tidings? Speak at once!

HIGH PRIESTESS: Did you my bidding? Spoke you with the Queen?

AMAZON: Forgive me, holy one, I came too late.
Ever swarmed round by cheering soldiery,
Flitting now here, now there, she eluded me.
But Prothoe I met for one brief space
And told her all your will: and she replied—
I know not—in the general turmoil I—
Mayhap, I heard her not aright.

HIGH PRIESTESS: Speak out!
What did she say?

AMAZON: Silent she sat her steed
And looked, methought her eyes brimming with tears,
After the Queen. I told her then, thou wert
Indignant that the war thus senselessly
Should be prolonged for one man's sake alone.
To which she thus replied: "Go to thy priestess
And bid her fall upon her knees and pray
That this one man may be her prize of battle;
Doomed otherwise are we and she together."

HIGH PRIESTESS: Oh, she runs steeply down to the abyss!
'Tis not to Achilles she will fall, when he
Encounters her, but to this inner foe.
And us she drags to ruin with her down;

The ship I see already cleaving the Hellespont,
That bears us captive, slaves, all gaily decked
With wreaths, in mockery of our hateful fate.
FIRST PRIESTESS: What matter now? Here comes the dreadful news.

# Scene 8

*Enter an Amazon officer.*
OFFICER: Flee! Bring the prisoners away! Oh, flee!
The Argive host e'en now bears down on you.
HIGH PRIESTESS: O all ye gods! What fearful thing has chanced?
FIRST PRIESTESS: Where is the Queen?
OFFICER: Fallen in battle! All
The army of the Amazons scattered!
HIGH PRIESTESS: Thou art mad! What word hath passed thy
[wanton lips?
FIRST PRIESTESS *(to the armed guard):*
Lead off the prisoners!
HIGH PRIESTESS: Tell us! Where? When?
OFFICER: Hear then in brief the whole disastrous tale!
Achilles and the Queen, with lances couched,
Rush to th' encounter, like two thunderbolts
That crash together in the vaults of space.
The lances, weaker than their breasts, are splintered.
He, Peleus' son, still stands: Penthesilea—
She sinks, o'erwhelmed by night, down from her horse.
And as she now, his vengeance' helpless prey,
Writhes in the dust before him, who could doubt
That he will send her straight to the nether world?
Yet, pale himself, he stands moved by strange thoughts,
Most like a shade of Orcus; then exclaims:
"Oh, what a look came from those dying eyes!"
Impetuous down he swings him from his steed,
And while her virgins stand, transfixed with horror,
Remembering too well the Queen's own word,
That none should raise her sword against that man,
Boldly goes to her where she lies, bends down
And calls to her "Penthesilea!" then
Raises her up and holds her in his arms,

Curses the deed that he has done and so,
Lamenting still, calls back her erring spirit.

HIGH PRIESTESS: He—What? Himself?

OFFICER:                                        "Leave her, thou impious
[man!"

The whole host thunders. "Death be his reward,"
Cries Prothoe, "if he'll not budge! Then send
The keenest shaft to find its mark in him!"
And with her stallion forcing him to yield,
Snatches the lifeless Queen from his arms; who then
—Oh, pitiful return to misery!—wakes
And is led off with shattered breast, gasping
For breath, her hair in shameful disarray,
That in the rearmost ranks she may recover.
But he, strange man, incalculable—a god
Has suddenly transmuted that fierce heart
Within the brazen-girdled breast with love—
He cries: "Wait, wait, good friends! I come in peace.
Never again shall war divide our nations!"
And casts his sword away, his shield away,
Strips all his harness from his body and limbs
And follows—with clubs we could have felled him, nay,
With our bare hands, had we not been forbid—
Follows the Queen undaunted through our ranks,
As though he knew already, mad as he is,
His life was sacred, safe from all our shafts.

HIGH PRIESTESS: Who gave this worse than senseless order?

OFFICER:                                        Who?
        The Queen! Who else?

HIGH PRIESTESS:                It is unspeakable!

FIRST PRIESTESS: Oh, see! She comes with feeble, tottering steps,
    Leaning on Prothoe! Oh, pitiful sight!

SECOND PRIESTESS: Ye gods in heav'n! Must I have eyes to see?

# Scene 9

*Enter Penthesilea, supported by Prothoe and Meroe; behind her
Amazons.*

PENTHESILEA *(in feeble voice)*:
    Set all the dogs upon him! Whip the elephants

With blazing faggots that they trample and crush him!
Drive over him with our steel-scythèd cars!
Mow down his sumptuous limbs and mangle them!
PROTHOE: Dearest! We all implore thee—!
MEROE:                                        Hear us!
PROTHOE:                                                        He,
  He himself, Achilles follows hard behind thee;
  Oh, flee, if life is anyway dear to thee!
PENTHESILEA:
  So crush and bruise this breast!—How could he do it?
  Oh, Prothoe! It is as wanton-cruel
  As though I were to rive the innocent lyre
  That hangs in the night breeze, whispering my name.
  At the bear's feet I would cower, nestling close,
  Would stroke and fondle the blotch'd panther, who
  Approached me with such feelings as I him.
MEROE: Wilt thou not move from here?
PROTHOE:                              Wilt thou not flee?
MEROE: Come! Save thyself!
PROTHOE:                    That thing unspeakable,
  Must it be done here before all our eyes?
PENTHESILEA: Is mine the fault that I must woo him thus,
  Here on the field of war must force his love?
  What is it I long for, when I strike at him?
  Is it to send him headlong to the shades?
  I long—ye gods above! I only long—
  To this warm breast I long to draw him close!
PROTHOE: She wanders!
HIGH PRIESTESS:        Hapless girl!
PROTHOE:                              Her wits are strayed.
HIGH PRIESTESS: She cannot think of aught but him.
PROTHOE:                                            The fall—
  Woe's me!—the fall has robbed her of all sense!
PENTHESILEA (*with forced calm*):
  Good then. Be it as you wish. I will be calm.
  This heart—Since it must be, I will command it
  And do with grace what hard compulsion bids.
  Oh, you are right! Why should I like a child
  Break with our ancient gods, because one wish,
  A passing whim's denied me? Come away.

This happiness—it would have been most pleasant.
But if it will not come to me, I'll not
Storm heaven to get it; rather let it go.
Help me away from here. Get me a horse.
Then I will lead you all back to your home.

PROTHOE: Thrice blessèd, noble lady, be this word
So queenly spoken from thy queenly heart.
Come! All is ready for our flight.

PENTHESILEA *(catching sight of the rose-wreaths in the
children's hands, in sudden anger):* How now!
Who gave command to start the rose-plucking?

FIRST GIRL: Dost thou still ask? Hast quite forgot? Who else
But only—

PENTHESILEA: But who?

HIGH PRIESTESS: Thyself didst give command
That we should celebrate the longed-for rites.
From thine own lips I had it. Hast thou forgot?

PENTHESILEA: Curses upon this beastly, wanton haste!
Curses on her that thinks but of the orgies
While war still rages, reeking of death and blood!
A curse on lusts that in my Amazons'
Chaste hearts like unleashed dogs do howl and quite
O'erwhelm the trumpet's brazen-throated voice
And all the leaders' cries of shrill command.
Victory—is that yet won, that you should thus
In fiendish mockery pluck triumphal garlands?
Away with them!
*(She slashes the wreaths to pieces.)*

FIRST GIRL: My Queen! What hast thou done?

SECOND GIRL: *(collecting the scattered roses):*
In all the valleys round for mile on mile
The spring has not a rose—

PENTHESILEA: Would God the spring
Should winter and die! Would God this planet Earth
Lay plucked and broken like these roses here!
Would I could tear apart the coronet
Of the circling globes as now this wreath of flowers!
—O Aphrodite!

HIGH PRIESTESS: Hideous, hideous fate!

FIRST PRIESTESS: Oh! She is lost!

SECOND PRIESTESS: Into the pit of hell
Her soul is cast, a plaything there for Furies!

A PRIESTESS *(on the hill):*
Ho, virgins! Save yourselves! The son of Peleus
Swiftly approaches scarce a bowshot off.

PROTHOE: Nay, then, I beg thee, I beseech thee: come!

PENTHESILEA: Oh, I am weary! Deadly, deadly tired!
*(She sits down.)*

PROTHOE: My Queen! This is stark madness!

PENTHESILEA: Flee, if you wish!

PROTHOE: Thou wilt—?

MEROE: Sit here?

PROTHOE: Thou wilt—?

PENTHESILEA: I will sit here.

PROTHOE: 'Tis madness!

PENTHESILEA: I am too weak to stand, I tell you.
Must I break all my bones? Let me alone.

PROTHOE: Most wretched of all women! Achilles comes
Now scarce a bowshot off!

PENTHESILEA: Good. Let him come.
Oh, let him plant his mail'd foot on my neck—
I have deserved no better. Why are these cheeks
In youthful loveliness still loath to mingle
With mud, the primal matter, from which they sprang?
Let him defile this body of mine, now full
Of pulsing life, drag me behind his car,
Shamefully cast me on the open field,
Give me to dogs and to the filthy clan
Of vultures to be mangled and devoured.
Much better dust than thus a woman scorned!

PROTHOE: Oh, Queen!

PENTHESILEA *(tearing the necklace from her neck):*
Off with these thrice-damned gewgaws!
[Off!

PROTHOE: Oh, gods above! Is that the calm command
Thy lips did but now promise? Calm thyself!

PENTHESILEA: From the head too—nodding follies! I curse
[you all,

More impotent even than arrow or blooming cheeks!
That hand I curse that decked me for the fight
This day, and that deceiving serpent-word
That told me I should conquer. Accursed! Accursed!
Oh, how they stood around me with their mirrors—
Flatt'rers!—on either hand and praised the form
Divine of my smooth limbs, molded in steel!
Pestilence smite you with your tricks of hell!

GREEKS *(off):* Go on, Achilles! Don't lose heart, man! Here,
This way she went. She can't be far off now.

PRIESTESS *(on the hill):*
O Artemis! Queen, fly for thy life! Or else
It is too late!

PROTHOE:         Sweet cousin! Dearest heart!
Wilt thou in sooth not flee?

            *(Penthesilea leans weeping against a tree.)*
                        Then, as thou wilt!
If thou canst not, wilt not—good! Dry thy eyes.
I'll stay beside thee. What's not possible,
What lies not in the precinct of thy will,
What thou *canst* not achieve: the gods forbid
That I should ask it of thee. Leave us, friends.
Go; get you back to our dear native plains.
Go—do not wait! The Queen and I stay here!

HIGH PRIESTESS: What, wretched girl! You aid her in this
                                        [madness?

MEROE: You say she *cannot* move from here?

HIGH PRIESTESS:                         Cannot!
Though nothing holds her, no fate binds her here,
Only her infatuate heart!

PROTHOE:                That is her fate!
You'd say steel fetters are unbreakable,
Would you not? I say: she *could* break them, perchance,
But never this feeling which you treat so lightly.
What darkly stirs within her, who can say?
A riddle is every heart's deep-flowing tide.
She longed to seize life's highest prize; almost
She touched it, grasped it. Now her hand will not

Be used to take some other, lesser thing.
Come, wait the end here leaning on my breast.
What is it? Wherefore weeping?

PENTHESILEA:                          Pain, oh, pain!

PROTHOE: Where?

PENTHESILEA:          Here.

PROTHOE:                          How can I help—?

PENTHESILEA:                                        No! Nothing,
[nothing!

PROTHOE: Now calm thyself. Soon it will all be over.

HIGH PRIESTESS *(aside):* Nay, this is madness!

PROTHOE *(aside to her):*                          Not a word, I
[beg!

PENTHESILEA: If 'twere my will to flee—if I did flee—
How might I calm myself? Tell me.

PROTHOE:                          You'd go to Pharsos.
There you would find the host, now scattered wide,
Drawn all together; thither I bade them go.
There you would rest, there you would tend your wound
And with the next day's light, if so it pleased,
You would renew the virgins' holy war.

PENTHESILEA: *If* it were possible—! *If* I had the power—
The utmost have I done that human strength
Is able—I have tried the impossible—
I have staked all upon one throw—all that I have.
The fateful die is cast—it lies before me:
And I must understand—that I have lost.

PROTHOE: Not so, my dearest heart! It is not so.
Surely you do not so contemn your strength.
That prize for which you strive—is it worth so little
That you should think, too arrogant, all had been done
That could be done—that it was worth no more?
What! Is this string of pearls, so white, so red,
That falls here from thy throat, the only wealth
That thy rich soul can summon to its aid?
So much of which thou'st never thought, could still
Be done to gain thy end, wert thou in Pharsos.
But now, 'tis true, almost it is too late.

PENTHESILEA *(with an uneasy gesture):*
  If I were swift—Oh, it will make me mad!
  Where stands the sun?
PROTHOE:                    There, straight above thy head.
  This day, before night falls, thou couldst be there.
  A treaty we could make, unknown to the Greeks,
  With Priam's stronghold; all unnoticed then
  We'd reach the seashore, where the Greek fleet lies.
  At midnight, on a signal, all their vessels
  Flame skywards, the camp is stormed, the Argive host,
  Crushed in from every side by two such foes,
  Torn into shreds, dissolved, tossed far and wide,
  Pursued, tracked down, then seized and garlanded
  Each lusty youth—we've but to take our pick!
  What bliss! What heavenly bliss, if this could be!
  I'd ask no rest could I but fight beside thee,
  Nor shun the sun's fierce heat. Untiring still,
  I would consume my latest ounce of strength,
  Until at last my sister had her wish
  And Peleus' son, the prize of infinite toils,
  Sank at her feet—her spoil, her prisoner!
PENTHESILEA *(who has all this time been looking fixedly at the
  sun):*
  That I could cleave the air with rushing pinions
  Far-spreading—!
PROTHOE:        What?
MEROE:                 What does she say?
PROTHOE:                               My Queen!
  What is it you see?
MEROE:              What do you gaze upon?
PROTHOE: Dearest, tell me!
PENTHESILEA:            Too high! I know, too high!
  Far off, in flame-rings unapproachable,
  He circles sporting round my longing heart.
PROTHOE: Who, dearest Queen? Who sports with thee?
PENTHESILEA:                               It is well.
  —How do we go?
          *(She collects herself and stands up.)*
MEROE:          Have you decided then?

PROTHOE: Will you get up? Well, then, my Queen, be strong,
  A giant in thy strength! Nor never sink,
  Not though all Orcus weigh thee to the ground.
  Stand, stand now firm; firm as the arch must stand,
  Because each stone longs but to crash to earth.
  Present thy head, the keystone of thy self,
  To God's lightnings and call to him: "Here! Strike!"
  Ay! let him split thee to the very ground,
  But never waver in thyself again
  As long as any grain of stone and mortar
  Still hold together in thy breast. Now come.
  Come. Give thy hand.
PENTHESILEA:           Is this the way?—Or that?
PROTHOE: Either the rocky ground there, which is safer,
  Or here the easier valley.
PENTHESILEA:         The rocky ground!
  By so much I am nearer him then. Follow me!
PROTHOE: Whom, dearest lady?
PENTHESILEA:           Lend me your arm, my friends.
PROTHOE: As soon as thou hast topp'd that hillock there,
  Thou art in safety.
MEROE:       Come now.
PENTHESILEA (*suddenly stopping as she is crossing a bridge*):
                Listen, though:
  One thing is still to do before I go.
PROTHOE: To do still?
MEROE:       What is that?
PROTHOE:             Oh, hapless woman!
PENTHESILEA: One thing still, friends; for I were mad,
  That you must grant yourselves, did I not try
  Everything possible to gain my end.
PROTHOE (*in great annoyance*):
  Would that the earth should open and swallow us!
  No hope now of escape!
PENTHESILEA (*startled*): What? What's the matter?
  Have I offended her? Friends! Tell me how.
HIGH PRIESTESS: Thou think'st—?
MEROE:               Here on this very spot thou
                    [wilt—?

PENTHESILEA: Nothing, my friends, nothing to make her angry!
  Just to pile Ida onto Ossa, then
  Quietly take my place upon the top.
HIGH PRIESTESS: Pile Ida onto—?
MEROE:                                   Ida onto Ossa?
PROTHOE (*turning away*): O all you gods, protect her!
HIGH PRIESTESS: Lost forever!
MEROE (*timidly*): This is a task for giants, Queen, not men.
PENTHESILEA: Well! What of that? In what do they excel me?
MEROE: In what excel thee!
PROTHOE:                       O gods!
HIGH PRIESTESS:                             But even then—?
MEROE: Granted thou hadst accomplished this, what then?
PROTHOE: Ay, granted that, what would'st thou—?
PENTHESILEA:                                       Foolish child!
  By his gold-flaming locks I'd draw him down,
  Down, down to me—
PROTHOE:             Whom?
PENTHESILEA:                   Whom but Helios,
  As he sweeps by me in his fiery car?
      (*The princesses look at each other in speechless horror.*)
HIGH PRIESTESS: Bear her away by force!
PENTHESILEA (*looking down into the stream*):
                                   Oh, foolish me!
  Why, there he is below me! Take me! I come—!
  (*She is about to throw herself into the stream; Prothoe and
  Meroe catch her as she falls.*)
PROTHOE: O wretched, wretched woman!
MEROE:                               Lifeless, see!
  Limp as a garment, in our arms she falls.
PRIESTESS (*on the hill*):
  Achilles is upon you! All in vain
  The virgins' phalanx strives to hold him off!
AN AMAZON: Save her, ye gods! Protect our Virgin Queen
  From desecrating hands!
HIGH PRIESTESS (*to the priestesses*):
                         Come hence! Away!
  We may not stay amid the clash of war.
      (*Exeunt High Priestess, Priestesses, and girls.*)

# Scene 10

*Enter a troop of Amazons with bows in their hands.*

FIRST AMAZON *(calling into the wings):* Back, impious man!

SECOND AMAZON: He does not hear us call.

THIRD AMAZON: Princesses, if we may not shoot at him,
There is no way to check his mad career!

SECOND AMAZON: What can we do? Say, Prothoe!

PROTHOE *(busy with the Queen):*                Let fly
Ten thousand arrows at him!

MEROE *(to the attendants):*        Bring us water!

PROTHOE: But still be careful that no wound is deadly!

MEROE: Bring me a helmet full of water!

A PRINCESS *(bringing water):*                Here!

THIRD AMAZON *(to Prothoe):*
You need not fear. We'll keep you safe!

FIRST AMAZON *(to the rest):*                Stand here!
We'll graze his cheeks and singe his golden hair;
So let him taste the transient kiss of death.
                *(They make ready their bows.)*

# Scene 11

*Enter Achilles, without helmet or weapons, some Greeks follow-
ing.*

ACHILLES: Whom would you welcome with these shafts, dear
girls?
Surely not my all unprotected breast?
Should I tear wide this silken shirt as well,
That you could see how innocent beats my heart?

FIRST AMAZON: Ay, if you will!

SECOND AMAZON:                There is no need!

THIRD AMAZON:                                Shoot now!
The arrow there, just where he holds his hand!

FIRST AMAZON: That it may pierce his heart and bear it onwards
In flight, like a dead leaf—!

MEROE:                          Shoot!
*(They shoot over his head.)*
ACHILLES:                              Foolish children!
  With your sweet eyes you hit more certainly.
  By all the gods, in very sooth and sadness,
  I feel your darts deep in my innermost breast,
  Disarmed in every sense, defenseless, here
  Before your delicate feet I lay myself.
FIFTH AMAZON *(pierced by a spear from behind the scenes):*
  Ye gods above!
                    *(She falls.)*
SIXTH AMAZON *(also smitten):* Alas!
                    *(She falls.)*
SEVENTH AMAZON *(also smitten):* Diana help me!
                    *(She falls.)*
FIRST AMAZON: Oh, fearful man! ⎫
MEROE *(busy with the Queen):*  ⎬ *Together.*
  Ah, thrice-unhappy girl!        ⎭
SECOND AMAZON:        And calls himself disarmed! ⎫ *Together.*
PROTHOE *(also busy with the Queen):* Oh! She is dead! ⎭
THIRD AMAZON: We stand here while his people ⎫
                          slaughter us! ⎬ *Together.*
MEROE: On every hand our virgins are cut down! ⎭
  What can we do?
FIRST AMAZON:      Bring out the scythèd car!
SECOND AMAZON:                              Bury him! Crush
                                              [him
  With huge stones flung from towering elephants!
A PRINCESS *(suddenly leaving the Queen):*
  It must be! I will see what a shot can do!
              *(She unslings her bow and strings it.)*
ACHILLES *(turning from one Amazon to another):*
  How should I credit it? So sweet, so silvery,
  Your voices still belie these ruthless words.
  Thou, blue-eyed beauty, sure it is not thou
  That would unleash the dogs on me to tear me?
  Nor thou whose glory is thy silk-soft locks?
  Think! If unchained upon your hasty word
  With fearful howl these savage beasts sprang on me,

With your own bodies you would interpose
'Twixt them and me, to save this heart, this stout
Man's heart, that glows with love for none but you!

FIRST AMAZON: Unbridled insolence!

SECOND AMAZON:                    Hark how he boasts!

FIRST AMAZON: He thinks with flattering words to lull—

THIRD AMAZON *(calling the first under her breath):* Oterpe!

FIRST AMAZON *(turning around):*
  Ah, look! 'Tis she who never yet has missed!
  Open your ranks a little!

FIFTH AMAZON:            For what purpose?

FOURTH AMAZON: No questions! You will see!

FIRST AMAZON:                      Here! Take this
  arrow!

PRINCESS *(setting the arrow to the string):*
  I will transfix his thighs and cripple him.

ACHILLES *(to a Greek at his side, whose bow is at the ready):*
  Shoot her!

PRINCESS:    Ye gods above!
                    *(She falls.)*

FIRST AMAZON:              Oh, dreadful man!

SECOND AMAZON: 'Tis she who's hit and falls!

THIRD AMAZON:                          The gods protect
                                              [us!
  Another band of Greeks bears down on us.

# Scene 12

*Enter Diomede with the Aetolians on one side, soon followed by
Odysseus with the army on the same side as Achilles.*

DIOMEDE: This way, my stout Aetolians! Follow me!
  This way!
              *(He leads them over the bridge.)*

PROTHOE:   O Artemis! Now save us all,
  Else are we quite destroyed!
  *(With the help of some Amazons she carries the Queen to
  the front of the stage.)*

AMAZONS *(in confusion):*      We are surrounded!

We are cut off! We are all prisoners!
Run! Get away while there is time!
DIOMEDE *(to Prothoe):*          Now yield!
MEROE *(to the fleeing Amazons):*
What! Are you mad? Will you not stand and fight?
Prothoe! Look!
PROTHOE *(still with the Queen):* Go after them! Rally them!
And when thou canst, come back and rescue us!
  *(The Amazons flee in different directions. Meroe follows.)*
ACHILLES: Now where is she? Where shines that lovely head?
A GREEK: There!
ACHILLES:       Diomede shall have ten kingly crowns.
DIOMEDE *(to Prothoe):*
Once more I call on you to yield!
PROTHOE:          To him
Who won her, not to thee, I yield. To thee?
She is Achilles' prize, belongs to him alone.
DIOMEDE: Then cut her down!
AN AETOLIAN:         Come on!
ACHILLES *(pushing the Aetolian back):*     He dies this instant
Who dares to lay a finger on the Queen!
Mine is she! Out of here! Take yourselves off!
DIOMEDE: Oho! She's thine? Well, by Zeus' inky locks!
Upon what reason? With what right, may I ask?
ACHILLES: For two good reasons—this right one and this left!
                *(to Prothoe)*
Give her!
PROTHOE:    Here, take! In thy big heart she's safe.
ACHILLES *(taking the Queen in his arms):* Safe, safe!
              *(to Diomede)*
                [Go now and smite the fleeing women.
I must stay here a moment. Do not stay!
For my sake, go. Do not oppose me! Hell
Itself I'd challenge for her, much more thee!
    *(He lays her reclining against the root of an oak.)*
DIOMEDE: Well, then! Follow me!
ODYSSEUS *(passing across the stage with the army):*
               Good luck, Achilles! Good luck!
Shall I send thy thund'ring war-car to thee there?

ACHILLES *(bent over the Queen):* There is no need. Not now.
ODYSSEUS: Good! As thou wilt.
   All follow me! Before these women can rally!
        *(Odysseus and Diomede with the army off.)*

# Scene 13

*Penthesilea, Prothoe, Achilles. Greeks and Amazons in attendance.*

ACHILLES *(unbuckling the Queen's armor):* No breath of life!
PROTHOE: Oh, may she nevermore
   Look on the pallid light of this drear day!
   I fear, I fear that she must still awaken.
ACHILLES: Where did I wound her?
PROTHOE: From that blow, which split
   Her breast, she by main force of will did rally.
   Thus far we led her, weak and tottering still,
   And were about to climb with her this rocky slope,
   But pain o'ercame her, whether of her body
   So wounded, or of her bruisèd heart: she could not
   Abide the thought that thou hadst overcome her.
   Her stumbling foot refused its service; vague,
   Meaningless babblings passed her anguished lips,
   And once again she sank into my arms.
ACHILLES: She stirred!—Did you not see?
PROTHOE: Ye gods above!
   Has she not yet drunk all her bitter cup?
   Look, look! Oh, piteous sight!
ACHILLES: I feel her breath.
PROTHOE: Great son of Peleus! If thou canst know pity,
   If any tender feeling stirs thy breast,
   If it is not thy will to slay her nor to entoil
   Her trembling senses in the web of madness,
   Then grant me this one boon!
ACHILLES: Say quickly!
PROTHOE: Leave her! Go off! Noblest of men, go off!
   Stand not before her face when she awakes.

Remove from here thy attendant company,
And ere tomorrow's sun cast his fresh light
On the far mountain's misty top, let no one
Greet her with that fell word, more bitter than death:
That she is prisoner to Peleus' son.

ACHILLES: So! Does she hate me?

PROTHOE: Ask not, generous man!
When she returns now to the light with joy
And delicate hope, let not her vanquisher
Be her first sight, killing both hope and joy.
How much is hidden in a woman's breast
It is not meet should see the light of day.
If she at last, since Fate has so ordained,
Must give thee hateful greeting as thy prisoner,
At least do not demand it, that I beg,
Until her spirit is strong to bear such grief.

ACHILLES: My will is, I would have thee know, to do
To her as I did to Priam's son.

PROTHOE: Oh, fearful man! Not that!

ACHILLES: Does she fear this?

PROTHOE: Thou wilt accomplish on her nameless shames?
This lovely body in the bloom of youth,
Decked out with beauties as a child with flowers,
Shamefully, like a rotting corpse thou wilt—?

ACHILLES: Say to her that I love her.

PROTHOE: How? Thou lov'st—?

ACHILLES: How, by the gods above? As men love women;
Chastely—and yet with longing; in innocence—
And yet not loath to rob her of her own.
It is my will to take her for my Queen.

PROTHOE: O blissful words! Say them—say them once more!
It is thy will?

ACHILLES: Now may I stay?

PROTHOE: Oh, stay,
Thou godlike man! Let me but kiss thy feet!
Now, if thou were not here, I would go seek thee,
Even beyond the Pillars of Hercules!
But see! Her eyes are opening—

ACHILLES: She moves.

PROTHOE: Now is the time! Withdraw, you there; and thou
    Hide quickly from her sight behind that oak!
ACHILLES *(to Myrmidons)*:
    Move off, my friends! Away from here!
                *(Achilles' attendants off.)*
PROTHOE *(to Achilles, who hides behind the oak)*:
                              Hide well!
    And do not show thyself, I beg, until
    Thou hear'st me call. Achilles! Dost thou promise?
    I cannot tell how her poor mind will be.
ACHILLES: I will obey.
PROTHOE:             You may watch us unseen.

# Scene 14

*Penthesilea, Prothoe, Achilles. Attendant Amazons.*
PROTHOE: Penthesilea! What! Still lost in dreams?
    In what far paradise does thy swift spirit
    Still wheel and hover on its restless wings,
    Leaving its proper seat in strange disgust?
    While Fortune, like a young and lusty prince,
    Enters thy breast and, all amazed to find
    The lovely dwelling-place quite tenantless,
    Turns on his heel and makes again to bend
    His fleeting steps to heaven whence he came.
    Fond girl! Wilt thou not bind the sweet intruder?
    Come, raise thyself and lean on me!
PENTHESILEA:              Where am I?
PROTHOE: Dost thou not know the voice of thy own sister?
    This rocky slope, this narrow bridge, these wide
    And fertile-teeming plains—do you not know them?
    Look, here thy maidens all who wait upon thee:
    As though before the gates of some brighter world
    They stand and bid thee welcome. Dearest heart,
    Wherefore that sigh? What dost thou fear?
PENTHESILEA:              Oh, Prothoe!
    I dreamed, I dreamed—ah, what a fearful dream!

How sweet it is, sweet even to tears, to feel
This anguished heart, deadened with pain's excess,
Beat against thy strong heart, now I awake.
I dreamed that in the fiercest clash of war,
Smitten by Achilles' lance, I crash'd to the ground
And loud around me rang my brazen arms,
While Earth herself resounded to my fall.
And while the army in confusion flees—
I still with limbs entangled helpless there—
He has leapt down from off his charger, springs
With triumphant strides towards me, stoops
And seizes me, half swooning as I am,
Raises me up in his strong arms and holds me:
Vainly I seek to find and draw my dagger:
His prisoner I, and with fierce, mocking laughter
He bears me off by force to his hateful tents.

PROTHOE: Ah no, dear Queen! Not that! Not mocking laughter.
His noble generous heart could never mock thee.
If it indeed should hap, what they dream told,
Truly that were for thee a blissful hour:
I doubt not, in the dust, upon his knees
Before thee as thy slave thou'dst see Achilles.

PENTHESILEA: Accursèd I, if that should ever be!
Accursèd, should I yield my maidenhead
To any man not prisoner of my sword!

PROTHOE: Calm thyself, dearest lady!

PENTHESILEA: Calm! Why calm?

PROTHOE: Dost thou not lie here safe upon my
bosom? } *Together.*

Whatever fate hang poised above thy head,
We will endure together: calm thyself.

PENTHESILEA: But I was calm, my Prothoe, as the sea
That lies landlocked between craggy shores; not one
Feeling that roused a ripple on my heart,
But now this "Calm thyself!" suddenly whips
The unsheltered oceans of my mind to fierce turmoil.
What has befall'n that I must needs be calm?
You stand and look so strangely, so uneasy,
And throw such fearful glances, by the gods,
Behind me there, as though some dreadful thing

With wild, contorted face stood threatening me.
I told thee, it was but a dream, it is not—
Or is it? What? Oh tell me! Is it real?
Where's Meroe? And Megaris?
> *(She looks behind her and sees Achilles.)*
>                         Oh, horrible!
Most dreaded to my eyes! He stands behind me.
But now my hand is free—
> *(She draws her dagger.)*

PROTHOE:                         Stop, senseless girl!

PENTHESILEA: Shameless! Betrayer! Would you thwart me still?

PROTHOE: Achilles! You can save her!

PENTHESILEA:                         Are you mad?
His only thought to trample me to dust.

PROTHOE: Trample thee? Never!

PENTHESILEA:                         Away! Leave me, I say!

PROTHOE: But do but look at him, impetuous girl!
Does he not stand unarmed, defenseless there?

PENTHESILEA: Unarmed?

PROTHOE:                 Why, yes! And ready, if thou wilt,
To have thee chain him with these wreaths of love.

PENTHESILEA: It cannot be!

PROTHOE:                 Achilles! Speak thyself!

PENTHESILEA: My prisoner he?

PROTHOE:                 Why, yes! Why, yes! What else?

ACHILLES *(who has come forward)*:
In every way that's fair, thy prisoner I!
My only will to flutter out my life
In the soft durance of thy heavenly eyes.
> *(Penthesilea buries her face in her hands.)*

PROTHOE: So now, you have heard him say himself 'tis so.
At your encounter he too crashed to earth;
And while you lay lifeless upon the ground
He was disarmed—is't not so?

ACHILLES:                 Yes, disarmed.
And then led captive here before thy feet.
> *(He falls on one knee before her.)*

PENTHESILEA *(after a short pause)*:
Welcome—fair greeting then—fresh sweetness of life,
Thou lovely god with the bright cheeks of youth!

And oh, my heart, be rid of that stored blood
That, waiting on his coming, stagnant lies
Oppressive in the chambers of my breast.
You messengers of pleasure, eager-wing'd,
Sap of my youth, life's liquor, stir yourselves,
Flood through my veins, leap, shout for lusty joy,
And let the empurpled banner, steeped in gules,
Flaunt from the imperial watch-tower of my cheeks.
Achilles' self, the goddess-born, is mine!

*(She rises.)*

PROTHOE: My dearest Queen, be moderate in thy joy!

PENTHESILEA *(stepping forward):*

Come, then, you victory-crownèd virgins, come,
You daughters of Mars, from head to foot still thick
Encrusted with the blood-caked dust of battle,
Come, leading each by the hand that Argive youth
That she has vanquished on the field of war.
You younger maids draw near that keep the roses;
You have not wreaths enough to deck each brow?
Out then and seek o'er all the fields! And if
The niggard spring refuse me roses, breathe,
Breathe on the plain and it will burgeon for me!
Diana's priestesses! Take up your office,
That wide the thund'ring portals of her house,
Light radiant, with heady incense sweet,
May open to me like the gates of heaven.
First now the ox, well fattened, short of horn,
Here to the altar; thus the axe strikes home,
Fells him without a sound, and all the vast
And holy building trembles at his fall.
You temple serving-women, strong of limb,
The blood! The blood! Where are you?—Quick! To work!
Wash clean of blood the marble pavement, spread
The fragrance of burned Persian unguents here.
And all you fluttering kirtles, kilt you high!
You golden goblets, overflow with wine!
Bugles, shrill out! Horns, blare your resonant thunder!
Let heaven's firm-planted vault reverberate
To our melodious peals of heady joy!—

O Prothoe! Help me give rein to this
Fierce ecstasy of bliss! Invent, discover,
How I may celebrate a festival
More heavenly than heav'n's own joyous pomps—
The wedding-feast of the dread brides of war,
The seed of Inachus, daughters of Mars!
O, Meroe, where are you? And you Megaris?

PROTHOE *(with suppressed emotion):*
I see joy is no less thy bane than sorrow;
No matter which, it straight will make you mad.
You think yourself, fond fool, in Themiscyra.
Oh! When you thus break bounds and range at large,
I am sore tempted to pronounce that word
That lames your wing and tumbles you to earth.
Poor self-deceived, look round thee, where thou art?
Where is the host? The priestesses? Thy friends?
Asteria? Meroe? Megaris? Where are they?

PENTHESILEA *(on her breast):*
Not harsh, my Prothoe! Let my poor heart
Like a dirt-dabbled, happy child, sink deep
One wondrous moment in the stream of joy.
With every splash in those exultant waves
A stain is washed from my sad, sinful breast.
They flee at last, the dread Eumenides;
I feel the approach of godlike presences
And I would join my voice to their happy choir.
Ne'er was I half so ripe for death as now.
Yet one thing before all: I am forgiven?

PROTHOE: My Queen and lady!

PENTHESILEA: Good! I know, I know!
Thou hast the nobler part of our kindred blood.
They say misfortune purifies the soul,
But I, my love, have never found it so.
Bitterness still, rage against gods and men,
Unseeing passion, are its fruits in me.
With strange perversity I then have hated
On others' faces every mark of joy;
The blithe child playing in its mother's lap
Seemed but conspired to mock my sullen grief.

But now how gladly would I see each thing
Content and happy round about! Dear friend,
Man can be great in grief, ay, even a hero,
But only in happiness is he a god.
But now, much is to do. Without delay
The host shall make all ready for the march.
Soon as the companies both man and beast
Are rested, with the prisoners the whole
Breaks camp and moves to our far native vales—
Where is Lykaon?

PROTHOE:　　　　Who?

PENTHESILEA (with tender reproach): You ask me, who?
That fair Arcadian, of heroic form,
Whom thy sword won thee. Why is he not here?

PROTHOE (embarrassed):
My Queen, he lies with all the captive Greeks,
There in the woods, close guarded like the rest.
I pray you grant, as ancient law demands,
That I not see him till the city is reached.

PENTHESILEA: Call him before me! Close guarded in the woods!
Here at my Prothoe's feet is his right place.
Dearest, let him be called, I beg of you!
You stand so blighting there as frost in May,
Congealing all my springs of vernal joy.

PROTHOE (aside):
Unhappy girl!—Good, then! Go one of you
And do what you have heard the Queen command.
　　　　　(She signs to an Amazon, who exits.)

PENTHESILEA: Now, who will fetch the rose-girls to me here?
　　　　　(catching sight of roses on the ground)
Look! Here are blossoms—Ah! So sweet to smell!
Here on the ground—
　　　　　(passes her hand over her brow.)
　　　　　　　　Oh, My evil dream!
　　　　　(to Prothoe)
Was not the Priestess of Diana here?

PROTHOE: I do not think so, gracious Queen. Mayhap—

PENTHESILEA: But how do the roses come here?

PROTHOE *(quickly):* Ah! I know.
  The girls, when they were searching all the plain
  For roses, left one basket here forgotten.
  Now this is a most lucky accident!
  Look, I will wind thee from these scented blooms
  A wreath to honor Achilles. Shall I do it?
        *(She sits down against the oak.)*
PENTHESILEA: Thou dearest! Kindest! Now you touch my heart!
  Good, then. These hundred-petaled buds I'll wind for thee
  To be thy wreath of victory for Lykaon.
    *(She too gathers up some roses and sits down by Prothoe.)*
  Music, my friends, music! I am not calm.
  Let your clear song sound out and bring me peace!
A VIRGIN: What should we sing?
ANOTHER: The triumph song?
PENTHESILEA: The Hymn.
VIRGIN: So be it! (Deluded still!) Sing, then, and play!
CHOIR OF VIRGINS *(with music):*
  Ares withdraws!
  See how his gleaming white team,
  Trailing vapor to Orcus, sweeps afar!
  The loathly goddesses open, the Eumenides,
  Then shut to the portals once again behind him.
A VIRGIN: Hymen! Why tarriest thou?
  Kindle the torch-flame and light us! Light us!
  Hymen! Why tarriest thou?
CHOIR: Ares withdraws!
  See how his gleaming white team,
  Trailing vapor to Orcus, sweeps afar!
  The loathly goddesses open, the Eumenides,
  Then shut to the portals once again behind him.
  *(Achilles moves stealthily up to Prothoe during the singing.)*
ACHILLES: Where does this lead me? Speak! I will be told!
PROTHOE: Patience one moment more, great-hearted man.
  I beg you—patience. Then you shall have your will.
    *(When the wreaths are made, Penthesilea and Prothoe
    exchange wreaths, embrace each other, and examine them.
    The music ends. The Amazon returns.)*

PENTHESILEA: Well, did you do it?
AMAZON: Lykaon, gracious Queen,
 The young Arcadian prince, will soon be here.

# Scene 15

PENTHESILEA: Come now, my own Achilles, goddess-born.
 Come, lay thee at my feet. Nay, closer yet!
 No shame nor coyness! Sure, thou dost not fear me?
 Nor hate me neither?
ACHILLES *(at her feet):* As flowers the spring sunshine!
PENTHESILEA: Then thou canst look on me now as thy sun.
 Diana, gracious lady! See, he is
 Wounded!
ACHILLES: Grazed by an arrow, that is all.
PENTHESILEA *(taking the wreaths):*
 I pray thee, son of Peleus, never think
 That I did ever wish to take thy life.
 'Tis true, when this arm smote thee, it was bliss;
 But when thus smitten thou didst fall, my heart
 Envied the dust that then was pressed beneath thee.
ACHILLES: Nay, if you love me, do not speak of it.
 You see, 'tis healing.
PENTHESILEA: Then I am forgiven?
ACHILLES: With all my heart!
PENTHESILEA: Good. Now I would be taught
 What wiles the Queen of Love must use, when she
 Would bind with silken chains the shag-maned lion.
ACHILLES: With her soft hand she strokes his horrid cheeks;
 Then he is still.
PENTHESILEA: 'Tis well. Then thou wilt not
 Move more than does the tender turtle-dove
 When round her neck her mistress lays soft cords.
 For know, sweet youth, the emotions of this breast
 Play round thee still like soft caressing hands.
   *(She lays garlands round him.)*
ACHILLES: Who art thou, strange and wondrous woman?
PENTHESILEA: So!—

I said keep still! Soon I will tell thee all.
But first thou must be bound, thus lightly bound,
With ropes round thy head and round thy throat
—Then down around thy arms, thy hands, thy feet,
Thence back up to thy head—Now, it is finished.
What do you breathe so?

ACHILLES:            Scent of thy warm lips.

PENTHESILEA *(straightening herself a little)*:
It is the roses. Their scent fills the air.

ACHILLES: Would I might taste those roses where they grow.

PENTHESILEA: At the appointed time my love shall pluck them.
     *(sets one last wreath on his head and lets go of him.)*
So it is finished! See, my Prothoe!
Suffused with delicate rose, is he not handsome?
The Day new-sprung, I swear it, when from the hills
The light-foot Hours come leading him along—
His swift feet shedding pearls and diamonds—
Look not more gentle nor more tenderly.
Would you not say his eye held back a tear?
In sooth, one well could doubt, when he looks so,
That it is he.

PROTHOE:      Who, sister?

PENTHESILEA:        Who? Achilles!
That man that slew old Priam's greatest son
Before the walls of Troy—Say! Was it thou?
And didst thou truly, thou, with these thy hands
Pierce his fleet ankles, then behind thy car
Drag him headlong around his native city?
Speak! What's the matter? Why art thou so moved?

ACHILLES: I am that man.

PENTHESILEA *(looking at him sharply)*: He says 'tis he.

PROTHOE:                             My
                                      [Queen,
Here by his fine-wrought armor thou cast know him.

PENTHESILEA: How?

PROTHOE:          This is that famed harness—nay, look
                                      [close—
That Thetis, his dread mother, suppliant,
Begged of divine Hephaestus, lord of fire.

PENTHESILEA: So, then, I seal thee with this kiss, of all
    Mankind the most rebellious, mine! 'Tis I
    Who am thy mistress, youthful war-god thou!
    Should any ask thee of the people, name my name.
ACHILLES: O thou, who with soft, heavenly radiance,
    As though the realms of light had oped their doors,
    Descendest on me, strange beyond wit: who art thou?
    How do I name thee, when my own soul asks,
    In sudden rapture who her mistress is?
PENTHESILEA: When thy soul asks, then name these features, that
    Be all the name of me dwells in thy mind.
    This golden ring indeed I give to thee,
    Whose marks are surety to thee I am I;
    Show it to any, all will know it mine.
    Rings may be lost, a name may be forgotten.
    My name forgot, this ring quite lost, couldst thou
    Still find my living image in thy heart?
    Canst thou, eyes closed, create it in thy mind?
ACHILLES: Clear, true it stands, as graved in diamond.
PENTHESILEA: I am the Queen of all the Amazons;
    My race claims Ares as its first begetter;
    Otrere was my noble mother; me,
    My warlike people calls: Penthesilea.
ACHILLES: Penthesilea.
PENTHESILEA:        Thus I said to thee.
ACHILLES: Dying, my swan shall sing: Penthesilea.
PENTHESILEA: Thou hast thy liberty. Through all the host
    Freely, where'er it pleases, thou may'st walk.
    Quite other chains, more delicate than flowers,
    As brass unbreakable I mean to wind
    About thy heart and bind thee fast to me.
    But till they, link on link, are hammered out
    In passion's heat and adamantine forged,
    No more destructible by time or chance,
    Thou wilt return of right to me again,
    To me, my friend, no other; for 'tis I
    Will serve thee in thy every need or wish.
    Tell me, wilt thou return?

ACHILLES:                 As do young stallions
  To that sweet-scented manger where they feed.
PENTHESILEA: Good. I shall trust thy word. Now we begin
  The long march back to our city, Themiscyra.
  Take from my stables what horse suits thy whim.
  Thou shalt have purple tents to dwell in; nor
  Shall slaves to serve thee as befits and do
  Thy royal will in everything be lacking.
  But since upon the march I shall be bound
  By cares of leadership, thou wilt consort
  Still with the other Argive prisoners.
  At home in Themiscyra, not till then,
  Shall I be free to give thee all my heart.
ACHILLES: So it shall be.
PENTHESILEA *(to Prothoe):* But tell me now, dear friend,
  Where can thy young Arcadian be?
PROTHOE:                 My Queen—!
PENTHESILEA: I would so gladly see thee set the wreath
  Upon his head, my Prothoe.
PROTHOE:             He will
  Soon come. Indeed, he shall not lose his wreath.
PENTHESILEA *(preparing to rise):*
  Good, then. A thousand duties call me, friend.
  So let me go.
ACHILLES:       What!
PENTHESILEA:        Let me rise, I say.
ACHILLES: Thou wilt be gone? Wilt leave me here? Though still
  Thou hast not satisfied my longing breast's
  Untaught surmise and baffled questioning?
PENTHESILEA: In Themiscyra, friend.
ACHILLES:                  No, here, my Queen!
PENTHESILEA: In Themiscyra, friend, in Themiscyra!
  Let me go!
PROTHOE *(restraining her, troubled):*
  Why? What wilt thou do, dear lady?
PENTHESILEA: Strange question! I must order the companies,
  Consult with Meroe and Megaris.
  By heaven, have I nought else to do but chatter?

PROTHOE: The army still pursues the fleeing Greeks.
　　Leave Meroe, who leads the van, that work.
　　You still have need of rest. Soon as the foe,
　　Both horse and foot, is back behind Scamander
　　Shall the victorious host parade before you.
PENTHESILEA *(considering)*:
　　Ah! Here, where I am standing? Is that sure?
PROTHOE: Certain. I promise it.
PENTHESILEA *(to Achilles)*: 　　　Well, then, be brief.
ACHILLES: What is the cause, thou strange and wondrous woman,
　　That, Pallas-like, queen of a host in arms,
　　Thou fling'st thyself, all unprovoked, a bolt
　　From heaven, into our quarrel here with Troy?
　　What urges thee, in steel caparisoned,
　　Full of insensate rage, most like a Fury,
　　To fall thus headlong on the tribes of Argos?
　　Thou who dost need but to reveal thy sweet
　　Person in quiet loveliness and straight
　　All men will fall before thee worshipping!
PENTHESILEA: Son of the dread sea-goddess! Not for me
　　The common arts of gentler womanhood!
　　When to the games the lusty youths rejoicing
　　Throng to make trial of each other's strength,
　　I may not, as do your maids, choose my love
　　And draw him to me with shy downward eyes
　　Or with bright wanton nosegay, here or here;
　　I may not in the dark-leaved orange grove,
　　Where nightingales throb out the forenoon's heat,
　　Sink on his breast and tell him it is he.
　　No, on the bloody field of war must I go seek him,
　　That youth my heart has chosen for its own,
　　And clip him to me with harsh arms of brass,
　　Whom rather I would press to this soft breast.
ACHILLES: But whence can spring, how ancient is that law,
　　Unwomanly, forgive me, nay, unnatural,
　　A custom strange to all the tribes of men?
PENTHESILEA: From the remotest urn of things revered,
　　O youth, down from remotest peaks of time,
　　Unknown, untrodden, wrapped eternally

In divine mystery as in a cloud.
The ban was laid by word of our first mothers,
And we are dumb before it, son of Thetis,
As thou before thy first forefathers' words.
ACHILLES: Speak plainer.
PENTHESILEA:         Be it so, then! Hearken well.
  In that far land where the Amazons now dwell,
  Lived once, obedient to the gods, a tribe
  Of Scythians, warlike, subject to no lord,
  Not different from other tribes of men.
  For centuries past counting they had called
  The high, flower-cradled Caucasus their own;
  At whose foot Vexoris, the Ethiop king,
  Appearing suddenly, slew all the men
  Who stood in arms against him, thence unhindered
  Poured through the valleys, slaughtering every male,
  Old men and boys, where'er his sword might find them,
  Earth's splendor with that race was blotted out.
  The victors then, brazen barbarians,
  Took to themselves our huts, dwelt in them, fed
  Their hateful bodies from our fields' fat crops,
  And, that our cup of shame might quite o'erflow,
  Forced on our women vile embrace of love.
  They tore us, still lamenting our dead menfolk,
  From those sad graves into their loathsome beds.
ACHILLES: Crushing in sooth, Queen, was that fate to which
  Your woman's nation owes its timely birth.
PENTHESILEA: Yet man rebels, shaking his shoulders free
  Of all that gyves his heart beyond endurance;
  Ills must be moderate, or he'll not bear them.
  Long nights on end, in deepest secrecy,
  The women lay in Ares' house and wept,
  Graving with passionate prayer the altar steps.
  Their beds, by ruffian force defiled, began
  To fill with daggers needle-sharp, rough-forged
  In the hearth's homely flame from ornaments,
  From bodkins, rings, and brooches: only still
  They waited on the nuptials of King Vexoris
  With Tanais, their Queen, to kiss with these

Keen love-tokens their ravishers' swart breasts.
And when the wedding hour was now at hand,
Into his heart the Queen drove home her blade,
Mars in his stead fulfilled the solemn rite,
And all that race of murderers with knives
In that one night was tickled to the shades.

ACHILLES: Ay! Women's vengeance! I can well believe it!

PENTHESILEA: And now in open folk-moot was decreed:
Free as the wind that sweeps the unsheltered fallow
Are women who have wrought so great a deed,
And to the male no more subservient.
A nation has arisen, a nation of women,
Bound to no overlord, in which no voice
Of arrogant, o'erweening man is heard;
A folk that gives itself its own just laws,
Obeys its own decrees, and can defend
Itself from foes; and Tanais is its Queen.
That man whose eye but looks upon this people
Shall straightway close his eye forever; where
A boy is the sad fruit of that forced mating,
No room for pity! He must straight below,
Down to the shades to meet his savage sire.
Thereon the house of Ares straight was thronged
With folk close-packed, to crown great Tanais
Queen, paramount defender of the state.
But just as she, at that most solemn moment,
Mounted the altar steps, to grasp the bow—
The mighty, golden bow of the Scythian realm,
Which none but kings till then had borne—and take it
From the rich-robed high priestess' hand, sudden
An awful voice was heard uttering these words:
" 'Twill but invite menfolk to mockery,
A nation such as this, and 'twill succumb
To the first onset of its warlike neighbors;
For never can weak women, hampered still
By the full-swelling bosom, learn to use
The taut bow's deadly swiftness, as can men!"
One moment long the Queen stood, pondering
What good might spring from counsel of the god.

But as base fear began to sweep the people,
She tore away her own right breast, baptizing
Thus all these women who would wield the bow
—Herself, ere she had finished, swooned away—
The Amazons, that is: the breastless ones!
This done, the crown was set upon her head.

ACHILLES: Why then, by God! She had no need of breasts!
  She could have been as well a queen of men,
  And from my heart I bow in reverence to her.

PENTHESILEA: My friend, upon this deed was utter stillness;
  No word, no sound was heard, save that the bow
  Fell whirring from the bloodless, lifeless hands
  Of the high priestess to the temple floor.
  It fell, the mighty golden bow of our race,
  Then rang aloud three times from the marble step
  With bell-like drone and settled slowly down
  And lay mute at her feet, silent as death.

ACHILLES: You women do not follow her, I hope,
  In this example?

PENTHESILEA:      Not? Indeed we do!
  Maybe not quite so eagerly as she.

ACHILLES (*astonished*): What? Then it is—? Impossible!

PENTHESILEA:                    What, then?

ACHILLES: The monstrous rumor then is true indeed?
  And all these lovely forms, that stand around thee
  In youthful bloom, the pride of womanhood,
  Each one decked out with charms, a holy altar
  Before which we must bow the knee for love—
  Are barbarously, inhumanly, deformed—?

PENTHESILEA: Was that indeed unknown to thee?

ACHILLES (*hiding his face on her breast*):
                    My Queen!
  The seat of all youth's tenderest, sweetest feelings
  Thus criminally, thus wantonly—

PENTHESILEA:             Fear not!
  Here in this left breast they have taken refuge
  And are, by that much, nearer to my heart.
  Not one shalt thou find lacking, friend, in me.

ACHILLES: In sooth, a dream that's dreamed at gray of dawn

Seems truer far than does this here and now.
But now, proceed.
PENTHESILEA:      What?
ACHILLES:                There is more to come.
  For this too daring-proud nation of women
  That without help of men arose, how still
  Can it without men's help renew itself?
  Does old Deucalion from time to time
  Toss you a rock or two from his magic store?
PENTHESILEA: Whenever, following yearly reckonings,
  The Queen thinks fit to replace whate'er the state
  Has lost through death, she calls the blossoming prime
  Of all the women—
           *(stops short and looks at him)*
           Why do you smile?
ACHILLES:                        Who? I?
PENTHESILEA: Did you not smile? It seemed so.
ACHILLES:                    For thy beauty
  My thoughts had strayed. Forgive me. I was wond'ring
  If thou wert not come down to me from the moon.
PENTHESILEA *(after a pause)*:
  Whenever, following yearly reckonings,
  The Queen thinks fit to replace whate'er the state
  Has lost by death, she calls the blossoming prime
  Of all the women from her whole realm together
  To Themiscyra. There, in Diana's temple,
  She prays for all: that their young wombs may teem
  With the sweet fruit of Ares' chaste embrace.
  This festival of gentle hope we call
  The Feast of Flowering Virgins, and we wait
  Until the mantling snow's breathed all to shreds
  And spring has pressed his kiss on Earth's cold breast.
  The Queen's prayer made, Diana's holy priestess
  Passes into the temple of great Mars
  And there, prone on the altar steps, she lays
  The mothers' wish before the all-seeing god.
  The god, then, if he inclines to hear her prayer
  —For often he'll not have it: niggardly
  Of sustenance are these our snow-capped hills—

The god makes known to us through his high priestess
A people chaste and lordly which shall do
Instead of him the service we have asked.
This people's name and habitation known,
A surging joy runs throughout city and land.
As Brides of Mars we greet the warrior-virgins,
Who from their mothers' hands receive their weapons,
Short sword and arrows; and their youthful limbs,
Joyously waited on by busy hands,
Are quickly cased in brazen wedding garb.
The day is set for their glad journeying;
Faint bugle calls are heard, whispered commands;
The bands of girls swing themselves into the saddle;
Noiseless and stealthy, as though woolen shod,
Under the moon they ride through valley and woodland
To the far burg where lies that chosen folk.
The land once reached, we halt upon its frontier,
Two days of rest for weary man and beast,
Then, like the fiery hurricano's blast,
We sweep into the forest of their menfolk,
Snatch up the ripest of the fallen fruit—
Seeds that are scattered from the thrashing treetops—
And bear them with us to our native plains.
Here we conduct them in Diana's temple
Through many a solemn rite, of which the name
Alone is known to me—the Feast of Roses:
Forbidden is it—death is his reward
Who dares approach, except the Brides of Mars.
The seed is sown, and when the crop is up,
We heap on them full measure of glorious gifts;
On steeds richly caparisoned we send
Them home. The Feast of Fruitful Mothers this,
In sooth a festival of little joy.
Ah, son of Thetis! Many a tear is shed,
And many a heart, fast gripped by dreary grief,
Must ask itself: is Tanais the Great
For every binding word so praiseworthy?
What do you muse on?

ACHILLES:                    I?

PENTHESILEA:                     Who else?
ACHILLES:                           My love!
  On more than I can yet find words to utter—
  And shall I in like manner be dismissed?
PENTHESILEA: I do not know, dear. Do not ask me!
ACHILLES:                           Strange!
                *(falls into thought)*
  But there is one thing I must understand.
PENTHESILEA: Willingly, friend. Speak freely.
ACHILLES:                     Tell me why
  Thy hot pursuit was aimed only on me?
  Was I then known to thee?
PENTHESILEA:             Ay, that thou wast!
ACHILLES: But how?
PENTHESILEA:       If thou'lt not smile at my foolishness.
ACHILLES *(smiling)*: I know not—thou must promise too.
PENTHESILEA:                   Well, then,
  I'll tell thee. Already I had seen the feast,
  The happy Feast of Roses, twenty times
  And three; but always only from afar
  Had heard the glad outcry where from the grove
  Of holy oaks the temple towers, when Mars
  Upon Otrere's, my dear mother's, death
  Chose me to be his bride. For you must know,
  It is not right that they of the royal blood,
  Princesses of our house, of their mere will
  Should join the Feast of Flowering Virgins; Mars,
  Should he desire, calls them with circumstance,
  Worthily, by the mouth of his high priestess.
  My dying mother, ashen-pale, lay there—
  I held her in my arms—when from the god
  They brought to me his solemn salutation
  And called on me forthwith to move on Troy,
  Thence to conduct him wreathed, in triumph, home.
  Now it so happened that never yet was named
  To do the god's work any race more welcome
  To the Brides of Mars than these Troy-girdling Greeks.
  The streets were filled with noise of jubilation;
  In every market-place the songs were heard

That tell the tale of that war's giant deeds:
Of Paris' apple and the Rape of Helen,
Of Atreus' sons, stout leaders of the host,
Briseïs, cause of strife, the ships in flames,
And then Patroclus' death, and with what pomp
Thou didst avenge and celebrate his end:
Those deeds and many others then were sung.
But I, consumed with grief and quenchless tears,
Heard but with half an ear the solemn message
Which the god sent me as my mother died.
"Oh, let me stay beside thee, Mother!" I cried.
"Use it once more, thy royal dignity,
—For the last time—and bid these women go."
But she, a queen to her last breath, who long
Had wished to see me in the field—for still
Without heir of the blood she left the throne,
Prey to the wanton greed of ambitious kindred—
She said to me: "Go, child! The god has called thee.
Thou wilt bring back the son of Peleus crowned:
Be thou a mother, proud and glad as I—"
Then gently pressed my hand and left me weeping.

PROTHOE: So then she named him by his name to thee?

PENTHESILEA: She named him, Prothoe. Why should she not,
Mother and daughter speaking privily?

ACHILLES: But why? What cause? Does the law then forbid?

PENTHESILEA: It is not fitting that a daughter of Mars
Should seek her opponent; she must be content
To take whome'er the god sends her in battle.
But it is well if she with eager spirit
Fights only where the noblest foemen stand.
Is that not so?

PROTHOE:                 So is it.

ACHILLES:                           Well—?

PENTHESILEA:                                      I wept,
Long, long I wept, a whole grief-laden month,
At my dear mother's grave, neglecting still
The crown that lay beside me masterless,
Until at length the oft-repeated cry
Of the people, who, eager for joyful war,

Impatient, lay encamped around my palace,
Dragged me by force to mount the throne. I came,
Still bowed by grief, with inward-warring heart,
To the temple of Mars; the bow—they gave it me,
The twanging bow of all the Amazons.
And as I look it in my hand I felt
My mother all about me; nought was holier
To me than to make good her dying will.
Then, having strewn upon her bier the sweetest,
Most heaven-scented flowers, I straight struck out
With all the puissance of the Amazons
For Ilium's towers—less honoring in that
Ares, the god of war, by whom I was elect,
Than that dear shade—my mother's, great Otrere's.

ACHILLES: Grief for the dead one moment sapped the fire
  That else runs coursing through thy youthful breast.

PENTHESILEA: I loved her.

ACHILLES:             Good. And then?

PENTHESILEA:                         As day by day
  Nearer I drew to old Scamander's stream,
  And every vale around through which I swept
  Echoed the clash of battle before Troy,
  So did my grief abate, and my wide soul
  Drank in the universe of joyful war.
  To myself I said: if they should all together,
  The mighty moments of the daedal past,
  Return for me, if all the company
  Of heroes, whom the songs of minstrels sing,
  Should step down from the stars, I should not find
  Not one more excellent, to crown with roses,
  Than that man whom my mother chose for me—
  So dear, so wild, so sweet, so terrible—
  The slayer of Hector! O thou son of Peleus!
  Ever my single thought when I awoke,
  Ever my dream in sleep wast thou! The world
  Lay stretched before me like a patterned web,
  And in each glorious, wide-gaping mesh
  One of thy deeds with craftsman's skill enwoven;
  Upon my heart, as on silk white and fine,

I burned each deed with colors steeped in flame.
Now I beheld thee smite him to the earth,
Though still he fled thee, there before Priam's towers.
Or now, enflamed in lust of victory,
Thou did'st turn back to look upon his head,
Bloody and battered by the ungentle ground.
Or then 'twas Priam, suppliant in thy tent—
And I wept scalding tears of joy to think
That some emotion yet, thou pitiless man,
Could penetrate and stir thy flinty bosom.

ACHILLES: My dearest Queen!

PENTHESILEA:                    But, oh, that moment, when
With these my eyes, I saw thee—thee thyself!
There in Scamander's vale thou didst appear,
Ringed round by all Achaea's mightiest—
Wan luminaries before the day-star paling.
Not otherwise would it have seemed to me
If he himself with his snow-gleaming team
Had thundered down upon me from Olympus,
Ares, the god of war, to greet his bride.
Blinded I stood long time, when thou wast gone,
By that swift apparition, as when at night
The lightning plunges down before the wanderer
Or heaven's groaning doors, all radiance,
Open before the soul—and close again.
I knew at once—how should I not, Achilles?—
Whence came the flooding turmoil in my breast:
The god of love had overtaken me.
Of two things then I swore that one should be:
Either to win thee or to perish here.
And now of these the sweeter is my lot—
What is the matter?

                    *(Clash of arms is heard far off.)*

PROTHOE:             Achilles! Listen to me!
You must declare yourself at once to her.

PENTHESILEA *(leaping up.):* The Achaeans come! Your weapons!

ACHILLES                              [Nay, sit still!
For sure, it is a band of prisoners.

PENTHESILEA: Of prisoners?

PROTHOE *(aside to Achilles):* I tell you, 'tis Odysseus!
  Your friends, hard pressed by Meroe, fall back.
ACHILLES *(into his beard):* God smite them all to stone!
PENTHESILEA:                                             What is
                                              [the matter?

ACHILLES *(with forced cheerfulness):*
  Queen! Thou shalt bear me soon the god of Earth!
  Prometheus shall arise from his hard bed
  And loud proclaim to all the tribes of men:
  This is a man, pure image of my thought!
  But not to Themiscyra will I go;
  No, thou shalt follow me to fertile Phthia:
  For when I have wound up the clue of war,
  In triumph I shall take thee home and set thee
  —Ah, too great bliss!—beside me on the throne.
                *(Clash of arms continues.)*
PENTHESILEA: What? How? What does he mean?
AMAZONS:                                O all ye gods!
PROTHOE: Achilles! Wilt thou—?
PENTHESILEA:                     What? What is the matter?
ACHILLES: Nothing, my Queen! Nothing! No need to fear.
  Thou seest, time forces us, and thou must hear
  What fate the assembled gods have doomed for thee.
  'Tis true, by Love's dominion I am thine,
  And never shall I cast these happy bonds.
  But by decree of arms thou art my prize:
  Before me in the dust thou didst sink down,
  Not I before thee, when there we met in battle.
PENTHESILEA *(starting back):* Oh, horrible!
ACHILLES:                          Not so, I beg,
                                    [beloved!

  Not Cronos' son can alter what is done.
  Master thyself and hear unflinching still
  The messenger who there draws near with some
  Ill-ominous word, I doubt not, for my ear.
  To thee—this understand!—he brings thee nought.
  Thy fate is fixed forever—locked and sealed.
  Thou art my prisoner; a hound of hell
  Would guard thee less implacably than I.

PENTHESILEA: Thy prisoner, I?
PROTHOE: Queen! It is even so!
PENTHESILEA *(raising her hands):*
 Eternal gods in heaven! You hear my cry!


# Scene 16

*Enter a Captain, also Achilles' attendants with his arms.*
ACHILLES: What news do you bring?
CAPTAIN: You must retire, Achilles.
 The chance of war, with veering April face,
 Once more calls out our foes to victory;
 Their headlong thrust's aimed at this very spot,
 Their savage warcry still: Penthesilea.
  *(Achilles stands up and tears off the wreaths.)*
 Bring me my weapons! The horses! Bring the horses!
 By God! My brazen car shall mow them down!
PENTHESILEA *(with trembling lip):*
 Oh! See him now, so terrible! So changed!
ACHILLES *(raging):* Are they far off?
CAPTAIN: Not far! Here in the valley
 Easily can be seen their golden crescent.
ACHILLES *(doing on his armor):* Get her away!
A GREEK: Whither?
ACHILLES: To the Argive camp.
 I will be with you in a little space.
THE GREEK *(to Penthesilea):* Stand up!
PROTHOE: Oh, my revered, my well-loved Queen!
PENTHESILEA *(beside herself):*
 Hast thou no bolt for me, great son of Cronos?


# Scene 17

*Enter Odysseus and Diomede with the Greek army.*
DIOMEDE *(passing across the stage):*
 Away! Away from here, my friend! Away!

The last way out—the last that still lies open—
Even while we talk, those women are cutting it!
Away!

(*Off.*)

ODYSSEUS: Bear off this queen from here, Achaeans.

ACHILLES (*to the Captain*):
Alexis! Be so good, my friend. Help her.

THE GREEK (*to the Captain*): She will not move.

ACHILLES (*to the Greeks attendant on him*):
My shield, ho! Where's my lance?
(*commandingly to Penthesilea, who is resisting.*)
Penthesilea!

PENTHESILEA: O great son of Peleus!
Thou wilt not follow me to Themiscyra?
Nor to that temple wilt thou not follow me,
That towers far off above the oak-grove's crowns?
Come to me; there is more that I would tell.
(*Achilles, now in full armor, goes up to her and gives her his hand.*)

ACHILLES: My Queen!—To Phthia!

PENTHESILEA:                         Oh! To Themiscyra!
My friend! my friend! We must to Themiscyra,
Where Dian's temple thrusts above the oaks!
Ay, though the Blest Abodes were there in Phthia,
Yet, yet, my friend, we must to Themiscyra,
Where Dian's temple thrusts above the tops!

ACHILLES (*taking her up*):
It cannot be. You must forgive me, dearest.
Just such a temple will I build in Phthia.

# Scene 18

*Enter Meroe and Asteria with the Amazon army.*

MEROE: Strike him down!
(*Achilles lets the Queen go and turns.*)

ACHILLES:                         What! Do they ride upon the storm?

THE AMAZONS *(thrusting themselves between Penthesilea and Achilles)*:
  Set the Queen free!
ACHILLES:  Never! By this right hand!
  *(He tries to drag the Queen off.)*
PENTHESILEA *(pulling him to her)*:
  Thou wilt not follow me? Wilt not?
ODYSSEUS:  Away!
  Thy stubborn folly will undo us all!
  *(He drags Achilles off. Greeks exeunt.)*

# Scene 19

*Enter the High Priestess of Diana with the Priestesses.*
THE AMAZONS: Triumph! Triumph! Triumph! Our Queen is
  [saved!
PENTHESILEA *(after a pause)*:
  Accursèd be this shameful cry of triumph!
  Accursèd every tongue that utters it,
  Accurs'd the servile air on which it swims!
  Was I not his by every use of chivalry,
  By fairest chance of war his lawful prize?
  When man on man makes war—not on the wolf
  Or ravening tiger but on his own kind—
  Show me the law—I say, show me!—which then
  Permits the prisoner who has yielded him
  To be set free again from his captor's bonds.
  Oh! Son of Peleus!
THE AMAZONS:  What are these words of madness?
MEROE: Most reverend Priestess of Diana, hear!
  Stand not aloof, I beg thee—
ASTERIA:  She is wroth,
  Because we set her free from shameful bonds.
THE HIGH PRIESTESS *(stepping forward out of the crowd of women)*:
  In sooth, worthily hast thou set, O Queen,
  I must confess, with these abusive words,

The crown of shame upon this day's doings.
'Tis not alone that thou with scant respect
For custom thus must pick and choose thy foe;
Nor that, rather than hurl him in the dust,
Thyself dost fall, too weak; nor yet that thou,
In thanks for this, dost crown him here with roses.
Thou dost revile as well thy loyal folk
That breaks thy shameful chains, dost turn away
And call the man that topped thee back again.
'Tis well then, daughter of Tanais, 'tis well—
It was an error, nothing more, for which
Too hasty deed I humbly beg forgiveness.
The blood then spilt for thee—we could have spared it;
And all our prisoners, lost for thy sake,
With all my soul I would we had them still.
Here in the people's name I do release thee;
The world is open to thee. Go thy way!
With fluttering kirtle thou canst now pursue
Him who has made thee captive and canst give him
Those chains, by us hewn through, to weld again:
Thy vaunted laws of war demand no less!
Us, gracious Queen, us wilt thou not forbid
Now to break off the war and to begin
At once the long march home to Themiscyra.
For we, at least, we cannot beg those Greeks
Who have escaped to stand and be recaptured;
Cannot as thou, the victor's wreath in hand,
Implore them to fall prostrate at our feet.

(Pause.)

PENTHESILEA (*reeling*): Prothoe!
PROTHOE:                     Dearest sister!
PENTHESILEA:                               Oh, do not leave
[me!

PROTHOE: Never! No, not in death! Why do you tremble?
PENTHESILEA: It is nothing—nothing. Soon I shall be strong.
PROTHOE: A great grief struck thee; show thyself as great.
PENTHESILEA: And they are lost?
PROTHOE:                      Who lost, my dearest lady?

PENTHESILEA: That glorious company whom we had reaped—
   All lost through me?
PROTHOE:                         It is no matter. Soon
   Thou shalt win others in another war.
PENTHESILEA *(on Prothoe's bosom):* Oh, never!
PROTHOE:                                        How, my Queen?
PENTHESILEA:                                       [Oh, never! Never!
   No! I must bury me in endless night!


# Scene 20

*Enter a herald.*
MEROE: A herald comes, my Queen.
ASTERIA:                              What is thy will?
PENTHESILEA *(with faint joy):*
   'Tis from Achilles!—Ah, what shall I hear?
   No, Prothoe, bid him go.
PROTHOE *(to the herald):* What is thy message?
HERALD: Most mighty Queen! Achilles sends me to thee,
   Son of the dread reed-wreathèd Nereid,
   And bids me, as his mouth, thus to declare:
   Since thou dost lust to carry him away,
   Thy prisoner, to thy far native fields,
   And he on his side lusts no whit the less
   To bear thee to the wide plains of his home;
   Thee now he challengeth once more to stand
   And face him in the field in mortal combat.
   Thus shall the sword, Fate's iron tongue, decide,
   Here in the watchful presence of the gods,
   Which of you twain is worthier, thou or he,
   By their revered, inexorable doom
   To lick the dust before his foeman's feet.
   Hast thou the heart to trip this measure with him?
PENTHESILEA *(with a momentary pallor):*
   Thy tongue be sundered by the levin-bolt,
   Glib recreant, before thou speak again!

More welcome to my ear the granite block
That hurtles from the towering crag and leaps,
Striking and bounding, into unfathomed depths.
*(to Prothoe.)*
Thou must repeat it to me word for word.
PROTHOE *(trembling):*
The son of Peleus, so it seems, has sent
Him here to call thee again into the field.
Refuse him out of hand with brief: I will not!
PENTHESILEA: It is impossible!
PROTHOE:                      What, then, my Queen?
PENTHESILEA: He challenges me—he—to mortal combat?
PROTHOE: I'll tell him thou wilt not and bid him go.
PENTHESILEA: He challenges me—he—to mortal combat?
PROTHOE: Ay, lady, as I said, he'll fight with thee.
PENTHESILEA: He, he, who knows I am too weak by far,
He sends this challenge, Prothoe, to me?
My faithful breast here moves him not a whit
Till he has crushed and split it with his spear?
Did all I whispered to him touch his ear
Only with the empty music of the voice?
Has he forgot the temple midst the oaks?
Was it a block of stone my hand did crown?
PROTHOE: Forget the unfeeling man.
PENTHESILEA *(with burning indignation):* Then be it so!
Now I do feel the strength to stand against him:
Now he shall down and grovel in the dust,
Thou Lapiths—ay, though giants fight to save him!
PROTHOE: Belovèd Queen!
MEROE:                    Hast thou bethought thee well?
PENTHESILEA *(interrupting her):*
You shall have all the prisoners again!
THE HERALD: Thou wilt in combat—?
PENTHESILEA:                        Fear not! I will meet him!
Ay, me he shall encounter; all the gods
—And Furies too—I do call down to witness.
*(Thunder.)*
HIGH PRIESTESS: If my hard words have stung thee, Penthesilea,
Thou wilt not cause me pain—

PENTHESILEA *(suppressing tears)*: Nay, holy dame!
   Not vainly, be assured, were those words spoken.
MEROE *(to the Priestess)*:
   Use thy dread office, name, and dignity.
HIGH PRIESTESS: Didst thou not hear his anger?
PENTHESILEA:                                        Him and all
   His thunders down upon my head I call!
FIRST OFFICER *(in agitation)*: Princesses all!—
SECOND OFFICER: It may not be!
THIRD OFFICER:                   Impossible!
PENTHESILEA *(in wild ecstasy)*:
   To me, Ananké! Keeper of the hounds!
FIRST OFFICER: We are dispersed, are weary!
SECOND OFFICER:                              Our ranks are
                                            [thinned!
PENTHESILEA: Thou, Thyrroe—the elephants!
PROTHOE:                                   My Queen!
   With dogs and elephants it is thy will—?
PENTHESILEA: And you, scythed chariots of glinting steel,
   You that endow war's harvest festival,
   Come, ghastly row on row of reapers, come!
   And you that thresh the crop of human corn,
   Trampling to nothingness both stalk and grain,
   Thronged squadrons, range your ranks about me now!
   Thou beauteous horror of war, hear me who call!
   Grim-visaged, fell destroyer, come! Oh, come!
*(She seizes the great bow of the Amazons from the hand of an attendant.
Enter Amazons with hunting dogs on leashes.*
               *Later elephants, flaming torches, scythed chariots, etc.)*
PROTHOE: Oh, my illustrious Queen! Hear me! Hear me!
PENTHESILEA *(turning to the dogs)*:
   Up, Tigris, up! I need thee. Up, Leäne!
   Up thou, Melampus, shaggy-maned and savage!
   Up, Aclé, bane of the mountain fox! Up, Sphinx!
   Alektor too, that runs the doe to ground.
   Up! Oxus, many a boar has felt thy fangs,
   And thou whom the lion daunts not, Hyrcaon!
                    *(Loud thunder.)*
PROTHOE: She is beside herself!

FIRST OFFICER:                                   Nay! She is mad!
  *(Penthesilea kneels with every sign of madness while the dogs
  set up a fearful howling.)*
PENTHESILEA: Thee, Ares, I invoke, thou terrible one!
  Thee, awful founder of our house, I call!
  Oh! Swiftly send me down thy brazen car
  In which the walls of cities and the gates
  Thou crushest, all-destroyer, and the ranks
  Of men, in blocked phalanx, dost trample down.
  Oh! Swiftly send me down thy brazen car
  That I may set my foot within its shell,
  Seize up the reins and, sweeping o'er the fields,
  Fall like a thunder-bolt from clouds of wrath
  Upon the head of yonder impious Greek!
                              *(She rises.)*
FIRST OFFICER: Princesses!
SECOND OFFICER:                    Up! Prevent her! She is mad!
PROTHOE: Hear me, great Queen, I beg!
PENTHESILEA *(drawing the bow)*: Ah! Here is sport!
  Now I can see if my shaft still flies true.
                    *(She aims at Prothoe.)*
PROTHOE *(dropping to the ground)*: Ye gods!
A PRIESTESS *(quickly moving behind Penthesilea)*:
                                    Achilles calls!
A SECOND *(doing the same)*: The son of Peleus!
A THIRD: Here, here behind thee!
PENTHESILEA *(turning)*:            Where?
FIRST PRIESTESS:                          Was it not he?
PENTHESILEA: No, no! The Furies are not yet assembled.
  Follow me, Ananké! Follow me, my friends!
      *(Exit with the bulk of the army amid violent claps of
      thunder.)*
MEROE *(raising Prothoe)*: O fearful fate!
ASTERIA:                              Go after her! Prevent
                                                        [her!
HIGH PRIESTESS *(deathly pale)*:
  Eternal gods! What doom hangs over us?
                    *(Exeunt omnes.)*

# Scene 21

*Enter Achilles and Diomede. Later Odysseus and finally the herald.*

ACHILLES: Listen, Diomede! Be a good comrade now,
 Don't say a word to that old Puritan,
 Sour-faced Odysseus, of what I'm going to tell you;
 I hate it worse than plague—it makes me sick—
 When he puts on that smug, censorious face.

DIOMEDE: Did you in truth send her the herald, Achilles?
 Did you in truth?

ACHILLES: Now listen, friend, one word:
 —But you keep quiet, do you understand?
 No comment! Not a word!—This wondrous woman,
 Half Fury, half goddess, she loves me; I—
 What care I for the Grecian women? I swear,
 By Hades! By the Styx!—I love her too!

DIOMEDE: What?

ACHILLES: Yes. But still a whim, to her most holy,
 Commands that I fall vanquished by her sword.
 That must come first; then love's work can begin.
 So then I sent her—

DIOMEDE: Madman!

ACHILLES: He'll not listen!
 What he has never seen, in all the world,
 In all his life, with those blue eyes of his,
 That he'll not grasp—he cannot—even in thought.

DIOMEDE: Then you—? You mean—? You will—?

ACHILLES *(after a pause):* What will I
                                        [do?

 What is this monstrous thing that I will do?

DIOMEDE: You mean, you've challenged her to mortal combat,
 Simply that she—?

ACHILLES: Now by cloud-shaking Zeus!
 She will not harm me, I tell you! Sooner far
 Would her mailed arm mangle her own fair bosom
 And cry: "Triumph!" when her heart's blood spurts forth,

Than it would rage against me! A month, no more,
I will do service to her hot desires,
A month, or maybe two, not longer: surely
In that time all your old, sea-chafèd isthmus
Will not crumble and melt away! Thereafter,
As from her own red lips I know, I am free—
Free as the roe upon the heath. If she
Will follow me then, it were bliss pure and boundless,
If I could set her on my fathers' throne.

*(Enter Odysseus.)*

DIOMEDE: Odysseus! Here a moment!

ODYSSEUS:                            How now, Achilles?
  You have challenged the Queen into the field.
  Will you, all wearied as the companies are,
  Stake all once more upon the chance of war?

DIOMEDE: There'll be no chance of war, no fighting, friend;
  He will surrender himself her prisoner.

ODYSSEUS: What?

ACHILLES ( *flushing violently*):
                            Take your face away, for God's sake, man!

ODYSSEUS: He will—?

DIOMEDE:              Just so. Hack pieces off her helmet
  Like a gladiator, look ghastly and rage,
  Rattle upon his shield until sparks fly—
  Then mutely lay him, her devoted slave,
  Down in the dust before her little feet.

ODYSSEUS: Is this man raving mad, great son of Peleus?
  Did you not hear what he—?

ACHILLES *(controlling himself)*: I pray you, friend,
  Let it not curl, that upper lip—not curl!
  It makes me mad to see it, by the gods,
  A twitching madness even to my fist.

ODYSSEUS *(enraged)*:
  Now by Cocytus' flaming waves! I will
  Be told whether my ears hear right or no!
  You will now, son of Tydeus, be so good
  And swear upon your oath that what I ask
  Is so; I must and shall have certainty!
  He will surrender himself her prisoner?

DIOMEDE: Even so!

ODYSSEUS:           Will follow her to Themiscyra?

DIOMEDE: That too.

ODYSSEUS:           And all this war for Helen's sake
  Before Troy citadel, he will take a toy
  In his infatuation cast away
  Because some brighter plaything steals his fancy?

DIOMEDE: By Jupiter, 'tis so!

ODYSSEUS *(folding his arms):* I may not credit it.

ACHILLES: He speaks of the citadel of Troy.

ODYSSEUS:                               What?

ACHILLES:                                       What?

ODYSSEUS: Did you not say something?

ACHILLES:                       I?

ODYSSEUS:                           You!

ACHILLES:                                   I said:
  He speaks of the citadel of Troy.

ODYSSEUS:                       Why, yes!
  Rage in my heart, I asked if it were true
  That all this war for Helen's sake before
  Troy town were sheer forgot like a dream at dawn.

ACHILLES *(stepping up to him):*
  Son of Laertes! If the towers of Ilium
  Should sink from sight—you follow?—so that a lake,
  A blue lake, lay where once those towers had been,
  And hoary fisherfolk by the moon's pale light
  Made fast their skiffs to those drowned weathercocks;
  If a huge pike should rule in Priam's palace,
  Or in fair Helen's bed a pair of otters
  Or stinking water rats should breed and litter
  It were to me no less than it is now.

ODYSSEUS: By the Styx, friend Diomede! It is no jest!

ACHILLES: By the Styx! By the marsh of Lerna! Ay, by Hades!
  By all that's on the earth or under it
  Or in some third abode: it is no jest!
  It is my will to see Diana's temple.

ODYSSEUS: *(aside to Diomede):*
  See that he does not leave this spot, my friend—
  If you will be so good.

DIOMEDE:                      If I—! Why, surely!
  Yourself be but so good and lend me your arms.
                 *(Enter the herald.)*
ACHILLES: Ah! Will she fight? What news, friend? Will she fight?
HERALD: Ay, she will fight; already she comes on.
  But 'tis with dogs and elephants she comes
  And a whole savage host on horseback: what
  Their part in this single combat is yet dark.
ACHILLES: This is her tribute paid to custom. Come!
  Oh, she is full of tricks, by all the gods!
  —You say, with dogs?
HERALD:              Yes.
ACHILLES:                      And with elephants?
HERALD: Right terrible to see, great son of Peleus!
  Were it her intent to fall on Agamemnon
  In the walled camp before Troy, she could not come
  In darker nor more awful panoply.
ACHILLES *(to himself)*:
  Sure they will feed from your hand. Come, follow me!
  Oh! They are tame as she.
                 *(Exit with his attendants.)*
DIOMEDE:                   Nay! He is mad!
ODYSSEUS: Come, we must seize and bind him! Up, you Greeks!
DIOMEDE: Here come the Amazons! We must away!
                 *(Exeunt omnes.)*

# Scene 22

*Enter the High Priestess, pale and anxious, and several other Priestesses and Amazons.*
HIGH PRIESTESS: Bring binding cords, you women!
FIRST PRIESTESS:                          What has
                                         [happened?
HIGH PRIESTESS: Drag her to the ground! Overpower her!
                                         [Bind her fast!
AN AMAZON: Do you mean the Queen?
HIGH PRIESTESS:                   That lewd she-dog I
                                         [mean!
  No more can she be held by human hands.

THE AMAZONS: Most reverend mother, you seem all distraught.
HIGH PRIESTESS: Three of her maids she trampled underfoot
 Whom we had sent to halt her; Meroe,
 For that she threw herself upon her knees
 Imploring her with every sweet endearment,
 She set the dogs on her and chased her away.
 And me—as I approached her still far off,
 Stooping straightway, darting hate-laden glances
 Upon me, she from the ground with both hands tore
 A mighty stone—that moment was my last
 But I withdrew among the common folk.
FIRST PRIESTESS: 'Tis fearful!
SECOND PRIESTESS:    Horrible it is to hear!
HIGH PRIESTESS: And now with maniac tread among her hounds
 With foam-flecked lip she goes and calls them sisters,
 Who howl and howl; most like a Maenad she,
 Dancing across the fields, her bow in hand,
 She urges on the pack that pants for blood
 Around her, bidding them seize the fairest prey
 That ever, so she tells them, ranged the earth.
AMAZONS: Gods of the dark! What fearful punishment!
HIGH PRIESTESS: Therefore with cords, you daughters of Ares,
               [quickly
 There where the ways meet, there lay snares for her,
 Covered with leaves, before her hurrying feet,
 And drag her down; when she is tripped and stumbles,
 Hold her and bind her like a rabid dog.
 When she is bound, we then shall bear her home
 And see if some way she may yet be saved.
THE AMAZON HOST (*off*):
 Triumph! Triumph! Triumph! Achilles falls!
 Captive the hero! Soon victorious
 The Queen shall wreathe his yellow head with roses!
       (*Pause.*)
HIGH PRIESTESS (*her voice half stifled with joy*):
 Did I hear aright?
PRIESTESSES AND AMAZONS: Oh! all the gods be praised!
HIGH PRIESTESS: Was this in truth the exultant shout of joy?
FIRST PRIESTESS: The cry of victory, most holy dame.
 A sound more blessèd never did I hear.

HIGH PRIESTESS: You maidens, who will bring me news?
SECOND PRIESTESS:                                    Terpé!
  Quick! Tell us what you see from yonder hill?
AN AMAZON (*who has mounted the hill, horror-struck*):
  You grim and ghastly gods of nether hell!
  Be witness to my words—Oh, fearful spectacle!
HIGH PRIESTESS: How now! How now! Has she beheld Medusa?
PRIESTESS: What do you see? Speak! Speak!
AMAZON:                                    Penthesilea—
  Groveling she couches by her grizzly hounds,
  She whom a woman's womb did bear, and rends—
  His limbs she rends and mangles into shreds!
HIGH PRIESTESS: Oh horror! Horror!
ALL:                                    Deed unspeakable!
AMAZON: See where it comes, bleached o'er with death's own hue,
  The word that solves for us the gruesome riddle.
          (*She descends from the hill.*)


# Scene 23

*Enter Meroe.*
MEROE: O you, Diana's holy priestesses,
  And you, Ares' chaste daughters, hear me speak:
  I am the Afric Gorgon and to stone—
  Behold!—Your bodies' warmth I freeze at once.
HIGH PRIESTESS: Oh, ghastly sight! Say what befell.
MEROE:                                    You know,
  She moved to meet that youth whom she so loves,
  —She who from this time forth no name can name—
  In the confusion of her youthful senses
  Arming with all the horrid terrors of war
  Her hot desire to seize and to possess him.
  Ringed round with howling hounds and elephants
  She strode before, the great bow in her hand:
  War that rages among the citizens,
  Fell form that drips with brothers' blood, when he
  Stalks through the land with giant strides of woe,

Swinging the torch of death o'er blossoming cities,
He looks not half so terrible as she.
Achilles, so 'tis said in all the host,
Had challenged her only that he—poor fool!—
Of his free will might yield to her in combat:
For he too—oh, all-powerful are the gods!—
He loved her too, stirred strangely by her youth,
And wished to follow her to Dian's temple:
He now approaches, dreaming of sweet delights,
And comes alone, his friends left far behind.
But now, as she with such heaped horror bears
Rumbling upon him, who half playfully
Is armed but with a spear and thinks no danger,
Sudden he stops, turning his slender neck,
Listens, then flees in horror, stops, then flees,
Like a young roe that in the rocky gorge
Hears from afar the shag-maned lion's roar.
He calls, "Odysseus!" but fear bates his voice;
Casts anxious eyes behind and calls, "Diomede!"
And still has hope to flee back to his friends
And stands, seeing his road already cut,
And throws his hands aloft and stoops and creeps
Into a pine tree's shelter—ah, poor wretch!—
That hangs heavy, drooping its branches down.
The Queen, meanwhile, unfaltering nears apace
—The dogs hard on her heels—and spies afar
With hunter's glance scanning the woods and hills;
And just as he, parting the close-grown boughs,
Is fain to sink a suppliant at her feet,
"His antlers still betray the stag!" she cries
And straight, with strength of madness born, she draws
The mighty bow till the ends touch and kiss
And raises up the bow and aims and shoots,
Driving the arrow through his throat. He falls;
The folk gives forth a barbarous shout of triumph.
But he still lives, most miserable of men;
The jutting shaft deep buried in his throat,
He staggers gasping to his feet, stumbles
Full length, is up again and seeks to flee.

But quick "On him!" she calls, "Tigris! On him, Leäne!
Dirké! Melampus! Sphinx! On him! Hyrcaon!"
And flings herself—herself with the whole pack!—
Upon him and by his helmet's plume, a bitch
In company of dogs—one grips his breast,
Another's jaws close on his neck—drags him
To earth, that far around the ground re-echoes.
He, writhing in a pool of his own gore,
Touches her delicate cheek and calls to her:
"Penthesilea! What dost thou? My belovèd!
Is this the Feast of Roses thou didst promise?"
But she—the lioness had been moved to hear,
Who ravening stalks over the barren snow,
And hideous howls, seeking some hapless prey—
She strikes, first tearing his armor from his limbs,
Strikes deep her teeth into his snowy breast,
She and the dogs in ghastly rivalry,
Oxus and Sphinx rending his right flank,
And with them she his left; as I appeared,
Black blood was dripping from her mouth and hands.
                    *(Pause of horror.)*
If ye have heard my words, O women, speak
And give some sign that ye still live and breathe.
                    *(Pause.)*
FIRST PRIESTESS *(weeping on the breast of the second):*
   Oh, such a virgin, Hermia! So modest!
   So deft in all the arts of women's hands!
   So lovely when she danced or when she sang!
   So full of wisdom, dignity, and grace!
HIGH PRIESTESS: Her never did Otrere bear! The Gorgon
   There in the palace whelped such monstrous brood!
FIRST PRIESTESS *(continuing):*
   The nightingale that dwells around Diana's
   High temple might have been her gentle mother.
   Rocked in the topmost branches she would sit,
   Fluting and warbling, warbling and fluting still
   The breathless long night through, that afar the wand'rer
   Hearkened and in his heart strange longing stirred.
   The mottled worm that sported in the dust

Before her delicate feet, she would not crush;
She would recall the shaft ere it could pierce
The savage wild boar's shoulder, and his eye,
Glazing in death, could drag her to her knees
Before him, melted quite in soft remorse.

*(Pause.)*

MEROE: And now she stands there mute, hedged round with
[horror,

Beside his corpse. The dogs snuff at her hands
While she stares stony out, her face an empty page
—The bow still laid triumphant on her shoulder—
Out into the infinite in awful silence.
We with our hair on end fearfully ask her:
What she has done? No answer. Does she know us?
No word. Will she go with us? Silent still.
I could endure no more and fled to you.


# Scene 24

*Enter Penthesilea, the body of Achilles covered with a red pall,
Prothoe and others.*

FIRST AMAZON: Look, look, my friends! See where she comes
[apace

Crowned all with nettles—oh, unhappy sight!—
That she has worked into the wreath of thorns.
This her victorious laurel! Now she walks
Behind his body, gaily, with bow on shoulder,
As though her mortal foe lay slaughtered there.

SECOND PRIESTESS: Her hands! Look at her hands—!

FIRST PRIESTESS:                                    Oh! Turn
[away!

PROTHOE *(sinking on the High Priestess' breast):*
My mother!—Oh!

HIGH PRIESTESS *(in horror):* Diana be my witness!
Not mine the blame for this most cruel deed!

FIRST AMAZON: Straight before the High Priestess now she
[stands.

SECOND AMAZON: She makes a sign.
HIGH PRIESTESS:                    Avaunt, thou ghastly
                                   [creature!
   Thou denizen of hell! Avaunt, I say!
   Take this my veil, take it and cover her!
   *(She tears off her own veil and throws it in Penthesilea's face.)*
FIRST AMAZON: A walking corpse, no more! Still quite
                                   [unmoved—
SECOND AMAZON: Still she makes signs—
THIRD AMAZON:                    She points and points
                                   [again—
FIRST AMAZON: Points always down, to the High Priestess' feet.
SECOND AMAZON: Look, look!
HIGH PRIESTESS:          What do you want of me?
                                   [Begone!
   Go to the ravens, shade! Go, fade away!
   That look will shrivel up my whole heart's peace.
FIRST AMAZON: Ah! Now she is understood—
SECOND AMAZON:                    Now she is calm.
FIRST AMAZON: Achilles—that was it!—he must be placed
   Before the feet of great Diana's priestess.
THIRD AMAZON: But why before the priestess' feet? Why there?
FOURTH AMAZON: What can her meaning be?
HIGH PRIESTESS:                    What *means* this,
                                   [pray?
   Why should the *body* stand before me here?
   Let mountains cover it, trackless, snow-crowned,
   Ay, and the memory of thy deed as well!
   Did I, thou—woman no more, how should I name thee?—
   Did I with inhuman tongue demand this murder?
   If a gentle rebuke from the kind mouth of love
   Can cause such monstrous deeds, then must we hope
   The Furies for their part will teach us kindliness!
FIRST AMAZON: Relentless still she gazes at the Priestess.
SECOND AMAZON: Straight in her face—
THIRD AMAZON:                    Unwavering, unwinking,
   As though she wished to look her through and through.
HIGH PRIESTESS: Come, Prothoe, I beg you, come, dear girl.
   I cannot bear the sight; lead her away.

PROTHOE *(weeping):* Oh, misery!

HIGH PRIESTESS: Be strong!

PROTHOE: The deed she did
  Is far too horrible; leave me alone.

HIGH PRIESTESS: Command thyself—And yet her mother was fair.
  Come, offer her assistance; lead her off.

PROTHOE: I will not ever look on her again!

SECOND AMAZON: That slim arrow—look how she ponders it—

FIRST AMAZON: Turns it this way and that—

THIRD AMAZON: Intently scans it!

FIRST PRIESTESS: It seems that is the shaft with which she felled
  him?

FIRST AMAZON: Ay, so it is.

SECOND AMAZON: Now she cleans it of blood,
  Busily wiping off each tiniest stain.

THIRD AMAZON: What might her thoughts be now?

SECOND AMAZON: And now the
  [feathers

  —She dries them, smooths them, gently teases them
  With delicate grace—now each lies properly.
  Oh, what a sight!

THIRD AMAZON: Tell us, is that her custom?

FIRST AMAZON: Does she always do so?

FIRST PRIESTESS: Arrows and bow
  She keeps with her own hand in proper order.

SECOND PRIESTESS: The bow was holy to her, no doubt of that.

SECOND AMAZON: And now she takes the quiver from her
  [shoulder

  And sets the arrow back where it belongs.

THIRD AMAZON: Now she is finished—

SECOND AMAZON: Now the job is done—

FIRST PRIESTESS: And now once more she looks into the world.

SEVERAL WOMEN: Oh, wretched, wretched sight! Oh, dreary waste,
  Barren as desert sands where no grass grows!
  Gay gardens which the lava flow has wasted,
  Seethed in the earth's dark womb and belched afar
  O'er all the blossoming paradise of her heart—
  More pleasant these to look on than her face.

  *(Penthesilea shudders violently and lets the bow fall.)*

HIGH PRIESTESS: What? What? Oh, dreadful!
PROTHOE *(startled):* Now what will she
[do?
FIRST AMAZON: Down to the earth she lets the great bow plunge.
SECOND AMAZON: See how it falters—
FOURTH AMAZON: Sways and clanging falls—
SECOND AMAZON: Writhes once more on the ground—
THIRD AMAZON: And dies
[at last,
As it was born at first to Tanais.
*(Pause.)*
HIGH PRIESTESS *(turning suddenly to her):*
Great Queen and lady! Oh, forgive, I pray!
Diana is full well content with thee.
I see thou hast atoned; her wrath is turned.
The mighty founder of our women's realm,
Tanais' self, I cannot well deny,
She did not wield the bow more worthily.
FIRST AMAZON: She is silent—
SECOND AMAZON: Her eyes are wet—
THIRD AMAZON: She lifts her
[hand,
All bloody still. What will she do?—Oh, see!
SECOND AMAZON: Heartrending sight, wounding more keen than
knives!
FIRST AMAZON: She wipes away a tear.
HIGH PRIESTESS *(sinking on Prothoe's breast):* O Artemis!
Oh, what a tear!
FIRST PRIESTESS: Ay, such a tear, most reverend,
As creeps into the bosoms of men and there
Wildly jangles the fire-bells of the heart
And cries "Havoc!" that all the teeming crowd,
Fickle and light to move, comes welling forth
Out of our eyes and, gathering then in lakes,
Weeps for the pitiless ruin of a soul.
HIGH PRIESTESS *(bitterly):*
Well, then—If Prothoe will not help the Queen,
She must soon perish here in her distress.
*(Prothoe, after signs of a violent inner struggle, goes up to her.)*

PROTHOE (*in a voice still broken by sobs*):
    Will you not rest awhile, my dearest Queen?
    Will you not lean against my faithful breast?
    This dreadful day has seen you oft in battle
    And brought you sufferings manifold; from these
    Come, seek repose upon my faithful breast!
        (*Penthesilea looks around as though seeking a seat.*)
    Quick! Bring a seat! You see it is her wish.
        (*The Amazons roll along a rock for her. Penthesilea sits*
        *down supported by Prothoe. Prothoe sits too.*)
    Surely you know me, sister-heart?
        (*Penthesilea looks at her; her face brightens a little.*)
                                  I am
    Prothoe, who loves you dearly.
               (*Penthesilea gently strokes her cheek.*)
                          Oh, dear heart!
    Before whom my heart falls on its knees to worship,
    How thou dost move me!
                (*kisses the Queen's hand*)
                       Sure, thou art very weary?
    No need to guess what thou hast been at. Ah, well!
    Vict'ry cannot always be cleanly won.
    The signs of his trade ever become the master.
    But now—would it not be well to clean thyself,
    Thy face and hands? Shall I get water for thee?
    My dearest Queen!
             (*Penthesilea looks down at herself and nods.*)
                 Good, then. It is her will.
        (*She signs to the Amazons, who go to fetch water.*)
    And gently thou shalt lie on cool, soft rugs
    And win repose from thy too hard day-labor.
FIRST PRIESTESS: Be careful! If you sprinkle her with water,
    She will remember.
HIGH PRIESTESS:      Surely. 'Tis my hope.
PROTHOE: Thy hope, most holy one? For me, I fear it.
HIGH PRIESTESS (*seeming to consider two courses*):
    But why? Wherefore? That way is too much danger,
    Unless indeed the body of Achilles—
        (*Penthesilea flashes a terrible glance at the High Priestess.*)

PROTHOE: Oh, silence!

HIGH PRIESTESS:  Nothing, my Queen! Nothing, nothing!
All shall remain as thou wilt—nothing be changed.

PROTHOE: Take off your laurel-crown, so full of thorns;
We all do know you were victorious.
Undo this button here—now you can breathe.
And look!—A wound, a deep gash! Ah, poor dear!
You have not spared yourself, indeed you have not,
And so 'tis just that you should triumph now.
O Artemis!

*(Two Amazons bring a great shallow marble basin, filled with water.)*

Here! Set the basin down.
Now, shall I sprinkle water on your head?
You'll not be startled? Why, what are you doing?

*(Penthesilea drops from her seat onto her knees before the basin and drenches her head with water.)*

Why, look at that! You are right strong again!
That makes you feel better?

PENTHESILEA *(looking around her):* Oh, Prothoe!
*(again drenches herself with water)*

MEROE *(joyfully):* She speaks!

HIGH PRIESTESS:  Now all the gods be praised!

PROTHOE:  Good, good!

MEROE: So she is given back to us!

PROTHOE:  Wonderful!
Right under water with your head, dear! There!
There! And again! Again! Like a young swan!

MEROE: The darling!

FIRST PRIESTESS:  Look how she hangs her pretty head!

MEROE: And how she lets the water trickle down.

PROTHOE: Now—are you done?

PENTHESILEA:  Wonderful! Wonderful!

PROTHOE: Then we must put you back onto your seat.
Quick, let me have your veils, you priestesses,
That I may dry her dripping locks with them.
Here, Phania, yours! And Terpé's. Help me, sisters!
We'll cover all her head and neck with them.
That's right! And now we set you back on your seat.

*(She covers the Queen, lifts her on to the seat, and draws*
*her close to her breast.)*

PENTHESILEA: I feel—Oh!—

PROTHOE:              Better, dear?

PENTHESILEA *(lisping):*          Blissfully well!

PROTHOE: My sister-heart! Sweet darling! Dearest mine!

PENTHESILEA: Oh, tell me! Am I in Elysium?
  Art thou one of those ever-youthful nymphs,
  That seemly wait upon our heavenly Queen,
  When she steps down to the crystalline pool
  While the hushed oak-leaves whispering hold their breath?
  Dost thou but counterfeit, to give me joy,
  My Prothoe's loved features? Tell! Oh, tell!

PROTHOE: No, dearest Queen! No, no! It is not so.
  I am indeed thy Prothoe, who hold
  Thee here embraced, and what thy eyes behold,
  It is the world, our transient, brittle world,
  Oh which the gods look down but from afar.

PENTHESILEA: Good, good. That too is good. It is no matter.

PROTHOE: What, dearest lady?

PENTHESILEA:            I am well pleased, I say.

PROTHOE: My love, explain thyself. We cannot guess—

PENTHESILEA: I am glad that I still am. Now let me be.
               *(Pause.)*

MEROE: Strange, strange!

HIGH PRIESTESS:      A change most unaccountable!

MEROE: If it were possible to make her tell—

PROTHOE: What was it stirred in thee this strange belief
  That thou didst walk already with the shades?

PENTHESILEA *(after a pause, in a sort of ecstasy):*
  I am so happy, sister! More than happy!
  Quite ripe for death, Goddess, I feel myself.
  'Tis true, I do not know all that befell,
  And yet I could believe and, trusting, die,
  That I had overcome and won Achilles.

PROTHOE *(aside to the High Priestess):*
  Quick now, take off the body!

PENTHESILEA *(sitting up eagerly):* Prothoe!
  Whom do you speak with?

PROTHOE *(as the bearers still hesitate):* Quickly! Go!

PENTHESILEA: Diana!
  Great goddess! Is it true?

PROTHOE: What true, my dear one?
  Stand close together! So!
  *(She signs to the Priestesses to hide the body which is being picked up.)*

PENTHESILEA *(her hands before her face, joyfully):*
  O all ye gods!
  Oh, give me courage now to look around!

PROTHOE: Why, Queen! What do you think? What can you hope?

PENTHESILEA *(looking around)* Dearest! You play with me.

PROTHOE: No, no, by Zeus!
  I do not play with thee!

PENTHESILEA *(with rising impatience):* Most holy dames!
  Do me the pleasure! Stand apart!

HIGH PRIESTESS *(pressing close together with the other women):*
  My Queen!

PENTHESILEA *(rising):* Diana! Wherefore should I not? Diana!
  Once—once already he stood close behind me.

MEROE: Oh, look! How horror creeps upon her!

PENTHESILEA *(to the Amazons, who are carrying the body):*
  Hold!
  What is it you carry? I must know it! Stop!
  *(She thrusts the women aside and pushes her way to the body.)*

PROTHOE: Oh, Queen! My Queen! No further! Look no further!

PENTHESILEA: Is it he, my maidens? He?

ONE BEARER *(as the body is set down):* Who is that he?

PENTHESILEA: 'Tis not impossible; I see that now.
  A swallow's wing now—that I might have crippled
  And it might still be healed and fly again;
  The stag I lure into my park with arrows.
  But greased and treacherous is the marksman's art;
  Our master shot into the heart of happiness
  Envious and tricky gods turn all awry.
  What? Was my blow too deadly? Is it he?

PROTHOE: Oh, by the awful powers that rule Olympus,
  Ask not—!

PENTHESILEA: Stand back, I say! E'en though his wound

Gape at me like the frantic jaws of hell:
Yet I will see him!

*(draws back the pall)*

Oh, monstrous women! Who has done this thing?

PROTHOE: Can *you* ask that?

PENTHESILEA:                    O Artemis! Holy Queen!
Now is the end come for thy child!

HIGH PRIESTESS: She falls to the ground!

PROTHOE:                              Ye gods in heaven
                                          [above!

Why didst not let her be, as I counseled?
Much better had it been for thee, poor soul!
To wander still in the mind's dim eclipse,
Forever and forever, than to see
Once more the dreadful light of this sad day.
Hear me, beloved sister!

HIGH PRIESTESS:          Hear, my Queen!

MEROE: We all—all thy people—do share thy pain.

HIGH PRIESTESS: Raise thyself up!

PENTHESILEA: *(half rising):*        Ah, all these bleeding roses!
Ah, this red wreath of gashes round his head
Whose buds, scattering scent—fresh scent of graves—
Go down to make a festival for worms!

PROTHOE: *(tenderly):* And yet it was her love that wreathed him
                                          [thus.

MEROE: Ay, all too firm—!

PROTHOE:                With thorns among the roses,
So eager was she it should be forever!

HIGH PRIESTESS: Get thee away!

PENTHESILEA:                   But one thing I must know:
Who was my rival in such godless love?
I do not ask who struck him down while yet
He lived; I swear by our eternal gods
He shall go from me free—no bird more free.
But who thus slew the slain—that would I know;
On that thou must give answer, Prothoe.

PROTHOE: What, gracious lady?

PENTHESILEA:                   Understand me well!
I will not know who thus from out his breast

Stole the sweet spark of life; I will not know it
—Because I will not; so my whimsy jumps.
He is forgiven; free he is to flee.
But who to do this robbery could shun
Thus cruelly the open door and must
Through every snow-white alabaster wall
Break in upon this temple; who could thus
Horribly mar this youth, the high gods' image,
That life no more disputes with foul corruption
Which shall be lord; who thus hath done to him
That Pity hath no tears for him, and Love
—Love the immortal, now a harlot grown—
Faithless must turn away from him in death:
Whoe'er he be, my vengeance smites him. Speak!

PROTHOE *(to High Priestess)*:
    What answer can we give to such delusion?

PENTHESILEA: What? Must I wait to hear?

MEROE:                            O most dread Queen!
    If it can bring thee ease in thy distress,
    Thy vengeance fall on which of us thou wilt;
    Here we all stand, each glad to be thy victim.

PENTHESILEA: Mark me! They'll say that it was I who did it!

HIGH PRIESTESS *(timidly)*:
    Who else, unhappy girl, but only—

PENTHESILEA:                     Thou
    Black queen of hell in borrowed robes of light!
    To my face thou darest—?

HIGH PRIESTESS:           Artemis be my witness!
    And all this company that here surrounds thee
    —They must confirm my words! It was thy arrow
    That smote him first—ah, had it been but that!
    But thou, in the wild turmoil of thy rage,
    Didst throw thyself, as he sank to the ground,
    With all thy dogs upon him and didst sink—
    Oh, my faint lip rebels!—It will not utter
    What thou hast done. Ask not! Come, we must go!

PENTHESILEA: My Prothoe must say if this is true.

PROTHOE: My Queen and lady! Do not ask me that!

PENTHESILEA: What? I? I did—? With all my dogs about me?

With these my tiny hands they say I could—?
And this too gentle mouth, so soft for love—?
Made for quite other service than to tear—!
These two, for sport helping each other on,
Mouth now and hand, now hand, now mouth again—?
PROTHOE: O Queen! No more!
HIGH PRIESTESS:                    I cry woe! Woe upon thee!
PENTHESILEA: Nay, look! Of that you never can persuade me.
  Not though 'twere graved in flame upon the night,
  Not though the vast voice of the storm should cry it,
  Even so to both I still would cry: Ye lie!
MEROE: Let this faith stand, unshakable as the hills;
  Not we who will do aught to make it totter.
PENTHESILEA: How came it he would not defend his life?
HIGH PRIESTESS: He loved thee still, O hapless girl! He came
  To give himself to thee, thy prisoner.
  That his intent when he did challenge thee!
  He came to thee, dreaming sweet dreams of peace,
  Eager to follow thee to Dian's temple.
  But thou—
PENTHESILEA: Was it so?
HIGH PRIESTESS:          Didst smite him,
PENTHESILEA:                              And then tore him?
PROTHOE: Oh, do not ask me, Queen!
PENTHESILEA:                         Or was it not so?
MEROE: She is fearful!
PENTHESILEA:          I did kiss him dead?
FIRST PRIESTESS:                         O Heavens!
PENTHESILEA: Surely I kissed him? Or did I tear him? Speak!
HIGH PRIESTESS: Woe! Woe upon thee! Hide thyself!
  Eternal darkness cover thee from sight!
PENTHESILEA: So—it was a mistake. Kissing—biting—
  Where is the difference? When we truly love
  It's easy to do one when we mean the other.
MEROE: Help her, ye gods!
PROTHOE (*taking her arm*): Away now! Come!
PENTHESILEA:                              Nay! Leave me!
  (*disengages herself and falls on her knees before the body*)
  Poor man, of all men poorest, you forgive me?

It was a slip—believe me!—the wrong word—
I can't control my too impetuous lips.
But now I tell you clearly what I meant:
This, my belovèd, this—and nothing more.
                    *(She kisses him.)*

HIGH PRIESTESS: Get her away!
MEROE:                                    She must not stay here longer.
PENTHESILEA: How many a girl, her soft arms fast entwined
    About her man's neck, says that she loves him so
    Beyond words she could eat him up for love.
    And then, poor fool, when she would prove her words,
    Sated she is of him—sated almost to loathing.
    Now, my belovèd, that was not my way.
    Why, look: when my soft arms were round thy neck,
    I did it word for word; it was no pretending.
    I was not quite so mad as they would have it.
MEROE: Oh, monstrous and more monstrous! What a word!
HIGH PRIESTESS: Lay hold of her! Bring her away!
PROTHOE:                                              My Queen!
PENTHESILEA *(allowing Prothoe to help her up)*:
    Good, good! Look, I am here.
HIGH PRIESTESS:                    You will go with us?
PENTHESILEA: With you? No!
    Go back to Themiscyra and be happy,
    If you are able—
    My Prothoe above all—
    All of you—
    And—now a word in secret, none must hear:
    Tanais' ashes, scatter them to the winds!
PROTHOE: And thou? What wilt thou do, my sister-heart?
PENTHESILEA: I?
PROTHOE:        Thou!
PENTHESILEA:            Look, I will tell you, Prothoe:
    I do renounce the law that binds us women
    And I will follow him, this youth.
PROTHOE: My Queen, what do you mean?
HIGH PRIESTESS:                              Unhappy girl!
PROTHOE: You will—?
HIGH PRIESTESS:        You mean—?

PENTHESILEA:                     What? Why, of course!

MEROE:                            O heaven!

PROTHOE: One word then, sister-heart, here in your ear—
     *(Prothoe tries to take her dagger from her.)*

PENTHESILEA: What then? What do you seek there in my belt?
  Oh, that! Wait, wait! I had not guessed your thought—
  Here is the dagger.
     *(takes the dagger from her belt and gives it to Prothoe)*
                Will you have the arrows?
     *(takes the quiver from her shoulder)*
  The whole quiver—look, how I pour it out.
     *(pours all the arrows on the ground)*
  'Tis true, in one way it would be very sweet—
     *(picks up one or two of them)*
  For this one—was it not? Or was it this one?
  Yes, this one! Right! But never mind! Take them!
  Take all these shafts and keep them.
     *(She gathers up the whole bundle and gives it to Prothoe.)*

PROTHOE:                    Give me them.

PENTHESILEA: For now I will step down into my breast
  As into a mine and there will dig a lump
  Of cold ore, an emotion that will kill.
  This ore I temper in the fires of woe
  To hardest steel; then steep it through and through
  In the hot, biting venom of remorse;
  Carry it then to Hope's eternal anvil
  And sharpen it and point it to a dagger;
  Now to this dagger do I give my breast:
  So! So! So! So! Once more! Now, it is good.
     *(She falls and dies.)*

PROTHOE *(lifting the Queen)*: She's dead!

MEROE:                   Ay, she has followed
                                [him.

PROTHOE:                    'Tis well!
  For here there was no place for her abiding.
     *(She lays her back on the ground.)*

HIGH PRIESTESS: A brittle thing, ye gods, is humankind!
  She that lies broken here, a few hours since
  Swept proudly on her course among the peaks.

PROTHOE: Her blooming was too proud and glorious!
   Vainly the gale will shake the withered oak,
   But with a crash he flings the living down,
   Grasping with ruffian hands her copious locks.
             (*Curtain.*)

                    *Translated by Humphry Trevelyan*

# PRINCE FREDERICK OF HOMBURG

*A Play*

## CHARACTERS

FREDERICK WILLIAM, *Elector of Brandenburg*

ELECTOR'S WIFE

PRINCESS NATALIE OF ORANIEN, *his niece, and chief of a regiment of dragoons*

FIELD-MARSHAL DÖRFLING

PRINCE FREDERICK ARTHUR OF HOMBURG, *General of the Cavalry*

COLONEL KOTTWITZ, *of the regiment of the Princess of Oranien*

HENNINGS
COUNT TRUCHSS } *Infantry Colonels*

COUNT HOHENZOLLERN, *of the Elector's retinue*

CAPTAIN GOLZ
COUNT GEORGE OF SPARREN
STRANZ } *Cavalry Captains*
SIEGFRIED MÖRNER
COUNT REUSS
A SERGEANT

OFFICERS, CORPORALS *and* CAVALRYMEN. COURTIERS. LADIES-IN-WAITING. PAGES. HAIDUCKS. SERVANTS. PEOPLE OF EVERY AGE.

# Act I

## SCENE 1

*Fehrbellin. Garden in traditional French style. In the background a castle, from which a ramp leads down into the garden.*

*It is night.*

*Bareheaded and with an open shirt, the Prince of Homburg, half-awake, half-asleep, sits under an oak tree, weaving himself a wreath. The Elector, his wife, Princess Natalie, the Count of Hohenzollern, Captain Golz, and others step secretly forth from the castle and look down from the balustrade of the ramp upon Homburg.*

HOHENZOLLERN: The Prince of Homburg, our courageous cousin,
  Who has led our cavalry the past three days
  And given the elusive Swedes an eager chase,
  Appeared again today, quite out of breath,
  At our commanding post in Fehrbellin:
  Were your orders to him then that he remain
  For food and rest a mere three hours, then quick
  Approach the Hackel Mountains once again,
  To face our enemy Wrangel, who has tried
  To entrench himself along the River Rhyn?
ELECTOR: 'Tis so!
HOHENZOLLERN:  Now, having readied all his squadrons
  For breaking camp, as planned, at ten tonight,
  He sprawls exhausted, panting like a hound,
  To rest his weary limbs upon the straw,
  Before the battle facing us at dawn.
ELECTOR: So I'm told!—Well?

HOHENZOLLERN:                    But as the hour strikes,
 And our horsemen are already in the saddle
 And stamp the ground outside the city gates,
 Who's missing?—Cousin Homburg, their commander!
 With torches he's been sought, with lights and lanterns,
 Only to be found?—
                    *(takes a torch from a page)*
                    Somnambulating!
 On that bench! You would never have believed it!
 Enticed here by the moon, asleep but busy,
 He dreams with the eye of his own posterity,
 Weaving his own splendid wreath of fame.
ELECTOR: What?
HOHENZOLLERN: It's true! Just look there—where he sits!
                    *(lets the torchlight fall upon Homburg.)*
ELECTOR: Deep in sleep? Absurd!
HOHENZOLLERN:                    Yes, fast asleep!
 Call him by his name and down he'll fall.
                    *(Pause.)*
ELECTOR'S WIFE: As sure as I'm alive, the youth is ill.
PRINCESS NATALIE: He needs a doctor . . . !
ELECTOR'S WIFE:                            Yes, one ought to
                                              [help him,
 Not spend the moment making sport of him.
HOHENZOLLERN *(handing back the torch)*:
 Ill he is not, most sympathetic ladies,
 No more than I, by God! Tomorrow the Swede
 Shall feel that when we meet him in the field!
 It's nothing graver, take me at my word,
 Than a wayward habit of his fancy.
ELECTOR: A strange nocturnal fancy, I would say!
 Friends, come with me and let us look more closely.
                    *(They descend from the ramp.)*
COURTIER *(to the pages)*:
 The torches! Back!
HOHENZOLLERN:      No, leave them, let them stay!
 If the grounds were going up in flames
 It would make no more impression on his senses
 Than on that diamond there upon his finger.

*(They surround him, the pages providing light.)*

ELECTOR *(bent over him)*: What leaf is he entwining? Is it willow?

HOHENZOLLERN: The willow? O! Sire! It is the laurel
As he has seen it in the heroes' portraits
Hanging in the armory in Berlin.

ELECTOR: Where found he that in Brandenburger sand?

HOHENZOLLERN: That the gods alone would know.

COURTIER: It could be from the garden there behind us
Where the gardener raises other foreign plants.

ELECTOR: Strange, by Heaven! Yet, I think I know
What inflames the breast of this young fool?!

HOHENZOLLERN: Oh—quite! Tomorrow's slaughter, my
[Commander!

He already sees astronomers, in his fancy,
Winding suns into a victory wreath.

*(The Prince looks at his wreath.)*

COURTIER: Now he's finished!

HOHENZOLLERN: And it's such a pity,
That there's no looking glass nearby!
He'd sidle toward it, vain as any girl,
And try his garland on, this way and that,
As though it were a brand-new flowered hat.

ELECTOR: By God! I've got to see how far he'll go!

*(The Elector takes the wreath out of his hand; Homburg reddens and stares at him. The Elector loops his own necklace around the wreath and gives it to Natalie. Homburg leaps up. The Elector and Natalie, who raises the wreath into the air, step backward. With outstretched arms, Homburg follows her.)*

PRINCE *(whispering)*: Natalie! My tender maid! My bride!

ELECTOR: Hurry! Away!

HOHENZOLLERN: What did he say, the fool?

COURTIER: What were his words?

*(They all ascend the ramp.)*

PRINCE: Frederick! My liege! My
[father!

HOHENZOLLERN: Hell and damnation!

ELECTOR *(stepping backwards)*: Open me that gate!

PRINCE: O my mother!

HOHENZOLLERN: He's gone mad!

ELECTOR'S WIFE:                    Whom names he so!?
PRINCE *(reaching for the wreath)*:
   O dearest! Why withdraw from me? Natalie!
      *(He just manages to snatch a glove from her hand.)*
HOHENZOLLERN: In heaven's name! What has he got?
COURTIER: The wreath?
NATALIE:               No, no!
HOHENZOLLERN: *(opening the gate)*:
                              Quick! In here, my liege!
   Away, that the whole vision disappear!
ELECTOR: Into the void with you, Sir Prince of Homburg!
   Back into the darkness! If you please,
   We'll meet again upon the field of battle!
   It's not in dreams you'll capture such as these!
         *(All exeunt. With a rattle the gate slams shut
         in front of the Prince. Pause.)*


## SCENE 2

*Prince stands for a moment, wondering, in front of the doors,
then descends the ramp, brooding, with the hand holding the glove
pressed to his brow. As soon as he arrives below, he turns and
looks back up at the doors.*


## SCENE 3

*Hohenzollern enters from below through a grated door. He is fol-
lowed by a page. The Prince of Homburg.*
PAGE *(softly)*: My Lord, a word with you! Most gracious Count!
HOHENZOLLERN *(resisting)*: Hush, Cicada! Well, what's up!?
PAGE:                                        I'm
                                       [sent . . .
HOHENZOLLERN: Don't wake him with thy chirping now! Well?
   What is it?
PAGE:         Sir, the Elector sends me here!
   His orders are: the Prince, upon awakening,

Shall not hear a word about the joke
He's just allowed himself to play upon him!
HOHENZOLLERN: Away! Go lay thy head down in a wheatfield
And sleep thy fill! I knew that all along!
                    *(Exit the page.)*


## SCENE 4

*The Count of Hohenzollern and the Prince of Homburg. Hohen-
zollern places himself, at a good distance, behind Homburg, who,
still absorbed, looks up the ramp.*
HOHENZOLLERN: Arthur!
                *(Homburg falls to the ground.)*
    He's down! A bullet could have struck no better!
                *(approaching him)*
    I'm eager for the story he'll invent
    To explain to me why he's been here asleep.
                *(bending over him)*
    Arthur! Hey! Are you possessed? What ails you?
    How come you're here at night in such a place?
PRINCE: Alas, dear friend,—!
HOHENZOLLERN:                Really now, I say!
    The cavalry, whose commander you should be,
    Has been on the march an hour, and you—
    You're lying in the garden here asleep.
PRINCE: What cavalry is that?
HOHENZOLLERN:                The Mamelukes!—
    Sure as I live and breathe, he's quite forgot
    He leads the squadrons of the House of Brandenburg!
PRINCE *(standing up)*: My helmet, quick! My armor!
HOHENZOLLERN:                                And where
                                            [are they?
PRINCE: To the right, Hal, to the right—upon the stool!
HOHENZOLLERN: Where? What do you mean, upon the stool?
PRINCE: Yes. At least I think it's there. I . . .
HOHENZOLLERN *(staring at him)*:
    So get them from the stool again yourself!

PRINCE: . . . What glove is this?
   *(He stares at the glove, which he still holds.)*
HOHENZOLLERN:                    But how should I know?
                    *(aside)*
                                        Damned!

   He stripped it off unnoticed from her arm!
                    *(breaking off)*
   Quick! Be off! What's keeping you? Away!
PRINCE *(throwing away the glove):*
   At once! Hey, Frank! That sluggard should have waked me!
HOHENZOLLERN *(staring at him):* He's really raving mad!
PRINCE:                              Upon
                                      [my word!

   I know not, dearest Henry, where I am.
HOHENZOLLERN: In Fehrbellin, you muddleheaded dreamer!
   On a garden path that runs behind the castle.
PRINCE *(aside):* O that Night would swallow me! Again,
   Unwittingly, I've wandered in the moonlight!
                    *(trying to regain his composure)*
   Pardon! I now recall. The heat, you know,
   Made sleeping really difficult last night.
   I slipped into this garden, exhausted,
   And because the night enveloped me so sweetly,
   Her blond hair shedding such soft fragrances,
   Just as the Persian bride receives her bridegroom,
   So I lay me down here in her lap.—
   What hour just struck?
HOHENZOLLERN: But half an hour to twelve!
PRINCE: And all the cavalry, you say, have left?
HOHENZOLLERN:
   What else? At ten o'clock, as planned, of course!
   No doubt the Princess' forces, in the lead,
   Have reached the heights of Hackelwitz already,
   Where, facing Wrangel, on the morrow they
   Shall camouflage our silent deployment.
PRINCE: No matter, then. Old Kottwitz is in charge,
   And he knows every object of this march.
   What's more, at two o'clock tomorrow morning
   I'd have to come again to Fehrbellin

Because it's here that we're to have our briefing:
It's better that I stay behind in camp.
Come, let us go. The Elector doesn't know?
HOHENZOLLERN: Who, he? He's long been in his bed asleep!
*(They are about to go. Homburg stops short, turns around and*
*retrieves the glove.)*
PRINCE: What a strange and wondrous dream I've had!
  It seemed as if a royal palace, radiant
  With gold and silver, opened sudden portals,
  And down a lofty marble ramp
  There came to me a stately ring of dancers,
  The people who are nearest to my heart:
  The Elector and his Consort and . . . the . . . third
  . . . Oh, what's her name!
HOHENZOLLERN:            Who!?
PRINCE *(as if groping in search of her)*:
                         She!—The one I fancy!
  The deaf-and-dumb could call her by her name!
HOHENZOLLERN: Lady Platen?
PRINCE:            Hardly!
HOHENZOLLERN:            Baroness Ramin?
PRINCE: No, never!
HOHENZOLLERN:    Lady Bork or Winterfeld?
PRINCE: I beg of you! You overlook the pearl
  For the ring in which the pearl is held! No, no!
HOHENZOLLERN: O blast it, speak! Do you recall the features?
  What lady do you mean!?
PRINCE:           I say, no matter!
  Now I'm awake, the name has slipped my mind
  And matters little in this explanation.
HOHENZOLLERN: Enough! Continue!
PRINCE: Well, don't interrupt!—
  And he, the Elector, with a brow like Zeus,
  Held a wreath of laurel in his hand:
  He steps up close before my very eyes;
  As if to inflame my whole soul, he winds
  The chain from his own neck about the wreath
  And hands it, to be pressed upon my locks . . .
  O Henry!

HOHENZOLLERN: To—
PRINCE: O Henry!
HOHENZOLLERN: Well, speak up!
PRINCE:—It must indeed have been the Lady Platen.
HOHENZOLLERN: The Lady Platen? What? Who's now in Prussia?
PRINCE: Lady Platen. Quite. Or Baroness Ramin.
HOHENZOLLERN: Ah, Baroness Ramin! The redhead, what?—
    The Lady Platen, with those teasing violet eyes!
    Everybody knows it's she you like.
PRINCE:                      It's she I like.—
HOHENZOLLERN: So, and she's the one who handed you the
                                               [wreath?
PRINCE: High above me, like the muse of glory,
    She lifts the garland with its swinging chain
    As if about to crown a hero's head.
    I reach, with inexpressible emotion,
    I reach my hands out to possess the wreath:
    I want to sink before her at her feet.
    But, as in misty valleys, hung with flowers,
    A chilly breath of wind dispels the scent,
    These forms evade me, moving up the ramp.
    Its length extends, as I begin to mount it,
    Infinitely high to heaven's gate.
    I grope now to the left, now to the right,
    Anxious to retain one precious shape.
    In vain! The palace opens suddenly;
    A piercing bolt of light annihilates them;
    Rattling, the doors fly shut again:
    Only a glove, in passionate pursuit,
    I steal from the lovely spirit's arm:
    And now, almighty gods, as I awake
    A glove it is I'm holding in my hand!
HOHENZOLLERN: Upon my word!—And now you mean, that glove
    Belongs to her?
PRINCE:           To whom?
HOHENZOLLERN:                Why, Lady Platen!
PRINCE: Lady Platen. Quite. Or Baroness Ramin.
HOHENZOLLERN: Rascal that you are, with all your visions!
    Who knows from what sweet secret pastoral hour,

Enacted here awake, in flesh and blood,
The glove has been left clinging to your hand!
PRINCE: With me? What, here? O Love!
HOHENZOLLERN:                         Oh, what the deuce!
What's it to me! Let it be Lady Platen,
Or Baroness Ramin! The post for Prussia
Leaves on Sunday. That's the shortest way
To learn if your fair damsel's lost this glove.—
Away! It's twelve o'clock. We're wasting time.
PRINCE *(dreamily, with lowered eyes)*:
—You're right, of course. Let us to bed.
But one thing more, dear fellow. Are they still
In camp, the Elector's lady and her niece?
The lovely Princess of Oranien,
Who recently arrived in our encampment?
HOHENZOLLERN: But why? *(aside)* I do believe the fool—
PRINCE:                                          But
                                                    [why?
I'm bound, you know, to furnish thirty horsemen
To be their escort from the battle area.
I asked Ramin to make arrangements for me.
HOHENZOLLERN: What? Long departed! Gone, or on their way!
At least, Ramin stood ready at the gate
For imminent departure, all night long.
But come! It's twelve o'clock, and I'd prefer
To rest a little 'ere the fight begins.
                    *(Exeunt.)*


SCENE 5


*Fehrbellin. Hall in the castle. Distant shooting is audible.*

*Enter the Elector's Wife and Princess Natalie in travel clothes, escorted by a courtier. They are seated to one side. Ladies-in-waiting follow, then the Elector, Field-Marshal Dörfling, the Prince of Homburg (with the glove tucked inside his coat), the Count of Hohenzollern, Count Truchss, Colonel Hennings, Captain Golz, and various other generals, colonels and officers.*

ELECTOR: What's that shooting, Marshal? Is that Götz?
FIELD-MARSHAL: Colonel Götz indeed, my sovereign lord.
   He led the vanguard out to reconnoiter
   And already sends us back a messenger
   To give you reassurance in advance:
   A Swedish outpost of a thousand men
   Has broken forward to the Hackel Mountains,
   But Colonel Götz can guarantee these mountains
   And sends me word that you should carry on
   As if they had been captured by his vanguard.
ELECTOR *(to the officers):*
   Sirs, the Marshal knows the strategy of battle.
   I pray you, take your pencils, and record it.
*(They gather in a circle around Dörfling, taking out their tablets,
on the side of the stage opposite the ladies.)*
ELECTOR *(to the Courtier):* Ramin is at the entrance with the
   coach?
COURTIER: In a moment, Sire. They're harnessing the horses.
ELECTOR *(sitting down behind his wife and Natalie):*
   Ramin will be my dear Elisa's escort
   And thirty able horsemen follow him.
   He'll take you to my Chancellor Kalkhuhn's castle
   At Havelberg, across the Havel River,
   Where never a Swede would dare to show his face.
ELECTOR'S WIFE: And have they put the ferry back in service?
ELECTOR: At Havelberg? Arrangements have been made.
   What's more, it will be dawn before you reach it.
                  *(pause)*
   Natalie is so quiet, my sweet maid?
   —What is the matter, child?
NATALIE: I'm frightened, Uncle.
ELECTOR: And yet my little daughter's so secure,
   She was no safer in her mother's womb.
                  *(Pause.)*
ELECTOR'S WIFE: When do you think we shall meet again?
ELECTOR: If God grants me the victory, as he will,
   Perhaps as soon as in a few days' time.
      *(Enter pages to serve the ladies breakfast. Dörfling begins
   dictating. Homburg, pencil and tablet in hand, stares fixedly at
                  the ladies.)*

FIELD-MARSHAL: The illustrious plan of battle, ye commanders,
    Foresees the elusive Swedish army's ruin
    By severing all connections with the bridgehead
    That protects it from behind along the Rhyn.
    Now, Colonel Hennings—!
HENNINGS *(writing):*        Here!
FIELD-MARSHAL:        Who, by his Highness' wish
                               [today
    Commands the right flank of our combat forces,
    Shall try by quietly moving through the brush
    To sneak around the left flank of the Swedes,
    Then fling himself between them and the bridges
    And, supported by Count Truchss,—
    Count Truchss!
TRUCHSS *(writing):* Here!
FIELD-MARSHAL:        And, supported by Count Truchss,—
                *(pause)*
    Who, facing Wrangel meanwhile from the heights,
    Has fortified an outpost with his cannon,—
TRUCHSS *(writing):*
    —Has fortified an outpost with his cannon,—
FIELD-MARSHAL: Do you have it?
                  *(continuing)*
    Attempt to drive the Swedes into the marsh
    That lies behind their right flank.
A HAIDUCK *(entering):*
    The coach awaits you at the entrance, Madam.
             *(The ladies rise.)*
FIELD-MARSHAL: The Prince of Homburg—
ELECTOR *(also rising):*        And Ramin is ready?
HAIDUCK: He waits on horseback at the gates below, Sire.
      *(The family take their leave of one another.)*
TRUCHSS *(writing):* —That lies behind their right flank.
FIELD-MARSHAL: The Prince of Homburg—
  Where is the Prince of Homburg?
HOHENZOLLERN *(whispering):*    Arthur!
PRINCE *(with a start):*        Here!
HOHENZOLLERN: What's wrong with you?
PRINCE:                What is my Marshal's
                       [bidding?

*(His face reddening, he assumes his pose with pencil and paper and writes.)*

FIELD-MARSHAL: To whom our illustrious lord again entrusts
　The glorious command, just as at Rathenow,
　Of the entire cavalry of Brandenburg—
　　　　　　　　*(hesitates)*
　But assuming Colonel Kottwitz, notwithstanding,
　Shall assist him at all times with his advice.—
　　　　　　*(aside to Captain Golz)*
　Is Kottwitz here?

GOLZ: 　　　　　No, General, as you see,
　He has delegated me instead
　To hear the battle orders from your lips.
　　　*(The prince again stares over at the ladies.)*

FIELD-MARSHAL *(continuing)*: —Shall wait upon the plain at
　　　　　　　　　　　　　　[Hackelwitz,
　Facing from afar the Swedes' right flank,
　But well beyond the reach of cannonfire.

GOLZ *(writing)*: —But well beyond the reach of cannonfire.
　*(The Elector's wife binds a kerchief around Natalie's neck.*
*Natalie, about to put on her gloves, looks around as if searching*
　　　　　　　　*for something.)*

ELECTOR *(stepping towards her)*:
　What's the matter, little daughter?

ELECTOR'S WIFE: 　　　　　　Is something missing?

NATALIE: —My glove, dear aunt, I do not know . . .
　　　　　*(They all look around.)*

ELECTOR *(to the ladies-in-waiting)*: 　　　　O ladies!
　Gracious ladies, would you kindly see to this?

ELECTOR'S WIFE *(to Natalie)*:
　You have it, child!

NATALIE: 　　　The right one; but the left?

ELECTOR: Perhaps forgotten somewhere in your chamber?

NATALIE: Dear Lady Bork!

ELECTOR'S WIFE *(to the lady)*: Quick!

NATALIE: 　　　　　　　On the mantelpiece!
　　　　*(Exit the lady-in-waiting.)*

PRINCE *(aside)*: Lord of my life! Dare I believe my ears?
　　　　*(He pulls out the glove.)*

FIELD-MARSHAL *(looking at the paper in his hand)*:
But well beyond the reach of cannonfire;
                    *(continuing)*
—The illustrious Prince—
PRINCE:                She's looking for the glove!
    *(He looks now at the glove, now at Natalie.)*
FIELD-MARSHAL: —Shall not, until our Lord's express
                          [command,—
GOLZ *(writing)*: —Shall not, until our Lord's express command,—
FIELD-MARSHAL: —No matter how the battle's tide may turn,
  Depart from the position given him—
PRINCE: Quick, I have to test if it's the one!
*(He drops the glove together with his handkerchief. He picks up the handkerchief again, but leaves the glove on the floor where everyone can see it.)*
FIELD-MARSHAL *(taken aback)*: What is his Highness doing?
HOHENZOLLERN *(whispering)*:             Arthur!
PRINCE:                         Here!
HOHENZOLLERN: Are you possessed?!
PRINCE:               What is my Marshal's
                          [bidding?
*(He takes pencil and tablet up again. Dörfling throws him an inquiring glance. Pause.)*
GOLZ *(having written)*: —Depart from the position given him—
FIELD-MARSHAL *(continuing)*: —Until, hard-pressed by Hennings
  and by Truchss—
PRINCE *(aside to Golz, while looking at his tablet)*:
  Who, dear Golz? What? I?
GOLZ:             Yes, you! Who else?
PRINCE: —From the position given me I shall not—?
GOLZ: Most certainly!
FIELD-MARSHAL:    Well? Have you got that down?
PRINCE *(aloud)*: —Depart from the position given me—
                *(He writes.)*
FIELD-MARSHAL: —Until, hard-pressed by Hennings and by
                          [Truchss,—
            *(stops short)*
The left flank of the Swedes, disorganized,
Falls upon its right, and all their forces

Stagger backwards toward that stretch of land
Where in the marshes, cut across by ditches,
It's our intent at last to rub them out.

ELECTOR: Pages, light! Your arms, my dears!

*(The Elector's Wife and Natalie prepare to leave.)*

FIELD-MARSHAL: Then he will let the trumpets sound the fanfare.

ELECTOR'S WIFE *(as officers make their adieux)*:
Goodbye, my lords! Don't let us interrupt!

*(The Field-Marshal also bows to her.)*

ELECTOR *(suddenly stopping)*:
Look there! The lady's glove! Quick! There it lies!

COURTIER: Where?

ELECTOR:          There! At the Prince our cousin's feet!

PRINCE *(gallantly)*:
At my . . . ? Why, does this glove belong to you?

*(He picks it up and takes it to Natalie.)*

NATALIE: I thank you, noble prince.

PRINCE OF HOMBURG *(confused)*:    Is this glove yours?

NATALIE: It's mine, the one I have been looking for.

*(She accepts it and puts it on.)*

ELECTOR'S WIFE *(to Homburg, in leaving)*:
Farewell, farewell! Good luck and God protect you!
See that we meet again both soon and joyously!

*(Elector leaves with the ladies. Ladies-in-waiting, courtiers, and
pages follow. Prince stands a moment, as if struck by lightning;
then returns with triumphant steps to the circle of officers.)*

PRINCE: Then he will let the trumpets sound the fanfare.

*(He makes as if writing.)*

FIELD-MARSHAL *(looks at his paper)*:
Then he will let the trumpets sound the fanfare.
His Highness, though, in order to prevent
The blow from being struck before its time . . .

GOLZ: —The blow from being struck before its time . . .

PRINCE *(aside to Hohenzollern, greatly moved)*: Henry!

HOHENZOLLERN *(angrily)*: Now what is it? What's the matter?

PRINCE: What? You didn't see?

HOHENZOLLERN:          No! Quiet, blast it!

FIELD-MARSHAL *(continuing)*: —Shall send a member of his
                                                            [retinue
To give, and note this well, the express command

For the Prince to launch his charge upon the foe.
Then only will the trumpets sound the fanfare.
       *(The Prince stares distractedly at the ground.)*
  Do you have that?
GOLZ *(writing):* —Then only will the trumpets sound the fanfare.
FIELD-MARSHAL *(raising his voice):*
  His majesty the Prince has noted that?
PRINCE: Your pardon, Sir?
FIELD-MARSHAL:        Have you made note of all?
PRINCE: About the fanfare?
HOHENZOLLERN *(aside, with angry emphasis):*
             Fanfare, be damned! No sooner
                 [than until . . . !
GOLZ *(similarly):* Till he himself . . .
PRINCE *(interrupting them):*
  Of course. No sooner than—
  But then he'll let the trumpets sound the fanfare.
             *(He writes. Pause.)*
FIELD-MARSHAL: Please note this, Baron Golz: tell Colonel
                       [Kottwitz
  That I desire, if he can manage it,
  To speak with him myself before the battle.
GOLZ *(with meaning):* I'll see to it. You may depend on me.
             *(Pause.)*
ELECTOR *(returning):* Now, generals and commanding officers,
  The morn is graying. Do you have it written?
FIELD-MARSHAL: It has been done, my lord; your strategies
  Have duly been assigned to your commanders.
ELECTOR *(taking his hat and gloves):*
  Sir Prince of Homburg, I recommend composure!
  Recently you've thrown away two victories
  In my campaigns along the Rhine, as well you know.
  Control yourself! Don't make me lose a third,
  Which means to me no less than throne and kingdom!
            *(to the officers)*
  Follow me! Hey, Frank!
STABLEBOY *(entering):*    Here!
ELECTOR:              My white horse! Quick!
  I want to reach the field before sunrise!
      *(Exit; the generals, colonels, and officers follow.)*

## SCENE 6

PRINCE *(stepping downstage):*
Now then, Prodigious One, upon your globe,
You, whose veil the wind lifts like a sail,
Draw you near!
Already, Fortune, you have touched my brow
And tossed a pledge to me as you rolled by,
Shook from your horn of plenty with a smile:
But today, elusive offspring of the gods,
I shall capture you upon the battlefield
And spill out all your blessings at my feet,
Even if, with iron sevenfold,
You're shackled to the Swedes' triumphal car!
*(Exit.)*

# Act II

## SCENE 1

*Battlefield near Fehrbellin.*

*Colonel Kottwitz, Count Hohenzollern, Captain Golz, and other officers, at the head of the cavalry.*

KOTTWITZ *(still from offstage):*
Horsemen, halt! Halt and dismount!
HOHENZOLLERN AND GOLZ *(entering):* Halt! Halt!
KOTTWITZ: Who'll help me off my horse, friends?
HOHENZOLLERN AND GOLZ:                              Here, old
                                                                          [man!
*(Exeunt.)*
KOTTWITZ *(still offstage):*
A plague upon me! Ouf! I thank you, Sirs!
For your help, a noble son to each of you
To do as much for you in your decline!
   *(He enters, followed by Hohenzollern, Golz and others.)*
On horseback, yes, I still feel full of youth;

But what a strain begins when I dismount,
As if my soul and body pull apart!
                    *(looking around)*
Where is the Prince, our most esteemed commander?
HOLLENZOLLERN: He shall return at once.
KOTTWITZ:                              Where is he then?
HOHENZOLLERN: He rode into the village you've just passed,
   The one behind the brush. He'll soon return.
KOTTWITZ: Last night, I hear, he tumbled from his horse.
HOHENZOLLERN: So I'm told.
KOTTWITZ:                        He fell?
HOHENZOLLERN *(turning toward him)*: Oh, nothing grave.
   Crossing at the mill, his charger shied;
   The Prince slid off and wasn't hurt at all.
   It's not worth noting. Set your mind at rest.
KOTTWITZ *(climbing the hill)*:
   Ye gods! What a beautiful day!
   The Lord of Life created such a day
   For sweeter business than our fighting here!
   The clouds are blushing with the fiery sun,
   And manly feeling, mounting like the lark,
   Rejoices in the freshly scented air!
GOLZ: Did you find Marshal Dörfling?
KOTTWITZ *(stepping back down)*:        Blast it! No!
   What does his Excellency think I am?
   Am I a bird, an arrow, an idea?
   That I should flit about the battlefield?
   I checked the vanguard on the Hackel Heights
   And then the rearguard in the Hackel Valley,
   But the Marshal, Sir, was nowhere to be found.
   Thereupon I joined my regiment again.
GOLZ: He'll take it very ill; it seems he had
   A matter of some consequence to tell you.
OFFICER: Here comes the Prince, our most illustrious leader!


SCENE 2


*Enter the Prince of Homburg, a black bandage around his left hand. The others.*

KOTTWITZ: Hearty greetings, young and noble Prince!
  Look here! While you were in the village,
  I stationed horsemen on the valley road.
  I think you will be satisfied with me!
PRINCE: Good morning, Kottwitz!—Friends, good morning to
                                        [you!—
  You know I honor everything you do.
HOHENZOLLERN: What were you doing in the village, Arthur?
  —You look so solemn.
PRINCE:                I . . . was in the chapel
  We'd glimpsed among the quiet village trees.
  As I was riding past, the bell rang out
  For worship, moving me to join the rest
  In humble prayer before the altar.
KOTTWITZ: A reverent young sovereign, I must say!
  The deed, believe me, that begins with prayer
  Shall crown itself in grace and fame and victory!
PRINCE: I meant to ask you something, Henry . . .
        *(draws him a little downstage)*
  What was it at the conference last night
  That Dörfling read aloud for me to do?
HOHENZOLLERN: You were distracted. I observed that.
PRINCE: Distracted . . . or divided; I don't know,
  Dictation of commands confuses me.
HOHENZOLLERN: By luck there wasn't much for you this time.
  Truchss and Hennings, with our infantry,
  Are designated to attack the Swedes.
  It's your assignment to remain down here
  With all your horsemen ready in this valley
  Until you receive the signal to attack.
PRINCE *(after a moment, in which he muses with lowered eyes)*:
  —A strange coincidence!
HOHENZOLLERN:            What, friend?
      *(He stares at him. Noise of cannonfire.)*
KOTTWITZ: Hallo, good Sirs! Hallo! Upon your horses!
  It's Hennings and the battle has begun.
        *(They all climb the hill.)*
PRINCE: Who is it? What?
HOHENZOLLERN:          It's Colonel Hennings, Arthur.

He's slipped around in back of Wrangel's forces.
Up here! You can command a view of everything!
GOLZ *(on the hill):* See how dreadfully they flank the Rhyn!
PRINCE *(shading his eyes):*
    What, Hennings on the right?
FIRST OFFICER:                 Yes, noble Prince!
PRINCE: Why, hang it, yesterday he had the left!
           *(Cannon salvos in the distance.)*
KOTTWITZ: By thunder! From a dozen flaming jaws
    Wrangel is letting fire on Hennings' men!
FIRST OFFICER:
Look what the Swedes have done! I call those ramparts!
SECOND OFFICER: By God, embankments to the very church
                              [spire
    That rises from the village there behind them!
           *(Gunfire close by.)*
GOLZ: That's Truchss.
PRINCE:               It's Truchss?
KOTTWITZ:                    Of course!
    He's coming from in front to help out Hennings!
PRINCE: How come today it's Truchss who's in the center?
           *(Heavy gunfire.)*
GOLZ: By heaven, look! The village is on fire!
THIRD OFFICER: Upon my life, it's burning!
FIRST OFFICER:                    Yes, it's burning!
    And now the flames are darting up the steeple.
GOLZ: Fie! How the Swedish aides fly right and left!
SECOND OFFICER: They're pulling back!
KOTTWITZ:                  Where?
FIRST OFFICER:                    On their right
                                  [flank!
THIRD OFFICER: Indeed! In whole platoons! Three regiments!
    It seems they want to reinforce their left.
SECOND OFFICER: My word, the cavalry are moving up
    To cover their maneuver on the right.
HOHENZOLLERN *(laughs):*
    Ha! Ha! How quickly they will clear the field
    When we're discovered hidden in this valley!
           *(Musketfire.)*

KOTTWITZ: Look, brothers, look!

SECOND OFFICER:                    Do you hear that?

FIRST OFFICER:                                        Musketfire!

THIRD OFFICER: They're fighting at the ramparts!

GOLZ:                                        God, I've

                                                                    [never

   Heard such a thunder of artillery!

HOHENZOLLERN: Shoot! Shoot! Earth's womb be blasted open!
   The crater be a grave for all your corpses!

             *(Pause. A cry of victory in the distance.)*

FIRST OFFICER: O Lord in heaven, You who grant the victory:
   Wrangel's men are showing us their heels!

HOHENZOLLERN:                                        No, tell me!

GOLZ: By heaven, friends! Look there, at his left flank!
   He's clearing his emplacements from the ramparts.

ALL: Hurrah! Hurrah! Hurrah! The day is ours!

PRINCE *(climbing down the hill)*:
   Up, Kottwitz, follow me!

KOTTWITZ:                        Easy, easy, children!

PRINCE: Let the trumpets sound the fanfare! Follow me!

KOTTWITZ: I say, go easy.

PRINCE *(wildly)*:                        No, by all Creation!

KOTTWITZ: At the briefing yesterday his majesty
   Gave orders to await an express command.
   Golz, recite your minutes to the gentleman.

PRINCE: Await commands! O Kottwitz, do you ride so slowly?
   Have you not felt the orders in your heart?

KOTTWITZ: Orders?

HOHENZOLLERN:    I beg you!

KOTTWITZ:                        In my heart?

HOHENZOLLERN: Listen to him, Arthur!

GOLZ:                                        Hear the Colonel!

KOTTWITZ *(insulted)*: Oho! Young sir, is that the way you see me?
   Press me, and I'll drag that jade of yours
   By the tail of mine. So! Forward, gentlemen!
   To battle! Sound the fanfare! I'm with you.

GOLZ *(to Kottwitz)*: No, never, Colonel! Never in my life!

SECOND OFFICER: Hennings' troops have not yet reached the Rhyn.

FIRST OFFICER: Divest him of his sabre!

PRINCE:                               What! My sabre?
                    *(shoves him back)*
  Arrogant stripling, you who do not know
  The ten commandments yet of Brandenburg!
  Here is your own together with its scabbard!
              *(He tears off his sabre and sabretache.)*
FIRST OFFICER *(staggering)*:
  My Prince, this deed! By God . . . I . . .
PRINCE *(stepping toward him)*:               Still protesting?
HOHENZOLLERN *(to the Officer)*:
  Are you insane? Be quiet!
PRINCE *(delivering the sabre)*: Orderlies!
  To Fehrbellin with him, a prisoner!
              *(to Kottwitz and the other officers)*
  And now the word is, men: a scoundrel, he
  Who disregards his general's battle call!
  Who among you stays?
KOTTWITZ:                   Yes! Why so anxious?
HOHENZOLLERN *(conciliatory)*:
  We were only trying to give you our advice.
KOTTWITZ: Take it on your own head! I follow you.
PRINCE *(appeased)*:
  I take it on my own head! Friends, follow me!
                    *(Exeunt.)*


SCENE 3


*Room in the village. Enter a courtier in boots and spurs. A farmer
and his wife are sitting at a table, working.*
COURTIER: God speed you, honest people! Have you room
  To put up guests upon these premises?
FARMER: Of course! With all my heart!
WIFE:                             May we ask whom?
COURTIER: None other than our country's noble mother!—
  At the village gate her coach's axle broke,
  And since we've heard that victory is ours,
  Our journey is no longer necessary.
BOTH *(rising)*: The victory ours? Thank heaven!

COURTIER:                                          You didn't
                                                        [know?
The Swedish army has been beaten back.
If not forever, then at least for now,
Our land is rescued from its fire and sword.
But look ye here!
Our illustrious lady is already come.


## SCENE 4

*Enter the Elector's wife, pale and distraught. Princess Natalie and
several ladies-in-waiting follow. The others.*

ELECTOR'S WIFE *(at the threshold)*:
  Bork! Winterfeld! Come: give me each your arm!
NATALIE *(hurrying to her)*: O Mother dear!
LADIES-IN-WAITING:                          My God! She pales!
                                                [She faints!
                    *(They support her.)*
ELECTOR'S WIFE: Lead me to a chair. I must sit down.
  Dead? Did he say dead?
NATALIE:                      Beloved mother!
ELECTOR'S WIFE: I'll hear misfortune's messenger myself!


## SCENE 5

*Enter Captain Mörner, wounded, helped by two cavalrymen. The
others.*

ELECTOR'S WIFE: What do you bring me, dreadful messenger?
MÖRNER: Alas, what, to my everlasting grief,
  These very eyes have witnessed, precious lady.
ELECTOR'S WIFE: Proceed! Tell all!
MÖRNER:                      The Elector is no more!
NATALIE:                                  O Heaven!
  Must we suffer such a monstrous blow!?
                  *(She covers her face with her hands.)*
ELECTOR'S WIFE: Give me an account of how he fell.
  —And as the lightning bolt, which strikes the traveler,

Lights up his world once more in sudden purple,
So be your words. May night, when you have finished,
Thunder down upon my head forever.
*(Mörner moves closer to her, helped by his two cavalrymen.)*
MÖRNER: The moment that the Swedes, hard-pressed by
[Truchss,
Had started drawing back, the Prince of Homburg
Pushed in front of Wrangel on the plain.
His cavalry had broken through two lines
And then annihilated them in flight,
When he was halted by a field redoubt.
Confronted by a deadly rain of iron
His men were snapped and flattened like a wheat crop
Between the brush and hills he had to stop
To gather up his scattered horsemen's strength.
NATALIE *(to the Elector's wife):*
Dearest! Brace yourself!
ELECTOR'S WIFE:        No, let me be!
MÖRNER: Then just as we are scrambling from the dust,
We see his Majesty amid the flags
Of Truchss's corps advance to meet the foe.
Superb astride the whiteness of his horse
He lights the path of victory like the sun.
We all gather at this sight upon the hill,
Trying to glimpse him in a field of flame,
When suddenly the Elector, horse and rider,
Bites the dust before our very eyes.
Two standard-bearers, falling over him,
Covered him from our view with both their flags.
NATALIE: O Mother dear!
FIRST LADY-IN-WAITING:   O Heaven!
ELECTOR'S WIFE:                Go on! Go on!
MÖRNER: At this dread sight, his heart in agony,
The Prince descends upon the enemy
In vengeful fury, like a baited bear:
We fly across the ramparts and the ditches;
Their men we scatter, slain, upon the field;
Cannons and standards, flags and kettledrums,
The Swedes' entire battle gear is captured:

And had there been no bridgehead on the Rhyn
To check our onslaught, no one would remain
To say beside his fathers' fireside:
I saw the hero fall at Fehrbellin!

ELECTOR'S WIFE: A much too precious gain! I like it not.
Give me again the prize that it has cost us.

*(She falls into a swoon.)*

FIRST LADY-IN-WAITING: O God in Heaven! Help! My lady's fainted!

*(Natalie weeps.)*


## SCENE 6


*Enter the Prince of Homburg. The others.*

PRINCE: Oh, my most precious Natalie!

*(Touched, he lays her hand on his heart.)*

NATALIE:                              So it's true?

PRINCE: Oh, would that I could tell you, no!
Oh, would that with the blood of my own heart
I could call his heart's blood back to life.

NATALIE *(drying her tears)*: Then they have found his body?

PRINCE: Alas, my only business in that moment
Was vengeance upon Wrangel. How could I
Devote myself to such a care till now?
I have, however, sent a band of man
To seek his body on the field of death:
By nightfall it will doubtless have arrived.

NATALIE: Now who in this terrifying struggle
Will check the Swedes? defend us from the foe,
That robs us of his fortune and his name?

PRINCE *(taking her hand)*:
O Lady! I shall undertake your charge!
I'll stand, an angel with a flaming sword,
Beside your orphan'd throne!
Before the year is out, he would have wished
To liberate our land; so let it be!
I'll act as champion of that last desire!

NATALIE: My dear, beloved cousin!

*(She withdraws her hand.)*

PRINCE:                    O Natalie!
          *(holds back a moment)*
  What lies ahead for you?
NATALIE:                  I do not know.
  Indeed, what can there, now this thunderbolt
  Has blown apart the ground beneath my feet?
  My father and dear mother are at rest
  In graves at Amsterdam; our patrimony
  Dordrecht lies in ruins. Prince Moritz,
  My cousin of Oranien, hard-pressed
  By armies of the mighty Spanish tyrant,
  Cannot shelter his own children: and now sinks
  The last support that held my fortune's vines.
  Today I'm orphan'd for the second time.
PRINCE *(fastening an arm around her waist):*
  Oh, my sweet friend! Were not this hour
  Devoted to our mourning, I would say:
  Entwine your branches here around this breast,
  This breast that has, for years, in lonely bloom,
  Desired the lovely fragrance of your flowers!
NATALIE: My dear, beloved friend!
PRINCE:                    Will you? Will you?
NATALIE: . . . If I may grow into its very core?
          *(She lays her head on his breast.)*
PRINCE: What? How was that?
NATALIE:                  Away!
PRINCE *(holding her):*          Into its core!
  Into its own heart's core, Natalie!
          *(He kisses her; she tears herself away.)*
  O God, were he but here, whom we lament,
  To witness this alliance! Would that we
  Could stammer: Father, give your blessing to us!
          *(He covers his face with his hands;*
          *Natalie goes over to the Elector's wife.)*


## SCENE 7


*Sergeant Major rushes in. The others.*
SERGEANT MAJOR: My Prince, how dare I, by the living God,

Report to you the rumor that is spreading!
. . . The Elector lives!
PRINCE:                    He lives!
SERGEANT MAJOR:                    Now by Olympus!
Count Sparren just arrived here with the news.
NATALIE: Lord of my life! Mother, did you hear?
        *(She throws herself at her feet and embraces her.)*
PRINCE: No, speak—! Who brings us news?
SERGEANT MAJOR:                    George, Count of
                                [Sparren,

Who saw him safe and sound with his own eyes
At Hackelwitz with Truchss's regiment.
PRINCE: Quick! Run, old man! Bring him here to me!
        *(Exit the Sergeant Major.)*


SCENE 8


*Count George of Sparren and the Sergeant Major. The others.*
ELECTOR'S WIFE: Oh, do not fling me twice into the abyss!
NATALIE: No, no! My cherished mother!
ELECTOR'S WIFE:                    Frederick lives?
NATALIE *(holding her erect with both hands)*:
    Again you're on the pinnacle of life!
SERGEANT MAJOR *(stepping up)*:
    Here is the officer, Sir!
PRINCE:                    Good Count of Sparren,
    You've seen his Majesty both safe and sound
    With Truchss's regiment at Hackelwitz?
COUNT:
    I saw him, illustrious Prince, inside the parsonage,
    Where, surrounded by his staff, he issued orders
    For burial of all the dead, both foe and friend.
LADIES-IN-WAITING *(embracing each other)*:
    O God!
ELECTOR'S WIFE: O Daughter!
NATALIE:                    It's almost too much bliss!
        *(She hides her face in her aunt's lap.)*
PRINCE: Did I not from afar, with all my men,

See him overwhelmed by cannonfire?
  Both him and his white charger bite the dust?
COUNT: Indeed, that stallion with its rider fell,
  But it was not our Lord, my Prince, who rode it.
PRINCE: What? Someone else!?
NATALIE:                        Miraculous!
PRINCE:                                      Speak! Tell how!
  Like gold, your word falls heavy on my heart.
COUNT: Oh, let me tell the most pathetic story
  The ear has ever heard!
  His Majesty, who, deaf to every warning,
  Chose to ride that dazzling white horse
  Which Froben lately bought for him in England,
  Became again, as always,
  The target of the enemy cannonball.
  The horsemen in his retinue could barely
  Come within a hundred feet of him.
  A welter of grenades and ball and grapeshot
  Rolled 'round him like a broadening wave of death,
  And everything alive made for the shore:
  Only that brave swimmer faltered not,
  But, signaling back at us, rowed ever hopeful
  Toward the heights from which the deluge poured.
PRINCE: Heavens, yes, it was a dreadful sight.
COUNT: Equerry Froben, nearest of the troops
  That followed him, called out these words to me:
  "Oh, damn me for the whiteness of this horse
  I purchased for a heavy purse of gold!
  I'd give another fifty ducats now,
  Could I but camouflage the white with gray."
  Nearing him with grave concern, he shouts:
  "Your horse is skittish, Sire; please permit me
  To put it through its paces once again!"
  Alighting from his chestnut with this warning,
  He grabs the bridle of the other steed.
  Dismounting with a smile, our lord replies:
  "By daylight it will surely never master
  The skill that you would teach it, my old man!
  Hide it away, I say, in yonder hills,

Where they'll take no further notice of its flaw."
Mounting the chestnut that was Froben's steed,
He turns again where duty summons him.
But Froben has no sooner made the change
Than deadly bullets from the field redoubt
Pound him, horse and rider, to the ground.
A victim of his loyalty, he falls,
And not another sound was heard from him.

*(Short pause.)*

PRINCE: He has been paid! And if I had ten lives,
  I could not use them better than did he.

NATALIE: O valiant Froben!

ELECTOR'S WIFE:          Excellent man!

NATALIE: A lesser man would still deserve our tears!

*(They weep.)*

PRINCE: Enough! Now to the point: where is the Elector?
  Has he his quarters now at Hackelwitz?

COUNT: Pardon! My lord has gone back to Berlin
  And all of his commanding officers
  He calls upon to follow him at once.

PRINCE: What? Berlin? The campaign then is over?

COUNT: That this could all be news to you astounds me!
  The Swedish general, Count of Horn, is come,
  And in the camp, as soon as he arrived,
  An armistice was called.
  If I've correctly heard from Marshal Dörfling,
  Negotiations have been undertaken.
  It's possible that peace will be declared.

ELECTOR'S WIFE: O God, how splendidly the skies have cleared!

*(She stands up.)*

PRINCE: Come, let us follow to Berlin at once!
  —For quicker expedition, would you grant me
  A place with you in your conveyance?
  —Just let me write a line or two to Kottwitz,
  And I'll be ready to depart with you.

*(He sits down and writes.)*

ELECTOR'S WIFE: With all my heart I'm happy to oblige you!
*(Prince, having folded his letter and given it to the
Sergeant Major, turns again to the Elector's wife and Natalie
and gently puts an arm around Natalie's waist.)*

HOMBURG: I have a wish to entrust you with in private;
   May I be eased of it along the way?
NATALIE *(breaking away from him)*:
   My handkerchief, Bork!
ELECTOR'S WIFE:          You? A wish of me?
FIRST LADY-IN-WAITING:
   You're wearing it around your neck, my lady.
PRINCE *(to the Elector's wife)*:
   What? Don't you know?
ELECTOR'S WIFE:          No, nothing.
PRINCE:                          Not a syllable?
ELECTOR'S WIFE *(cutting him short)*:
   Enough! Today there's not a suppliant
   On earth to whom I'd answer, no,
   And least of all, victorious one, to you!
   . . . Let us go.
PRINCE:          Were those your words? O Mother!
   Dare I understand them as I wish?
ELECTOR'S WIFE: Away, I say! Discuss it in the coach!
PRINCE: Come, let me take your arms!—O Caesar Divus!
   My ladder now I set against your star!
          *(He leads the ladies away. The others follow.)*


## SCENE 9

*Berlin. Pleasure garden in front of the old castle. In the back-
ground, the royal chapel with a stairway. Bells. The church is
strongly lit, so that we can see Froben's body being carried over
and placed on a magnificent catafalque inside.*
*Enter the Elector, Field-Marshal Dörfling, Colonel Hennings,
Count Truchss, and various other colonels and officers. Opposite
them several couriers with dispatches. In the church and on the
square people of all ages.*
ELECTOR: No matter who was in command that day
   And launched the horsemen's charge of his own will,
   Before I gave the word for him to move
   Or Hennings could destroy the enemy bridges,
   He's guilty of a capital offense

And shall be tried in military court.
The Prince of Homburg was not in command?
TRUCHSS: No, not he, your Highness.
ELECTOR:                                        Who confirms this?
TRUCHSS: Some horsemen can corroborate my words;
    They told me this before the fight began:
    The Prince had fallen from a shying horse.
    They saw him, injured on both head and thigh,
    As he was being bandaged in a church.
ELECTOR: No matter. Our success today was brilliant.
    Tomorrow I'll give thanks before God's altar.
    Yet were it ten times greater, that would not
    Excuse him, through whom fortune granted it:
    I must fight still other battles after this one,
    And I demand adherence to the law.
    Whoever the man who led them into battle,
    I say again, he's forfeited his head.
    I summon him to military court.
    —Come, my friends, and follow me to church.


## SCENE 10

*Enter Prince of Homburg, carrying three Swedish flags, Colonel Kottwitz with two more, Hohenzollern, Golz, and Reuss, each holding another. Then various other officers, corporals and cavalrymen with flags, kettledrums, and standards.*
FIELD-MARSHAL *(as soon as he sees the Prince)*:
    The Prince of Homburg! Truchss, what have you done?!
ELECTOR *(with a start)*: Whence come you, Prince?
PRINCE *(stepping forward a little)*: From Fehrbellin, my liege,
    To bring these victory trophies here to you.
        *(He lays the flags at his feet; the others follow suit.)*
ELECTOR *(taken aback)*: You are wounded, so I hear, and gravely?
    —Count Truchss!
PRINCE *(cheerfully)*: Forgive this little bruise!
TRUCHSS: I'm speechless!
PRINCE: My chestnut fell before the battle started.

This hand here, bandaged by an army surgeon,
Does not deserve your christening it "wounded."
ELECTOR: So it was you who led the cavalry?
PRINCE *(staring at him):*
Why, I indeed! Am I the first to tell you?
The proof was just deposited before you.
ELECTOR: Divest him of his sabre. He's under arrest.
FIELD-MARSHAL *(aghast):* Who?
ELECTOR *(stepping over the flags):*
Kottwitz! Hearty greetings!
TRUCHSS *(aside):*         Damnation!
KOTTWITZ: By God, I'm utterly . . . !
ELECTOR *(staring at him):*      What's that you say?—
Look, what a harvest reaped for our reknown!
The Swedish Guardsman's Standard, is it not?
      *(He picks up a flag, unfurls and admires it.)*
KOTTWITZ: My Elector?
FIELD-MARSHAL:     My Sovereign?
ELECTOR:             Yes, indeed it is!
In fact, from the age of Gustavus Adolphus!
—What's the inscription?
KOTTWITZ:         I think . . .
FIELD-MARSHAL:        "Per aspera ad astra."
ELECTOR: That pledge was not upheld at Fehrbellin.
               *(Pause.)*
KOTTWITZ *(timidly):* Sire, may I speak—!
ELECTOR:             I beg your pardon?—
Take everything, flags, kettledrums and standards,
And hang them on the pillars of the church.
I mean to use them at tomorrow's festival.
    *(He turns to the couriers, takes their dispatches, and*
                          *[starts reading.*
KOTTWITZ *(aside):* By the living God, that's just too harsh!
    *(After some hesitation, Kottwitz picks up his two flags.*
    *The others follow suit. Finally, because Homburg's*
    *flags remain lying on the ground, Kottwitz picks up*
    *those too, so that he now carries five.)*
OFFICER *(stepping up to the Prince):*
Prince, your sabre, if I may.

HOHENZOLLERN (*with his flag, stepping to his side*):

                                      Calm, friend.

PRINCE: Do I wake? Dream? Am I alive? Unconscious?

GOLZ: Prince, I'd submit my sabre and be still!

PRINCE: I, a prisoner?

HOHENZOLLERN:       So it is.

GOLZ:                     You hear correctly.

PRINCE: And may one know the reason?

HOHENZOLLERN (*with emphasis*):       No, not now!—

   You pressed us prematurely into battle,

   Although we tried to warn you. The order was,

   Not to leave the post without a signal.

PRINCE: Help, friends, help! I've lost my mind!

GOLZ (*interrupting*):                 Be calm.

PRINCE: Then was the House of Brandenburg defeated?

HOHENZOLLERN (*stamping his foot*):

   No matter! Obedience should be the rule.

PRINCE (*bitterly*): So!—so, so, so!

HOHENZOLLERN (*backing away from him*):

                       It shall not cost your head.

GOLZ (*also moving away*):

   Perhaps you'll be released again tomorrow.

       (*The Elector folds the letters again and returns*
       *to the circle of officers.*)

PRINCE (*after taking off his sabre*):

   My cousin Frederick wants to play the Brutus,

   Chalks a sorry likeness on a canvas

   Of himself already on a curule chair:

   The Swedish standards lying in the foreground,

   And on his desk the royal code of war.

   By God, in me he will not find a son

   To do him homage at the headman's block!

   A loving heart of good old German stock,

   I'm much more used to generosity.

   And if he chooses to confront me now

   With the stony rigor of antiquity,

   I'm sorry for him and must pity him.

       (*Exit, after surrendering his sabre to the officer.*)

ELECTOR: Take him to Fehrbellin, and there convene
   The military court to judge his case.
      *(Exit into the church. The standard-bearers follow him
      and hang their flags upon the pillars, while he and
      his retinue kneel down and pray at Froben's coffin.)*


# Act III

### SCENE 1

*Fehrbellin. A prison.*

*The Prince of Homburg. In the background two cavalrymen as
watch. Enter Hohenzollern.*

PRINCE: Hey, there! Henry! Welcome to you, friend!
   Well, I'm rid of the imprisonment?
HOHENZOLLERN *(astonished)*:
   The Lord above be praised.
PRINCE:                              What's that you say?
HOHENZOLLERN: You're free? He's sent your sabre back to you?
PRINCE: Me? No.
HOHENZOLLERN: He's not?
PRINCE:                    No!
HOHENZOLLERN:                       How, then, rid of it?
PRINCE: I thought, you . . . you were bringing it.—No matter.
HOHENZOLLERN: I know of nothing.
PRINCE:                               No matter, hear? No
                                                    [matter!
   He must be sending someone else to tell me.
            *(turns and fetches some chairs)*
   Sit down!—So! Tell me all the news.
   —The Elector has returned to Fehrbellin?
HOHENZOLLERN *(distracted)*:
   Yes, last night.
PRINCE:             Did it occur as planned,
   The victory celebration?—But, of course!
   —And was the Elector present in the church?

HOHENZOLLERN: The Elector and his wife and Natalie.—
    The church was lighted in a fitting manner;
    During the Te Deum we could hear
    Tremendous cannon from the castle square.
    The flags and standards of the Swedes were flying
    As trophies from the pillars, and the victory,
    Upon our sovereign's express command,
    Was mentioned from the pulpit in your name.
PRINCE:
    I've heard!—And now, what else? What's on your mind?
    —Your face, I'd say, is hardly cheerful, friend!
HOHENZOLLERN: With whom have you already spoken, then?
PRINCE: Just recently, with Golz, up at the castle,
    Where I—as well you know—was standing trial.
               *(Pause.)*
HOHENZOLLERN *(observing him anxiously)*:
    Arthur, what's your view of your position,
    Since all these strange developments have changed it?
PRINCE: I? What you and Golz . . . the court itself,—
    The Elector acted as his duty bid him,
    And now he'll do the bidding of his heart.
    "You've blundered," he shall tell me earnestly,
    Then drop a word of death and prison:
    "But now I give you back your liberty . . ."
    Around the sword that won for him the victory
    He winds perhaps some token of his blessing;
    —If not, all right; since that I don't deserve!
HOHENZOLLERN: O Arthur!
               *(He stops short.)*
PRINCE:               Well?
HOHENZOLLERN:             Are you so sure of that?
PRINCE: I'm sure of it! I'm dear to him, I know it,
    Dear as a son; his heart, since early childhood,
    Has shown it to me in a thousand ways.
    What sort of doubt is it that agitates you?
    Did he not seem to revel in my growth
    To youthful glory almost more than I?
    Am I not everything I am through him?
    And he, should he, suspicious and unloving,

Now want to crush and trample in the dust
The plant that he himself has raised, and only
Because it bloomed too quickly and luxuriantly?
I'd not believe it from his greatest enemy,
Much less from you, you who know and love him.

HOHENZOLLERN: You've stood trial in military court
And still believe this?

PRINCE:                     For that very reason!
No one would go as far as this, by God,
Who didn't meditate an act of pardon!
Right there, in fact, before the bar of judgment
I found my confidence in him again.
Was it then a crime deserving death,
Two moments earlier than commanded,
To grind the Swedish might into the dust?
What other mischief am I guilty of?
How could he summon me before this bench
Of heartless judges, sitting there like owls,
Hooting a dirge of firing squads at me,
Unless he meant, serenely, with his veto,
To step into their circle like a god? '
No, friend, he conjures up this night of clouds
Around my head, in order, like the sunrise,
To break all radiant through their murky sphere:
And this caprice I surely can permit him.

HOHENZOLLERN:
And yet the court, they say, has passed its sentence?

PRINCE: So I've heard. For death.

HOHENZOLLERN (*astounded*):    You know already?

PRINCE: Golz was present for the final verdict
And told me later what the outcome was.

HOHENZOLLERN:
Well then, by God . . . ! The sentence doesn't move you?

PRINCE: Me? Oh, not at all.

HOHENZOLLERN:             You're raving mad.
Upon what do you base your confidence?

PRINCE: Upon my sense of him!
                    (*standing up*)
                        Don't, I pray you!

Why should I plague myself with groundless doubts?
      *(considers and sits down again. Pause)*
The judges' sentence had to be for death;
So reads the law that has to guide their judgment.
But sooner than have that sentence carried out,
Or by the signal of some handkerchief
Expose this heart that loves him to a bullet,
Look you, he'd sooner open his own breast
And spill his own heart's blood into the dust.

HOHENZOLLERN: Well, Arthur, I assure you . . .

PRINCE *(resistant):*              O dear friend!

HOHENZOLLERN: The Marshal . . .

PRINCE *(still determined):*      Friend, enough!

HOHENZOLLERN:                   Hear two
                                  [more words!
If they mean nothing, then I'll hold my tongue.

PRINCE *(turning toward him again):*
I know it all, you hear?—Now, what is it?

HOHENZOLLERN: It's strange; a little while ago the Marshal
Presented him the sentence at the castle,
And he, instead of granting you a pardon,
An option even given him on paper,
Asked that it come to him for signature.

PRINCE: So what, I say!

HOHENZOLLERN:      So what?

PRINCE:               For signature?

HOHENZOLLERN: Upon my honor! That I can assure you.

PRINCE: The sentence?—No! The minutes—?

HOHENZOLLERN:              The death sentence.

PRINCE: Who told you that?

HOHENZOLLERN:      He himself, the Marshal!

PRINCE: When?

HOHENZOLLERN: Just before I came.

PRINCE:              On his return?

HOHENZOLLERN: As he was coming down the stairs from him!—
Observing how dismayed I was, he added
That all was not yet lost, and that tomorrow
Held yet another chance to pardon you;
But his pale lips denied their very words,
And seemed to say: I fear it is not so.

PRINCE (*standing up*):
  How could—no!—how could such atrocious
  Resolutions welter in his breast?
  For a flaw upon the diamond just received,
  A flaw that's barely visible with spectacles,
  To have the donor trampled in the dust?
  A deed that purges white the Algerian Dey,
  Adorns Sardanapalus with silver wings,
  All cherub-like, and, as if innocent,
  Cradles in God's right hand all Roman tyrants
  Like babes who've perished at their mothers' breasts!
HOHENZOLLERN (*standing up*): You, friend, had better be
                                    [convinced.
PRINCE: And then the Marshal stood there and said nothing?
HOHENZOLLERN: What should he say?
PRINCE:                          O Heaven! All my hopes!
HOHENZOLLERN: Have you by any chance done anything,
  Be it on purpose or unconsciously,
  That might have hurt his pride?
PRINCE: Never!
HOHENZOLLERN: Think it over!
PRINCE:                    Heavens, never!
  The very shadow of his head was sacred to me!
HOHENZOLLERN: Arthur, don't be angry if I doubt you.
  Count Horn, the Swedish envoy, has arrived.
  His mission, I've been led to understand,
  Concerns Natalie, Princess of Oranien.
  A word your aunt, the Elector's wife, let fall
  Chagrined his Highness in the acutest way,
  They say she has already made her choice.
  You aren't involved in this in any way?
PRINCE: Oh, God! What are you saying?
HOHENZOLLERN:                        Well? Then are you?
PRINCE: I am, my friend; now all is clear to me;
  My courtship of her plunges me to ruin:
  Know that I'm to blame for her refusal,
  Because the Princess is betrothed to me.
HOHENZOLLERN: You rash, unthinking fool! What have you done?
  How often have you heard my faithful warnings!
PRINCE: O friend! Help, rescue me! Or I am done for.

HOHENZOLLERN: There must be an escape from this dilemma!
  Perhaps you should discuss it with your aunt.
PRINCE *(turning):* —Hallo, Guard!
CAVALRYMAN *(in the background):* Here!
PRINCE:                                     Call your officer!—
  *(The Prince hurriedly takes a coat from the wall and*
  *puts on a plumed hat that has been lying on the table.)*
HOHENZOLLERN: Wisely used, this step may bring salvation.
  For if our sovereign and the Swedish king
  Can, for that conscious price, make peace at last,
  You'll see, his heart will soon be reconciled,
  And in a few short hours you shall be free.


SCENE 2


*Enter an officer. The others.*
PRINCE *(to the officer):*
  Stranz, I am entrusted to your custody!
  Allow me, on some very urgent business,
  To leave the prison for an hour.
OFFICER:                              But, Sir,
  You're not entrusted to my custody.
  The orders I've been given simply say,
  To let you go wherever you desire.
PRINCE: Strange! Then I am not a prisoner?
OFFICER: Excuse me, Sir! Your word should be the fetter.
HOHENZOLLERN *(interrupting):*
  Good enough! It's all the same!
PRINCE:                              Farewell!
HOHENZOLLERN: These fetters follow hard upon his heels.
PRINCE: I go up to the castle, to my aunt.
  Two more minutes, and I shall return.
                        *(Exeunt.)*


SCENE 3


*Chamber of the Elector's wife. Enter the Elector's wife and*
*Natalie.*
ELECTOR'S WIFE: Come, my daughter, come! Your hour strikes.

Count Gustav Horn, the Swedish emissary,
And all his company have left the castle;
In your uncle's room I see a light:
Bind your scarf on, softly go to him,
And see what you can do to save your friend.
                    *(They are about to leave.)*

## SCENE 4

*Enter a lady-in-waiting. The others.*
LADY-IN-WAITING: Prince Homburg, gracious lady, waits
                                        [outside!

—I wonder if my eyes are seeing things!
ELECTOR'S WIFE *(taken aback):* O God!
NATALIE:                        In person?
ELECTOR'S WIFE:                            He's in
                                        [custody!

LADY-IN-WAITING: He's standing just outside in hat and coat,
    Distraught and urgent, begging to be heard.
ELECTOR'S WIFE *(exasperated):*
    The rash, unthinking man! To break his word!
NATALIE: Who knows what's oppressing him.
ELECTOR'S WIFE *(after some consideration):* Admit him!
                    *(She sits down on a chair.)*

## SCENE 5

*Enter the Prince of Homburg. The others.*
PRINCE: O my mother!
                    *(He falls on his knees at her feet.)*
ELECTOR'S WIFE: Prince! What do you want here!?
PRINCE: O my Mother, let me clasp your knees!
ELECTOR'S WIFE *(with suppressed emotion):*
    A prisoner, Prince, and still you dare to come?
    Why add new misdemeanors to the old?
PRINCE *(urgently):* Do you know what has befallen me?
ELECTOR'S WIFE: I do, poor soul, but what am I to do?
PRINCE: O mother, would you speak that way if death

Chilled your trembling soul as it does mine?
You seem to me endowed with heavenly powers,
Redeemers! You, the Princess and the ladies!
I could fall upon the neck of anyone,
The lowest stableboy who tends your horse,
The meanest servant, begging him to save me!
Upon all God's wide earth I am alone,
Helpless, left behind and powerless!

ELECTOR'S WIFE:
　　You're quite beside yourself! What's happened to you?
PRINCE: Tonight along the path that led me here
　　I saw the grave, agape in sudden torchlight,
　　Which on the morrow shall receive my bones.
　　Look, Aunt, these eyes that gaze upon you now
　　They mean to cloak in darkness, and this breast—
　　They want to pierce this breast with deadly bullets.
　　Reserved already on the market square
　　Are windows that will face the dreary spectacle;—
　　And the man who upon Life's pinnacle today
　　Still views the future like a fairyland
　　Shall tomorrow rot between two narrow boards,
　　A tombstone there to testify: he was!
　　　　　*(Shaken by his words, Natalie, who has been*
　　　　　*leaning on the shoulder of a lady-in-waiting,*
　　　　*at some distance, sits down at a table and weeps.)*

ELECTOR'S WIFE: Hear me, my son! If such is Heaven's will,
　　You'll arm yourself with courage and restraint!
PRINCE: Oh, God's world . . . O Mother! . . . is so fair!
　　Oh, let me not, before the hour strikes,
　　Descend to those black shadows, I implore you!
　　If he must punish me for doing wrong,
　　Why must it be the bullet after all?
　　Let him relieve me of my offices,
　　Demote me, if the law requires it,
　　Discharge me from the army: God in heaven!
　　I ask for nothing honorable anymore!

ELECTOR'S WIFE:
　　Stand up, my son! Stand up! What are you saying?
　　You're overwrought. You must compose yourself.

PRINCE: Not before you've given me your word, Aunt,
   To take the step that rescues my existence,
   And, pleadingly, to brave his proudest look!
   Your girlhood friend, my mother, when she died,
   Entrusted me to you at Homburg, saying,
   "Be a mother to him when I'm gone!"
   Deeply moved, and kneeling at her side,
   You pressed her hand to you and answered her:
   "He'll be to me as if he were my son."
   Now I must remind you of that pledge!
   Go, as if I were your son, and say:
   "Be merciful, I beg you! Set him free!"
   Then . . . Ah! . . . come back to me and say: Thou art!
ELECTOR'S WIFE: My precious son, it is already done,
   But everything I pleaded was in vain!
PRINCE: I give up every claim to happiness.
   As for Natalie, don't forget to tell him
   I desire her no longer; in my breast
   All tenderness for her has been snuffed out.
   She's free, free as the doe upon the heath,
   To betroth herself with hand and mouth again,
   As if I'd never been, and if it be
   To Swedish Karl Gustav, I applaud her.
   I go to my estates along the Rhine,
   There to build and to destroy again,
   To sow and reap until I drip with sweat,
   Consume alone, as if for wife and child;
   And when I've harvested, to sow again;
   And thus pursue this life across the heavens,
   Till sinking down at evening, it expires.
ELECTOR'S WIFE:
   So be it! Now go back to your imprisonment;
   That is the first condition of my favor.
      *(Prince of Homburg stands up and turns toward Natalie.)*
PRINCE: You poor girl! You weep because the sun
   Lights all your hopes today the way to death.
   Your first affection was inclined toward me
   And now your expression tells me, true as gold,
   No other man shall ever have your love.

What comforts have I left, poor thing, to lend you?
Get thee to a convent on the Main, I say;
Go join your cousin Thurn, or search the mountains
For a boy with curls as fair as mine;
Buy him with gold and silver, show him how
To stammer "Mother!", press him to your breast,
And when he's bigger, then explain to him
How to close a dying person's eyes!
That's all the happiness that lies before you!

> *(Natalie stands up, bravely and encouragingly,
> and puts her hand in his.)*

NATALIE: Return to your imprisonment, young hero,
And on your way there, calmly look again
At the grave that has been opened for you.
It is no wider, no, nor any darker,
Than what you've faced a thousand times in battle!
In the meantime, true to you till death,
I'll try a saving word for you with Uncle.
Perhaps I shall succeed in moving him
And so deliver you from all affliction.

> *(Pause.)*

PRINCE *(entranced, folding his hands in prayer):*
Had you two wings, O Maiden, on your shoulders,
I would surely take you for an angel!—
Dare I believe my ears, O God? You speak for me?
Where was it hid, this quiver of persuasions,
Until today, dear child, that now you dare
To approach our lord in such a matter?—
O light of hope, that quickens me again!

NATALIE: God will furnish me with darts that strike!—
But if the Elector cannot change, can*not*,
The sentence of the court, so be it, then!
O brave one, you will bravely acquiesce.
He who has won a thousand times in life
Knows also how to die victorious.

ELECTOR'S WIFE: Go! The favorable moment slips away!

PRINCE: May all the saints defend you! Fare you well!
God speed you! And whatever you achieve,
Allow me at least a sign of your success!

> *(Exeunt.)*

# Act IV

## SCENE 1

*Chamber of the Elector.*

*Holding some papers, the Elector stands at a candlelit table. Natalie enters through the middle door and at some distance from him goes down on her knees.*

*Pause.*

NATALIE *(kneeling):* My noble uncle, Frederick of Brandenburg!
ELECTOR *(putting his papers aside):* Natalie!
                    *(He tries to raise her to her feet.)*
NATALIE:                              Let me be!
ELECTOR:                                      What do
                                  [you want, love?
NATALIE: In the dust here at your feet, as suits my station,
    To plead for Cousin Homburg's absolution!
    I do not want to save him for myself . . .
    My heart desires him, I confess to you,
    . . . I do not want to save him for myself . . .
    Let him wed whatever wife he will,
    I only want to see him live, dear uncle,
    Apart, free, independent, self-sufficient,
    Like the single flower that gives me pleasure.
    I entreat this of you, highest lord and friend,
    And know that you will hearken to my plea.
ELECTOR *(raising her):*
    My little maid! What kind of words were those?
    —You know of Cousin Homburg's recent crime?
NATALIE: O Uncle dear!
ELECTOR:                    Well, was it not a crime?
NATALIE: O this fair-haired, blue-eyed misbegotten son!
    Whom, even 'ere he stammers, "I implore you,"
    Forgiveness should be raising from the ground:
    You surely would not kick him from your side!
    If only for his mother's sake, who bore him,
    You'll press him to your heart and say, "Don't weep!
    You're dear to me as loyalty itself!"

Was it not ardor for your glorious name
That tempted him to violate the rules
At such a crucial moment in the battle?
And what a noble youth in his transgression!
Did he not manfully crush the serpent's head?
First crown him as the victor, then behead him?
That's not what history demands of you;
That looks so unfeelingly sublime
That one could almost label it inhuman:
And God made nothing gentler than you.
ELECTOR: My darling child! Behold! Were I a tyrant,
  Your words—I feel it keenly—would have melted
  The heart that's pounding in this brazen breast.
  But now I ask you: may I suppress
  The sentence that the judges have delivered?
  What would be the consequence of that?
NATALIE: For whom? For you?
ELECTOR:                 For me? Not just for me!
  Do you know nothing higher, maid, than me?
  Is such a sacred place unknown to you
  As what we call in camp the Fatherland?
NATALIE: Oh, Sire! Why this concern? The Fatherland?!
  It shall not—just because you're moved to mercy—
  Fall in pieces and sink into ruin.
  In fact, what you, who have been raised in camp,
  Would call a loss of order, willfully
  To suspend the judges' sentence in this case,
  To me inaugurates the fairest order:
  The battle code shall govern, that I know,
  But so shall tenderhearted feelings.
  The Fatherland that you established for us
  Stands, a solid fortress, noble uncle:
  It shall weather much more dangerous storms
  Than this unanointed victory.
  The future shall enlarge it wondrously,
  A grandchild's care will make it grow more lovely,
  With towers numerous, like a fairyland,
  A joy to friends, a terror to all foes!
  It does not need this mortar, cold and wasted,

From friendly blood, in order to outlive
The peace and splendor of my uncle's autumn.

ELECTOR: Does Cousin Homburg think so?

NATALIE:                           Cousin Homburg?

ELECTOR: Does he think it matters little for the Fatherland
If impulse governs, or the code of law?

NATALIE: Ah, this youth!

ELECTOR:            Well?

NATALIE:                 O Uncle dearest!
—In reply to what you ask, I've only tears.

ELECTOR *(disconcerted):*
Why, my little daughter? What has happened?

NATALIE *(hesitating):*
He thinks of nothing now but this, his rescue!
The rifle barrels on the sentries' shoulders
Look so fierce, that, stunned and nearly fainting,
He retains but one desire, to stay alive.
He could watch as all of Brandenburg
Were swallowed up in thunderclaps and lightning
And wouldn't even ask, "What's happening?"
Oh, what a hero's heart you've broken, Sir!
               *(She turns away, crying.)*

ELECTOR *(utterly amazed):*
My dearest Natalie, I don't believe it!
He begs for mercy? That's impossible!

NATALIE: Oh, would that you had never, never damned him!

ELECTOR: No, speak! He begs for mercy?—God in heaven!
What's happened, my dear child? Why are you weeping?
You've seen him? Spoken with him? Tell me everything!

NATALIE *(leaning against his chest):*
Just this moment in my aunt's apartments,
Where, picture to yourself, in hat and cloak,
He'd stolen under cover of the twilight,
Distraught and shy, in secret, quite unworthy,
A disenchanting sight! To be lamented!
No hero praised by history, I would say,
Could sink to such a miserable state.
Just look at me, a woman! I recoil
From the worm beneath my heel: but even death

In horrid lion-shape would never find me
So without resources, so depressed,
So utterly devoid of real courage.
—Oh, what is human greatness, human glory!
ELECTOR *(perplexed):* Well then, by the God of all Creation,
Take heart again, my child: he is free!
NATALIE: How, my gracious lord?
ELECTOR:                         I say, he's pardoned!
I'll issue him the proper form at once!
NATALIE: O dearest! Is it really true?
ELECTOR:                         You hear it!
NATALIE: He shall be forgiven? shall not die?
ELECTOR: Upon my oath! I swear to you! How could I
Oppose the stand of such a warrior?
His intuition, as you know full well,
I trust and honor in my inmost soul:
If he can hold the sentence for unjust,
I'll set aside the article: he's free!
                        *(brings her a chair)*
Here, won't you sit down for just a moment?
         *(He goes to the table, sits down, and writes.)*
NATALIE *(aside):*
O heart, why dost thou pound against thy house?
ELECTOR: The Prince is in the castle still?
NATALIE:                             Pardon!
He has returned to his imprisonment!
           *(The Elector finishes and seals the letter
           and goes over to Natalie with it.)*
ELECTOR: My Natalie! My little daughter weeps!
And I, to whom her joy has been entrusted,
Must cloud the heaven of her darling eyes!
            *( fastens an arm around her waist)*
Will you take this note to him yourself?
NATALIE: You mean, into the prison?
ELECTOR *(pressing the letter into her hand):* Why not? Haiduks!
                  *(Enter Haiduks.)*
Let the coach be brought around! The Princess
Has some business with Commander Homburg!
                *(Exit Haiduks.)*

So he himself can thank you for his life.
                    *(embraces her)*
Precious child! Now am I forgiven?
NATALIE *(after a pause)*:
    What stirred your grace so suddenly, my Lord,
    I do not know and do not mean to ask.
    But this I feel, look you, in my heart,
    That you would not unkindly sport with me:
    Let the note contain what it contains,
    But I believe in pardon—and I thank you!
ELECTOR: Indeed, my little daughter, yes, indeed!
    As sure as Cousin Homburg wishes it.
                    *(Exeunt.)*


## SCENE 2

*Enter Princess Natalie. Two ladies-in-waiting and Captain Reuss follow.*
NATALIE *(hurriedly)*: What do you bring, Count? From my
                                        [regiment?
    Is it important? Can it wait 'til morning?
REUSS *(handing her a written paper)*:
    A note from Colonel Kottwitz, gracious lady!
NATALIE: Quick! Give it here! What's in it?
                    *(She opens it.)*
REUSS:                              A petition,
    Straightforward, but respectful, as you see,
    Addressed to his illustrious Majesty,
    In favor of our Prince, Commander Homburg.
NATALIE *(reading)*: "A supplication humbly submitted
    By the Regiment of the Princess of Oranien."—
                    *(pause)*
    Who drew up this petition?
REUSS:                    As you can see,
    The untutored hand itself of Colonel Kottwitz.
    —Look you, his noble name begins the list.
NATALIE: The other thirty signatures that follow . . . ?

REUSS: The names of officers, most gracious one,
  Organized in order of their rank.
NATALIE: And now to me? the petition comes to me?
REUSS: My Princess, only humbly to request
  That you shall likewise sign your name, as chief,
  On that first line, the blank one at the top.
               *(Pause.)*
NATALIE: I hear, the sovereign, of his own accord,
  Intends the Prince my noble cousin's pardon,
  And such a step shall therefore not be needed.
REUSS *(overjoyed)*: How? Really?
NATALIE:              Never mind, I won't refuse it;
  If wisely used, this sheet may even lend
  More weight to tip the scales in his decision.
  May, in fact, provide a welcome pretext . . .
  And so, at your request, I place my name,
  Herewith, atop the others on the list.
            *(She is about to write.)*
REUSS: This shall bind us to you yet more warmly!
               *(Pause.)*
NATALIE *(turning toward him)*:
  I see none but my regiment, Count Reuss!
  Why don't I find the Bomsdorf cuirassiers,
  The Götz dragoons and those of Anhalt-Pless?
REUSS: Not, as you may fear, because their hearts
  Beat for him less fervently than ours!—
  Unfortunately for this supplication,
  Kottwitz has been stationed off in Arnstein,
  Divided from those other regiments
  Which lie encamped around the city here.
  This paper lacks a safe and easy way
  To unfold its power freely everywhere.
NATALIE: But thus, I think, it has too little weight?—
  Are you certain, Count, that if you stayed in town
  And asked the gentlemen assembled here,
  They too would lend support to this petition?
REUSS: Here in town, my lady? Man for man!
  The whole cavalry would pledge itself
  By signature; I do believe, by God,

Subscription could successfully be offered
To the entire army of the Brandenburgs.

NATALIE *(after a pause):*
Then why not send out several officers
To carry on the business here in camp?

REUSS: Forgive me, but the Colonel has refused!
He would not, he declared, do anything
That could be christened with an evil name.

NATALIE: Extraordinary man! Now bold, now timid!
—As luck would have it, pressed by other business,
The Elector gave me leave, I now recall,
To order Kottwitz's removal here,
As the Arnstein stabling is too limited.
I'll sit down straightaway and write the letter.
*(She sits down and writes.)*

REUSS: Excellent, my lady! No event
Could more favorably coincide with this petition.

NATALIE *(while writing):*
Use it to advantage, good Count Reuss.
*( finishes, seals the envelope, and stands up)*
In the meantime, understand, this letter stays
In your portfolio: you shall not leave
For Arnstein or deliver this to Kottwitz
Until I give more definite instructions.
*(She hands him the letter.)*

HAIDUK *(entering):* My lady, on my lord's command, the coach
Stands ready for departure in the courtyard.

NATALIE: Bring it to the gate! I'll be right down.
*(Pause. Pensively she steps up to the table and puts on her gloves.)*
Noble Count, perhaps you'd give me escort
To the Prince. I have to speak with him.
There would be room for you in my conveyance.

REUSS: Indeed I would, my lady! What an honor!
*(He offers her his arm.)*

NATALIE *(to her lady-in-waiting):*
Follow me, my friends! It may well be
That I'll decide about the letter there.
*(Exeunt.)*

## SCENE 3

*The Prince's prison cell.*
*The Prince of Homburg hangs up his hat and slumps down onto
a floor cushion.*
PRINCE: Life's a journey, says the holy man.
   Admittedly, a short one. From six feet
   Above the ground to six feet under it.
   I wish that I could rest me halfway there!
   Who bears his head today upon his shoulders
   Hangs it tomorrow trembling on his breast,
   And it lies the following day beside his heel.
   They say the sun in fact shines there as well
   And over even gayer fields. I'm sure!
   It's just a pity that the eye must rot
   Which should behold all that magnificence.

## SCENE 4

*Enter Princess Natalie, escorted by Reuss. Ladies-in-waiting fol-
low. A guide with a torch precedes them all. Prince of Homburg.*
GUIDE: Your Majesty, the Princess of Oranien!
PRINCE *(standing up):* Natalie!
GUIDE:                Here in person, Sir!
NATALIE *(bowing to Reuss):*
   Please leave us for a moment to ourselves.
          *(Exit Reuss and the guide.)*
PRINCE: My precious lady!
NATALIE:           Dear, beloved cousin!
PRINCE: Well, what brings you here? How looks it? Speak!
NATALIE: Good! All good! As I've already told you,
   You are pardoned, free. Here is a letter
   In his writing to corroborate it.
PRINCE: No! I must be dreaming! It's impossible!
NATALIE: Read it! Read the letter! Then you'll see!
PRINCE *(reading aloud):*
   "When I arrested you, my Prince of Homburg,
   For your untimely charge, too soon accomplished,

It seemed to me that I fulfilled my duty;
For this I reckoned on your own approval.
If you maintain you've suffered an injustice,
I beg of you to send me word at once,
And I will send your sabre back to you."
                    *(Natalie pales. Pause.*
          *The Prince looks at her questioningly.)*
NATALIE *(with an expression of sudden joy):*
    Well then, you see? You've only to send word . . . !
    O dear beloved friend!
                    *(She presses his hand.)*
PRINCE:                     My cherished lady!
NATALIE: O blessed hour to which I am the witness!
    Here! Take it! Here's a pen! Take it and write!
PRINCE: And here the signature?
NATALIE:                     The "F", his mark!
    O Bork! Oh, let us celebrate! I knew it,
    His gentleness is boundless as the sea!
    Get him a chair! He'll write to him at once!
PRINCE: He says, if I be of the opinion—?
NATALIE *(interrupting):*                     Surely!
    Quick! Sit down! I'll dictate your reply.
                    *(She offers him a chair.)*
PRINCE: —I want to read the letter one more time.
NATALIE *(tearing it out of his hand):*
    What for? You've seen the vault at the cathedral,
    Gaping up at you with open jaws?—
    You're wasting precious time. Sit down and write!
PRINCE *(smiling):*
    You're acting now, I say, as if that grave
    Were poised to spring upon me like a panther.
                    *(He sits down and picks up a pen.)*
NATALIE *(turning away and starting to weep):*
    If you don't wish to make me angry, write!
          *(The Prince rings for a servant; the servant enters.)*
PRINCE: Pen, paper, wax and signet ring!
          *(After the servant has fetched these, he exits.*
*The Prince starts writing. Pause. Prince tears up the letter he has
    just begun and throws it under the table.)*

PRINCE: A stupid start!
> *(He takes another sheet.)*

NATALIE *(retrieving the first)*:
> How? What did you just say?
My God, that's very good! That's excellent!

PRINCE *(murmuring into his beard)*:
Pah! A scoundrel's wording! Not a prince's!
I have to find a better turn of phrase.
> *(Pause. He reaches for the Elector's letter, which*
> *Natalie still holds in her hand.)*
What did he really say there in the letter?

NATALIE *(avoiding his hand)*: Nothing!

PRINCE:                          Give it here!

NATALIE:                                   You've read
[it!

PRINCE *(grabbing it)*:
I want to see how to express myself.
> *(He unfolds it and reads.)*

NATALIE *(aside)*: Almighty God! Now all is lost for him!

PRINCE *(disconcerted)*: Look there! Extraordinary! On my life!
You must have overlooked this part!

NATALIE:                          No!—Which?

PRINCE: He calls for my decision in the matter.

NATALIE: Well, so?

PRINCE:              That's gallant of him! Really noble!
The very words of magnanimity!

NATALIE: Oh, yes, his kindness, friend, is limitless!
—But now, you do your part too, and write,
As he desires. You see, it's just the pretext,
Just the outward form that he requires:
As soon as he's received it, the affair
Is over in a twinkling!

PRINCE *(putting aside the letter)*:
> No, my love!
I want to think about it overnight.

NATALIE: You unpredictable . . . ! What turn of mind . . . ?
What for? And why?

PRINCE *(rising impassioned from his chair)*:
> I beg you not to ask me!

You've not reflected on the letter's contents!
I cannot write him under these conditions
That he has wronged me. And if, in this mood,
You force me now to send an answer to him,
By God, I'll put, "You've dealt with me correctly."
*(He sits down at the table again with arms folded
and looks over the letter.)*

NATALIE *(pale)*: You're absolutely mad! What did you say?
*(She bends over him, touched.)*

PRINCE *(pressing her hand)*: Wait a bit! It seems to me . . .
*(He reflects)*

NATALIE:                                 What's that?

PRINCE: I've almost figured out what I shall write.

NATALIE: Homburg!

PRINCE *(picking up the pen)*:
                  I'm listening! What now?

NATALIE:                         My sweet friend!
I praise the impulse quickening your heart.
But this I swear: the regiment is ready,
Ready to perform your funeral rites
Tomorrow with a last salute of guns
Over the mound of your oblivious grave.
If, noble as you are, you still cannot
Oppose the sentence, still not countermand it,
Cannot do as he demands of you:
Then, I assure you, as the matter stands,
He shall treat you with sublime detachment
And, full of pity, have you shot.

PRINCE *(writing)*:                No matter!

NATALIE: No matter?

PRINCE:            Let him deal as he may!
It's proper here to do as I see fit!

NATALIE *(frightened, nears him)*:
You prodigious man, what have you written?

PRINCE *(finishing)*:
"Signed, Homburg; on the twelfth, at Fehrbellin—";
I'm finished.—Hey, Franz!
*(He encloses and seals the letter.)*

NATALIE:                O God in heaven!

PRINCE *(standing up)*:
   Take this to the castle to my sovereign!
                    *(Exit the servant.)*
   He faces me with so much dignity,
   I won't confront him totally unworthy!
   Guilt, important guilt, weighs on my breast.
   If I must argue with him for my pardon,
   I'd just as soon know nothing of his mercy!
NATALIE *(kissing him)*: Take this kiss! And if a dozen bullets
   Shot you down, I could not help but shout
   With joy and weep and say: You gladden me!
   —Meanwhile, if you can follow your heart's bidding,
   It's granted that I also follow mine.
   —Count Reuss!
            *(A guide opens the door. Reuss enters.)*
REUSS:          Here!
NATALIE:               Go now with the letter,
   Go to Arnstein and to Colonel Kottwitz!
   The regiment shall move, his Highness wills it.
   I want it here before the midnight hour.
                    *(Exeunt.)*

# Act V

## SCENE 1

*Hall in the castle.*

*Enter the Elector, half-dressed, from an adjoining chamber. Count Truchss, Count Hohenzollern, and Captain Golz. Pages with lights.*
ELECTOR: Kottwitz? With the Princess' troops? In town?
TRUCHSS *(opening the window)*:
   Yes, Majesty! They stand outside the castle.
ELECTOR: Well! Solve this riddle for me, won't you, Sirs?
   —Who called him here?
HOHENZOLLERN: I do not know, my lord.

ELECTOR: The station I assigned to him was Arnstein!
  Quick! Send someone down to bring him here!
GOLZ: He shall appear before you in a moment, Sire!
ELECTOR: Where is he?
GOLZ:               In the Council Hall, I hear,
  Where the entire force of officers
  Who serve the House of Brandenburg are gathered.
ELECTOR: Why? To what purpose?
HOHENZOLLERN:             That I do not know.
TRUCHSS: Permit us also, Sire, to proceed there.
ELECTOR: To the Council Hall?
HOHENZOLLERN:          The gathering of lords!
  We gave our word to put in our appearance.
ELECTOR *(after a brief pause):*
  You are dismissed.
GOLZ:            Come, worthy gentlemen!
               *(Exeunt officers.)*


## SCENE 2

*Elector. Later on, two servants.*
ELECTOR: Strange indeed!—Were I the Dey of Tunis,
  I'd sound the alarm in such an ambiguous case.
  I'd lay the silken cord upon my table,
  And at the gate, well blocked with palisades,
  I'd have them draw up howitzers and cannons.
  Yet, as it's old Hans Kottwitz from Priegnitz,
  Who comes unsanctioned here, of his own will,
  I'll act as it befits tradition here:
  Of those three last gray locks on that bald head
  I'll take firm hold of one and gently lead him,
  With all twelve squadrons, back to camp at Arnstein.
  Why arouse the city from its sleep?
    *(After stepping over to the window again for a moment,*
       *he goes to the table and rings; two servants enter.)*
ELECTOR: Run down and ask, as if in idleness,
  What's happening at the prison.

FIRST SERVANT:                    Yes, Sire!
                    *(Exit.)*
ELECTOR *(to the other one)*:
   But you, you go and bring my clothes to me!
*(The servant goes and fetches his regalia. The Elector dresses and
                    adorns himself with it.)*


SCENE 3

*Enter Field-Marshal Dörfling. The others.*
FIELD-MARSHAL: Rebellion, my Elector!
ELECTOR *(busy dressing)*:                    Easy, easy!
   I abhor it, as you are well aware,
   To have my chamber entered unannounced.
   —What do you want?
FIELD-MARSHAL:             Sire, an event (your pardon!)
   Of special gravity impels me here.
   Colonel Kottwitz moved without instructions
   Here to town; a hundred officers
   Gather with him in the Hall of Knights.
   A sheet is being passed around their ranks
   Intended to infringe upon your rights.
ELECTOR: I'm well aware of that!—What should it be,
   But a petition in the Prince's favor,
   Whom the Court has sentenced to the bullet?
FIELD-MARSHAL:
   That's it, by God! You've hit the mark exactly!
ELECTOR:
   Well, good! My heart is present there among them.
FIELD-MARSHAL:
   They say, they plan to come today, the madmen,
   To hand you their petition in the castle,
   And if you, with unreconciled fury,
   Insist upon the sentence—dare I tell you?—
   They'll free him from your custody by force!
ELECTOR *(somberly)*: Who told you this?
FIELD-MARSHAL:                    Who told me? Lady
                                        [Retzow,

A woman you can count on, my wife's cousin,
This evening at her uncle's house, the Bailiff's,
She heard some men who'd just arrived from camp,
Boasting of the daring enterprise.

ELECTOR: A man must tell us that, before I listen!
Then with my boot set firmly at his door,
I shall defend him from these youthful heroes.

FIELD-MARSHAL: Sire, I swear to you, if it's at all
Your design to grant the Prince a pardon:
Do it, before some odious step is taken!
You know how every army loves its hero:
Do not allow the spark that leaps within it
To kindle wicked and devouring flames.
Kottwitz and the group that he's assembled
Don't yet know I've loyally forewarned you;
Before he comes, return the Prince his sabre,
Send it back to him, as he deserves!
Give the journals one more noble deed
And one less criminal one to write about.

ELECTOR: First I have to know the Prince's mind.
Arbitrariness, as you must know,
Did not arrest him and cannot release him.—
When the gentlemen arrive, I'll speak with them.

FIELD-MARSHAL *(aside):*
He is proof against each arrow, damn it!


## SCENE 4

*Enter two Haiducks, one holding a letter. The others.*

FIRST HAIDUCK:
Sire, Colonel Kottwitz, Hennings, Truchss, and others
Entreat an audience.

ELECTOR *(to the other Haiduck, taking an envelope from him):*
From the Prince of Homburg?

SECOND HAIDUCK: Yes, your Highness!

ELECTOR:                                    Who gave it to you?

SECOND HAIDUCK:
The Swiss who now stands watch before the gate,
Who received it from the Prince's orderly.

*(The Elector steps up to the table, reads, then turns and calls a page.)*

ELECTOR: Prittwitz! The death sentence! Bring it here to me!
—And the passport for Count Horn, the Swedish envoy!
*(Exit the page. To the first Haiduck)*
Let Kottwitz and his followers come in!


## SCENE 5

*Enter Colonel Kottwitz, Hennings, Count Truchss, Hohenzollern, Sparren, Reuss, captains Golz and Stranz, and other colonels and officers. The others.*

KOTTWITZ *(with the petition)*:
Suffer me, my most exalted lord,
On behalf of your entire army,
Humbly to submit to you this paper.

ELECTOR: Before I take it, Kottwitz, please explain:
Who summoned you this evening to the city?

KOTTWITZ *(staring at him)*:
With the dragoons?

ELECTOR:         With the regiment!—
I had assigned you Arnstein as your station.

KOTTWITZ: Your orders summoned me, your Highness!

ELECTOR: How?—Show me the paper!

KOTTWITZ:         Here, my lord!

ELECTOR *(reading)*: "Signed, Natalie—Fehrbellin—by order
Of my most exalted uncle, Frederick."—

KOTTWITZ: By God, my liege and lord, I dare not think
This order is unknown to you.

ELECTOR:         No, no!
Please understand me—Who delivered this?

KOTTWITZ: Count Reuss!

ELECTOR *(after a moment's pause)*:
What's more, . . . I'd like to welcome you!—
To Colonel Homburg, who has heard his sentence,
You and your twelve squadrons are appointed
To do him final honors in the morning.

KOTTWITZ *(frightened)*: How, my illustrious lord?

ELECTOR *(giving back the order):*                    The regiment
  Still stands in night and fog outside the castle?
KOTTWITZ: The night, forgive . . .
ELECTOR:                              Why hasn't it moved in?
KOTTWITZ: It has moved in, my lord, as you commanded.
  It already has its quarters in the city.
ELECTOR *(turning toward the window):*
  How? Two moments back . . . Well now, by heaven!
  You found your stabling quickly. All the better!
  Again I bid you welcome. Now, what news?
KOTTWITZ: Sire, this petition from your faithful army.
ELECTOR: Present it!
KOTTWITZ:                 But that word your lips let fall
  Has dashed my hopes.
ELECTOR:                        Another word can mend them.
                *(reads)*
  "Petition, begging most supreme reprieve
  For our leader, capitally indicated,
  General Frederick, Prince of Hessen-Homburg."
            *(to the officers)*
  A noble name, gentlemen! Not unworthy
  That you should intercede with such support!
         *(looks at the sheet again)*
  Who drafted this petition?
KOTTWITZ:                    I did, Sire.
ELECTOR: The Prince has been instructed of its contents?
KOTTWITZ: Not in any way! It was conceived
  Among us and concluded there as well.
ELECTOR: Give me your patience for just one more moment.
  *(steps up to the table and reads over the sheet. Long pause)*
  Hm! Unusual!—Veteran though you are,
  You defend the Prince's action? justify
  His charge on Wrangel, prior to the signal?
KOTTWITZ: So stands Kottwitz! Yes, my illustrious lord!
ELECTOR: But this was not your opinion in the field.
KOTTWITZ: I judged it far too hastily, my lord!
  I should have yielded more complacently;
  The Prince is highly competent in battle.
  While the Swedish forces faltered on the left,

Their right flank was engaged in reinforcement.
Had he awaited your explicit orders,
They would have gained new footholds in the gorges,
And you never would have won the victory.

ELECTOR: So! It pleases you to see it that way, does it?
I sent off Colonel Hennings, as you know,
To burn the bridgehead guarding Wrangel's rear.
If you had not infringed upon my orders,
Hennings' blow would surely have succeeded.
In two hours' time he would have burned the bridges
And established new positions on the Rhyn.
And Wrangel would have been, lock, stock and barrel,
Demolished in the marshes and the ditches!

KOTTWITZ: But only a bungling amateur, not you,
Has got to have the highest wreath of Fate!
You've taken, till today, what it can grant you.
The haughty dragon, threatening our land,
Is driven from it with a bloody pate:
What more could happen in a single day?
What's it to you, if, for two more weeks,
He licks his wounds, exhausted, in the sand?
Now we've learned the art of beating him,
We crave the chance to take him on again.
Let us meet with Wrangel one more time,
In all our vigor, man to man! We'll finish them,
And send them flying back into the Baltic!
Rome was not erected in a day.

ELECTOR: With what assurance, fool, can you assert that,
When anyone upon the battle chariot
May take the reins from me, of his own will?
You mean to say, that Luck may always be there
To grant a wreath for insubordination?
I want no illegitimate victory,
Fortune's bastard child; I want the law,
The upright mother of my crown, secure
To bear me an entire race of victories.

KOTTWITZ: Sire, the most supreme legality
Your generals' breast should feel, and hearken to,
Should not be the letter of your will;

It is the Fatherland, it is the crown,
It is yourself, upon whose head that garland rests.
I ask, what do you care about the rule
By which he's routed, if the enemy
Still sinks with all his banners at your feet?
The rule that beats him, that's the most supreme!
Should the fiery troops that cleave to you
Become a simple tool, like the sword,
That hangs there lifeless in your golden belt?
The wretched soul, the unprophetic mind,
Who was the first to teach that! How myopic
The statesmanship that, based on one example,
Where pure emotion proves itself disastrous,
Forgets ten others in our history,
Where only true emotion brings salvation!
Do I shed my blood for you in battle
For pay, be it in honor or in coin?
God forbid! It's much too good for that.
For myself alone, in quiet independence,
I take delight in your magnificence,
The growth and glory of your splendid name!
That is the wage for which my heart is spent.
Assume now, that for this unbidden victory
You let the Prince be shot; and I tomorrow,
Likewise unbidden, glimpsed a victory,
And like a shepherd with his friends, surprise it
With all my men somewhere among the hills.
By God, I'd be a scoundrel if I didn't
Eagerly repeat the Prince's action!
And if, with battlecode in hand, you said:
"Kottwitz, you have forfeited your head!",
I'd say, "I knew that, Sire; take it! Here!
When I swore my loyalty to your crown,
My head was not excluded from the bargain.
I give you nothing that is not your own.
ELECTOR: With you, you wonderful old gentleman,
I'm never done. Each word's another bribe,
Tempting me with cunning oratory,
Me, who likes you, as you so well know.

To take my case, I call an advocate
Who'll end this argument.
               *(rings; Enter a servant.)*
                  The Prince of Homburg!
Bring him from his prison here to us!
               *(Exit the servant.)*
He shall instruct you, that I guarantee,
What battle discipline and duty mean!
The note I have from him reads otherwise
Than that sophistic principle of freedom
You recite before me like a schoolboy.
        *(He steps to the table again and reads.)*
KOTTWITZ *(startled):* Bring whom? Call whom—?
HENNINGS:                            The Prince
                            [himself?

TRUCHSS: Impossible!
   *(The officers, upset, disperse and talk among themselves.)*
ELECTOR: Who is the author of this second letter?
HOHENZOLLERN: I, my lord!
ELECTOR *(reading):*        "Proof, that Elector Frederick
  Himself the Prince's deed . . ." Well now, by heaven!
  I call that bold!
  What! You cast the blame on me, the motive
  For the crime committed in the battle?
HOHENZOLLERN: On you, my Elector! Yes, I, Hohenzollern!
ELECTOR: Well, that, by God, surpasses every fancy!
  The one man tells me that he's innocent,
  The next man tells me I'm the guilty one!—
  How do you intend to prove this thesis?
HOHENZOLLERN: Your Majesty, you will recall the night
  We came upon the Prince, so deep asleep
  Beneath the plane trees in the castle garden:
  He might have dreamed of victory on the morrow,
  For in his hand he held a laurel wreath.
  You, as if to probe his inmost soul,
  Took his wreath and, smiling, wound the chain
  You wear upon your neck, around its leaves.
  You gave the wreath, and necklace thus entwined,
  Into the hands of your illustrious niece.

Reddening at such a wondrous sight,
The Prince stands up to take such sweet rewards,
Offered him by such beloved hands:
But you, retreating quickly with the Princess,
Evade his grasp; the door receives you all;
All vanish, maiden, necklace, laurel wreath,
And, enveloped by the night, he's left alone,
Holding in his hand a glove he's snatched,
With no idea from whom.

ELECTOR: What glove was it?

HOHENZOLLERN:                 Sire, let me finish!
The thing was done in jest, but I soon learned
Just how significant it was for him.
For now, when through the garden's lower gate
I circle idly back as if to join him,
I waken him and he regains his senses,
The memory of it bathes him in delight.
You cannot imagine anything more moving.
Recounting it to me in perfect detail,
As if the whole thing had been a dream,
He says, he's never dreamed so vividly—:
A firm belief takes shape within his mind
That Heaven itself has given him a sign:
All the images his soul has seen,
Maiden, wreath and royal ornament,
God shall grant him on the day of battle.

ELECTOR: Very strange!—And what about the glove—?

HOHENZOLLERN: This fragment of his dream, stuck to his hand,
At once destroys and strengthens his conviction.
At first he stares at it with wondering eyes—
The color's white, the style and shape would suit
A lady's hand, but since he'd been with none—
Who might have left it with him in the garden—
But then I interrupt his fabulations,
And call him to the castle for the briefing.
So, forgetting what he cannot apprehend,
Distractedly he puts the glove away.

ELECTOR: And then?

HOHENZOLLERN:      Then with his tablet and his pencil,

He goes inside to hear the battle orders
With worshipful attention from the Marshal;
By chance, the Princess and your noble wife
Are also there, preparing to depart.
Yet who cannot imagine the amazement
That seizes him when she seeks the very glove
That's tucked inside his coat. Repeatedly
The Marshal calls to him, "The Prince of Homburg!"
"What is my Marshal's bidding?" he replies,
Trying to collect his thoughts. However,
Encircled by such miracles as these,—:
A thunderbolt from heaven could have fallen!
                    *(He stops short.)*
ELECTOR: Was it then the Princess' glove?
HOHENZOLLERN:                              Of course!
          *(The Elector looks more thoughtful.)*
He's like a stone, his pencil in his hand,
Standing there, apparently alive,
But every feeling, as if struck by magic,
Gone; and not until the following morning,
With cannonfire thundering in the ranks,
Does he return to life again and ask me:
"What was it at the conference last night
That Dörfling read aloud for me to do?"
FIELD-MARSHAL: My lord, I quite subscribe to this account.
The Prince, as I recall, did not perceive
A word of what I said. I'd often seen him
Distracted, but I don't think ever so
Enrapt and absent as upon this day.
ELECTOR: And now, if I correctly understand you,
Your towering syllogism reads as follows:
Had I not jested with him in his sleep
In such ambiguous fashion, he'd be guiltless:
He'd not have been distracted at the briefing
Or insubordinate on the battlefield?
HOHENZOLLERN: My Lord, I leave the inference to you.
ELECTOR: Fool that you are! Stupid Fool! Had you
Not called me down with you into the garden,
Would I, compelled by curiosity,

Have staged that harmless jest before his eyes?
Of course not! So, with fully equal right,
I say that you are guilty of his crime!—
The Delphic wisdom of my officers!
HOHENZOLLERN: Sufficient, my Elector! I'm convinced
My words have fallen heavy on your heart.


### SCENE 6

*Enter an officer. The others.*
OFFICER: The Prince, my lord, shall be here in a moment!
ELECTOR: Very good! Announce him!
OFFICER:                                    Two more minutes!—
He stopped, in passing, at the cemetery
To have the keeper open him the gate.
ELECTOR: The cemetery?
OFFICER:                    Yes, my lord and sovereign.
ELECTOR: What for?
OFFICER:              To tell the truth, I hardly know:
Apparently he wished to see the tomb
Made ready there for him at your command.
          *(The officers gather and talk among themselves.)*
ELECTOR: Never mind! When he arrives, admit him!
          *(He goes to the table and surveys the papers there.)*
TRUCHSS: I see the guard approaching with him now.


### SCENE 7

*Enter the Prince of Homburg. Officer of the watch. The others.*
ELECTOR: My young Prince, I ask for your assistance!
Colonel Kottwitz here, on your behalf,
Brings me this paper, look, with signatures
Of many noblemen in long succession.
The army, so it reads, desires your freedom,
Repudiates the sentence of the court.
Please, I pray you, read it for yourself.
          *(Prince of Homburg, after glancing at it, turns
          and looks around at the officers encircling him.)*

PRINCE: Kottwitz, dear old friend, give me your hand.
  You're doing more than I deserved from you
  Upon the day of battle. But now, go
  Back to camp and stabling at Arnstein
  And stay there; now that I have thought it over,
  I wish to die the death decreed for me!
                    *(He hands back the petition.)*
KOTTWITZ *(stunned)*:
  No, nevermore, my Prince! What are you saying?
HOHENZOLLERN: He wants to die—?
TRUCHSS:                          He must and shall not die!
SEVERAL OFFICERS *(rushing forward at once)*:
  Elector! Lord and sovereign! Will you hear us?
PRINCE: Be calm! It is my absolute desire
  To glorify the sacred code of battle,
  Broken by me before the entire army,
  With voluntary death. What do I care
  For one more victory, brothers, over Wrangel,
  In my much more glorious triumph over pride,
  That devastating enemy within us?
  Down with every foe who would enslave us!
  Let every Brandenburger keep his freedom
  On his maternal soil; for it is his,
  In all the splendor of its woods and fields.
KOTTWITZ: My son! My dearest friend! What shall I call you?
TRUCHSS: Almighty God!
KOTTWITZ:                Let me kiss your hand!
                    *(They gather around him.)*
PRINCE *(to the Elector)*:
  To you, my sovereign, whom I used to call
  A sweeter name, now cast away in folly,
  I throw myself before you, deeply chastened!
  Forgive me, if upon that crucial day
  I served you with untimely eagerness:
  Death now purges me of every guilt.
  Console my heart, which now is reconciled
  And cheerfully surrenders to your sentence,
  By saying you've relinquished every grudge:

In token of our final hour together
Let your gracious will permit one favor.
ELECTOR: Speak, young hero! What is your desire?
  I pledge you with my noble word of honor,
  No matter what it be, I shall concede it.
PRINCE: Do not purchase peace from Karl Gustav
  With your niece's hand. Send him away,
  The bearer of such infamous proposals!
  Inscribe your answer with a rifle volley!
ELECTOR *(kissing his forehead):*
  Be it as you say! Let this kiss
  Ensure your last request of me, my son!
  Indeed, what need is there of yet another
  Sacrifice to battlefield misfortune?
  A victory blooms from every word you speak,
  Fit to grind the foe into the dust.
  She is Prince Homburg's bride, I'll write to him;
  Condemned victorious, after Fehrbellin,
  His ghost still marches with the battle flags,
  And he who wants her must contend with him!
          *(Kissing him once more, he raises him.)*
PRINCE: Behold, you've given me my life again!
  Now shall I pray for you that every blessing
  From the cloudy porches of the seraphim
  Be showered on your heads in jubilation!
  Go and do battle, Sire; and subdue
  All the foes on earth—for you are worthy!
ELECTOR: Guard! You may escort him back to prison!


SCENE 8


*Natalie and the Elector's wife appear at the threshold. Ladies-in-waiting follow. The others.*
NATALIE: O Mother, don't! Why speak now of propriety!?
  The highest thing at such an hour is love!
  —My precious miserable friend!
PRINCE *(leaving):*                Away!

TRUCHSS *(holding him):* No, nevermore, my Prince!
                    *(Officers stand in his way.)*
PRINCE:                                        Take me
                                            [away!

HOHENZOLLERN: Can your heart, my Elector—?
PRINCE *(tearing himself free):*              Despots, would
                                        [you have me

Dragged in chains before the firing squad?
Away!—I've made my reckoning with the world!
                *(Exit, with the officer of the watch.)*
NATALIE *(leaning on her aunt):*
O Earth, receive me now into your bosom!
Why look upon the sunlight any longer!


## SCENE 9

*The others, without the Prince of Homburg.*
FIELD-MARSHAL: Almighty God! Must it then come to this?
    *(The Elector speaks urgently and in private with an officer.)*
KOTTWITZ *(coldly):*

My liege and lord, with all that has transpired,
Are we dismissed?
ELECTOR:              No, you are not! Not yet!
I shall tell you when you are dismissed!
*(He fixes him with his eyes, then gathers up the papers the page
                has brought him from the table
                and turns to the Field-Marshal.)*
Here is the passport of the Swedish Count!
Inform him of my cousin Homburg's wish
That I am bound in duty to fulfill:
The war begins again in three days' time!
            *(Pause. He glances at the death sentence.)*
Now judge ye yourselves, my lords! In just one year
The Prince, in wanton recklessness and spite,
Blocked two of my most splendid victories
And seriously lamed a third as well.

Schooled in the crises of these past few days,
Will you take your chances with him one more time?
KOTTWITZ AND TRUCHSS *(simultaneously):*
How, my divine . . . beloved . . . ?
ELECTOR:                              Will you? Will you?
KOTTWITZ: By God, you could be tottering at the abyss,
But, unsolicited, he would not even
Touch his sword to help you or to save you!
ELECTOR *(tearing up the death sentence):*
Then, follow, friends! Come with me to the garden!


SCENE 10


*Castle, with the ramp that leads down into the garden, as in Act
I. Again, it is night.*
*The Prince of Homburg, blindfolded, is led by Captain Stranz
through the lower garden gate. Officer of the watch. In the dis-
tance the drum rolls of a funeral march.*
PRINCE: Now, O immortality, you're mine!
Your light, intenser than a thousand suns,
Pierces the bindings of these earthly eyes.
Mighty pinions grow on both my shoulders,
My spirit soars into the silent aether;
And like the ship, abducted by the wind,
That sees the lively harbor shrink and vanish,
So below me life grows dark and fades away:
Colors I can still perceive, and forms;
Then all lies beneath me in a mist.
                    *(The Prince sits down on a bench
                    encircling an oak tree in the middle
              of the courtyard; Captain Stranz, withdrawing from him,
                         looks up the ramp.)*
Oh, what a lovely scent of damesworts here!
Do you not smell it?
                    *(Stranz comes back to him.)*
STRANZ:               Pinks and gillyflowers, no?
PRINCE: Gillyflowers? How come they to be here?

STRANZ: I don't know. It looks as if a maiden's hand
   Has planted them.—Here, would you like a pink?
PRINCE: Dear friend!—
   I'll take it home with me to put in water.


SCENE 11


*Enter the Elector, holding the laurel wreath slung with the golden
chain, his wife, Princess Natalie, Field-Marshal Dörfling, Colonel
Kottwitz, Hohenzollern, Golz, and the others. Ladies-in-waiting,
officers and torch-bearers. All appear on the ramp of the castle.
Hohenzollern, with a kerchief in his hand, steps up to the balus-
trade and signals to Captain Stranz, who leaves the Prince there-
with and withdraws upstage to speak with an officer of the watch.*
PRINCE: Friend, what is this spreading radiance?
STRANZ *(returning to him):*
   My Prince, would you be good enough to rise?
PRINCE: What is it?
STRANZ:                    Nothing that might frighten you!—
   I'm merely going to unbind your eyes.
PRINCE: Has it struck, my final hour of pain?
STRANZ: It has! Hail, and God bless you! You are worthy!
   *(The Elector gives the wreath and chain to Natalie,
   takes her by the hand, and leads her down the ramp.
   Lords and ladies follow. Natalie, surrounded by
   torch-bearers, steps up to the Prince, who
   jumps up in astonishment; she places the wreath
   on his head, hangs the chain around his neck, and
   presses his hand to her heart. The Prince faints.)*
NATALIE: Heavens! He'll die of rapture!
HOHENZOLLERN *(lifting him up):*          We must help him!
ELECTOR: Let artillery thunder waken him!
         *(Cannonades in the distance. A march.
         The castle suddenly lights up.)*
KOTTWITZ: Hail, hail, the Prince of Homburg!
OFFICERS:                              Hail, all hail!
ALL: To the victor of the day at Fehrbellin!
         *(Momentary silence.)*

PRINCE: No, tell me! Is it a dream?
KOTTWITZ:                               A dream, what else?
SEVERAL OFFICERS: To the battlefield!
TRUCHSS:                               The combat!
FIELD-MARSHAL:                                   And the
                                                [victory!

ALL: Down with all the foes of Brandenburg!

(*Curtain.*)

*Translated by Peggy Meyer Sherry*

## ACKNOWLEDGMENTS

We gratefully acknowledge permission to reprint material from the following publications:

*Amphitryon, A Comedy after Molière by Heinrich von Kleist,* translated by Charles E. Passage, from *Amphitryon: Three Plays in New Verse Translations.* Copyright © 1973 The University of North Carolina Press. Published for UNC Studies in Comparative Literature.

*Penthesilea, A Tragedy,* translated by Humphry Trevelyan, appeared in *The Classic Theater,* edited by Eric Bentley (New York: Doubleday, Anchor Books, 1959). Translation copyright © 1959 H. Trevelyan.